Freire

Research Methods for

The Civil Right
Study (2010)

Stambach & Becker
(2006)
Charter schools.

help ensure white economically
Bodine (2008) advantaged
group
Charter schools that
work with majority black
populace rely more on non-
accredited teachers & have
poorer working conditions

Research Methods for the Social Sciences

Jerry Wellington and
Marcin Szczerbinski

continuum

Continuum International Publishing Group
The Tower Building   80 Maiden Lane, Suite 704
11 York Road   New York, NY
London, SE1 7NX   10038

www.continuumbooks.com

British Library Cataloging-in-Publication Data
A catalogue record for this book is available from the British Library.

ISBN: 9780826485670 (paperback)
      9780826485663 (hardcover)

Library of Congress Cataloging-in-Publication Data
To come

Typeset by YHT Ltd, London
Printed and bound in Great Britain by
The Cromwell Press, Trowbridge, Wiltshire

Preface

The aim of this book is to provide an introductory but not simplistic guide to research in the social and behavioural sciences: we discuss its nature, its value, its limitations and its uses. The book sets out to tackle difficult issues and concepts in a scholarly but accessible manner, providing ample guidance and signposts to further reading. For some readers it will provide a 'stepping stone' to more detailed texts on research methods; for others, it will act as an initial guide in getting them started on their own research project. A third category will be those readers who wish to or, as a result of their job, need to examine critically the research carried out by others, e.g. in the medical profession, speech therapy, social work, education and so on. With this category in mind, one of our main aims is to suggest ways of 'reading research' in a critical (but not a scathing or a fault-finding) way.

The book is designed as much for the reflective, researching professional as for the professional researcher. Our intention is to explore a wide range of questions about research and research methods, including:

- What counts as 'good research'?
- Methods and methodology: what are they and what is the difference?
- Why do social scientists spend so much of their time arguing about methods and methodology (and writing books about it) while natural scientists just get on with their research?
- By what standards or criteria can we judge a piece of research?
- What is the so-called 'qualitative/quantitative' divide and what are research approaches and 'paradigms'?

- When and where is quantitative research indispensable?
- If one suggests that research should be 'scientific' or follow the scientific method, what does that mean?
- Should all good research be 'scientific'?
- What methods and methodologies are used in social research?
- What is the role of statistics in social and behavioural research? How should statistical evidence be interpreted?
- Can one method or methodology be deemed to be better than others? If so, by what standards or criteria are we making the judgement of 'betterness'?
- What are the ways in which research can, and should, be disseminated and presented?

We do our best to illuminate some of these questions and debates, we provide illustrations (vignettes) and we offer our own views when appropriate. At different points in the book we provide guidance on further reading and possible websites, a glossary of terms and a full list of references; these will enable readers to explore many of the issues we raise in the book at a broader and deeper level.

Contents

PART 1: INTRODUCTORY THOUGHTS   1

1   A Broad Introduction to Social Research   3

2   Approaches to Social Research   18

3   Considering the Quality of Research: Methodology, Theory and Location   33

4   The Researcher's Role and Responsibility   51

PART 2: QUALITATIVE APPROACHES: THEIR VALUE AND THEIR LIMITS   77

5   Some Qualitative Methods Considered   79

6   Dealing with Qualitative Data   100

PART 3: QUANTITATIVE APPROACHES: THEIR VALUE AND THEIR LIMITS   115

7   Dealing with Quantitative Data   117

8   Psychometrics: Measuring Traits and States   142

PART 4: PRESENTING AND DISSEMINATING RESEARCH   169

9   Presenting and Reporting Research   171

PART 5: EXTRAS

PART 5: EXTRAS 191

References 193
Glossary of Terms 214
Appendix 1 226
Appendix 2 228
Appendix 3 230
Index 231

List of Figures

1.1 Research in the Media   5

2.1 Linear/Traditional/Idealized Approach to Research   26

2.2 Cyclical/Realistic Approach to Research   26

2.3 The Action Research Spiral   27

2.4 The Quantitative Research Spiral   28

4.1 Difficult and Interconnected Decisions in
Social Research   58

5.1 A Way of Crudely Classifying Methods in
Social Research   79

5.2 A Spectrum of Observation   80

7.1 Parallels Between a Judicial Process and the
NHST   129

8.1 First of the Ten Cards of the Rorschach
Inkblot Test   145

8.2 Converting Raw Scores into Normalized
Standard Scores   159

List of Tables

2.1 Contrasting Research 'Philosophies'   19

2.2 Practitioner/Insider Research: Potential Advantages
     and Possible Problems   24

2.3 Research Process Framework   29

3.1 Methodology: Questions to Consider   34

4.1 Ethically Problematic Research Situations   61

4.2 Principles to Follow in Ethical Research   62

4.3 Some Types of Probability Sampling   65

4.4 Some Types of Non-Probability, 'Purposive'
     Sampling   66

5.1 Styles of Interviewing   84

5.2 Forming Interview Guides and Interview Schedules   85

5.3 Five Types of Questions to Avoid   86

5.4 Tape-recording versus Notetaking   87

5.5 A Checklist for Conducting Focus Group Interviews   90

5.6 What Might Count as a Case Study?   92

5.7 Data collection in Case Study: A Summary of
     Commonly Used Techniques   93

5.8 Case Study: Strengths and Weaknesses   94

5.9 Ways of Maximizing Response Rate to a
     Questionnaire   96

5.10 Some Guidelines on Questionnaire Design and
     Layout   99

6.1 Degrees of Access and Examples of Different
     Types of Documents   110

6.2 Questions Which Might be Posed in Analysing
     Documents   113

7.1 Descriptive versus Inferential Statistics 119

7.2 Results of BAS and Schonell Tests 132

7.3 Examples of Null and Significant Results 140

9.1 Main Types of Research Publication 172

9.2 A Checklist for Good Reporting of Research 174

9.3 How to Submit a 'Perfect Book Proposal' 181

Part 1: Introductory Thoughts

1 A Broad Introduction to Social Research

Doing Research and Reading Research

Doing research which involves people – or 'social research' – can be very enjoyable. Travelling around, meeting different people, encountering different organizations such as schools or businesses, hearing new accents, meeting employers, seeing 'how the other half live' are all part of the fun.

Doing 'people research' can involve an almost infinite range of activities: asking people questions; listening and observing; administering performance tests; evaluating resources, schemes, programmes or teaching methods; performing brain scans and monitoring physiological responses (changes in heart rate, blood pressure or dilation of pupils) in response to various stimuli.

Research rarely goes according to plan – it can be messy, frustrating and unpredictable, and we discuss this in our book: conducting focus groups in which only one person turns up; arranging to meet a group of apprentices 90 miles away and arriving to find that their 'mentor' had mistakenly sent them home; visiting a school to find it closed for a 'Baker Day'; arranging to interview a 'very busy' employer for half an hour who in the event talks for two hours; a child refusing to complete your carefully constructed test, which she calls 'boring' (while her other classmate calls it 'trivial'). All these things have happened to us.

These are the differences between social research, which deals with humans, their society and culture and their organizations, and research in physics, which deals with inanimate, idealized entities such as point masses, rigid bodies and frictionless surfaces.

These differences also imply a different code of conduct in

contrast to the physical sciences, simply because social research involves the study of human beings. The physical sciences do have their own canons and ethics, but social research has additional ethical demands. Concern for ethics should start at the outset of any research project and continue through to the write-up and dissemination stages. Morals and ethics in research are considered at different times in this book.

As well as considering how people 'do' research we also look at how one might 'read' research. By what standards should we judge the research we read about? How can we distinguish good research from bad, assuming that it is more than simply a matter of taste? Are the conclusions drawn justified from the evidence or data collected? These are issues that we will consider, not least in the vignettes that are included in this book.

Research in the Media

For most people who are not researchers, their most common encounter with research is in the media. Research, of course, is constantly in the media. Research involving human beings, like politics or the selection of the national rugby, tennis or soccer team, is a subject on which everyone feels they are an expert, simply because we are all humans.

The collage of newspaper cuttings in Figure 1.1 shows some of the old chestnuts which have been media favourites for decades (see Baker, 1994). Some of the other questions and headline statements from social and medical research that have caused considerable media activity are:

- Can MMR cause autism?
- Do teachers make any difference?
- Regular exercise can ward off dementia.
- Drinking wine is good for your heart.
- Inequality in society causes crime.
- Infants are better off if they stay with their mothers.

A more recent controversial topic has been the under-achievement of boys, which received a huge volume of newspaper coverage in early-1998 and has recurred regularly since (incidentally, one wonders if the media spotlight would

Figure 1.1 Research in the Media

have been as strong if girls' GCSE results had fallen significantly below boys').

As well as the usual suspects, the occasional zany or off-the-wall item of research makes headlines. For example, the observation that 'women's brains shrink during pregnancy' was first put forward in 1997 and said by certain newspapers to be based on new scientific evidence. In 1998, music lessons were reported for the first time to be the 'key to a better memory' – based on a 'controlled' experiment in Hong Kong with 30 female students who had received them and 30 who had not. This topic of research continued to attract wide newspaper interest, with (for example) a *Times* article in 2006 (20 September, page 9) reporting an experimental study with only 12 children, displaying the headline 'Why music lessons are good for the memory'. Perhaps, we would speculate, these studies received media interest because they involved a controlled experiment which was perceived to have higher or 'scientific' status. As it turned out, the initial findings of the beneficial effects of classical music on memory and learning were not replicated. While the media hype beyond this so-called 'Mozart effect' does return occasionally it is fuelled by little evidence – as is much of the media hype about research, generally speaking. This is perhaps inevitable: the media goes for novelty, while establishing scientific consensus takes a great deal of systematic, unglamorous replication and follow-up.

Indeed, a systematic research programme which carried out an in-depth study of current media selection, filtering and portrayal of social research would make an interesting study. It might well reveal a media bias towards research which is seen as 'scientific', objective and value-free and *against* studies which are qualitative and therefore deemed to be value-laden and subjective – but this is speculation.

A Brief History of Social Research: Recurrent Debates

We cannot give a detailed account of the history of social research here but we can trace some of the key features and past definitions which have shaped its history. This brief history will help to highlight some of the recurring debates about research and research methods.

From the Laboratory Approach to the 'Natural' Setting

The location of social research has gradually shifted from the laboratory or the clinic to the real-life or 'natural' context. For example, one of the hot topics at the end of the nineteenth century was the study of 'individual differences' between human beings, most notably with the work of Galton, which was largely laboratory based and dependent on the statistical techniques of that era; this is an area which was to return in 1973 with Arthur Jensen and many other players in this large and diverse field (discussed further in Chapter 8).

Similarly, Thorndike's work in the first quarter of the last century is often noted as a key influence in the years to come. His famous slogan 'whatever exists at all exists in some amount' (Thorndike, 1918, p. 16) inspired and influenced subsequent researchers to mimic the 'scientific method' and rely exclusively on quantitative methods. His work on testing and academic achievement was very much laboratory research, divorced from the messy reality of homes, schools and classrooms.

Despite his apparent obsession with the quantitative and distance from a natural setting such as a home or the classroom, Thorndike's work in one area remains a live issue. He argued that training (or learning) in one situation would not readily transfer to another situation or context. His scepticism over 'transfer of training' is ironic in that his own conclusions on the difficulty of transfer have been extended and generalized from the clean, clinical world of laboratory to the complex, unpredictable worlds of school education and youth training. Nowadays, the transfer debate is as live as ever but is studied in natural settings, i.e. in context, rather than in labs. The transfer debate reappeared prominently in the 1970s with the emergence of 'generic' or 'transferable' skills in both schooling and youth training based on the belief that they would make young people more employable. Skills of a similar nature were given further prominence by the 'core skills' movement in the 1980s and their rechristening as 'key skills' at the end of the last century. Thorndike's original scepticism about 'transfer' reappeared with the 'situated cognition' movement of the last era which argued persuasively that skill, knowledge and understanding is context dependent, i.e. 'situated'. All of this work focused on skills development in real-life contexts such as apprenticeships and the workplace (see Lave's 1986 work on cognition in practice, and many other books). A similar impulse led to the calls for the 'ecological validity' (i.e. real-life relevance) of psychological research.

Ethics, from Jenner to Burt

Debates on social issues or problems, and arguments over *how* they should be researched, have a habit of recurring. Debates on the code of conduct governing research form one perennial example, though we do seem to have made some moral progress. In 1796, a doctor called Edward Jenner borrowed an 8-year-old Gloucestershire schoolboy named James Phipps and infected him with cowpox. Jenner later infected him with smallpox and (fortunately) James recovered. This 'scientific' experiment (incidentally with a sample of one) led eventually to widespread vaccination.

Similar examples have occurred in social research. In the two examples cited briefly below, one involves unethical *methods* and the second unethical *analysis of data*:

- The first, like Jenner's in employing unethical methods, was reported by Dennis in 1941. He was involved in the raising of two twins in virtual isolation for a year in order to investigate infant development under conditions of 'minimum social stimulation' (Dennis, 1941).
- A better-known name, Cyril Burt, who is renowned for his testing of 'intelligence' and the assessment of ability, has been accused of twisting, manipulating and even fraudulently misrepresenting his data (see Flynn, 1980), and probably also fabricating them, though that is controversial (see Joynson, 1989).

Ethical issues are a common feature in the history of both scientific and social research.

The 'Jump' from Data to Theory

Approaches to research have changed and we consider the possibilities now available in a later chapter. One issue that has not changed is the connection between a researcher's ideas and theories and the data they have collected. In some ways this is still a mystery, mainly because it seems to rely on some sort of 'creativity', act of faith or blind leap from data to conclusions in certain cases.

Are the ideas directly derived from their research data by some sort of process of induction? Or do they stem from creative insights, hunches and imaginative thinking? Probably a combination of both, one would suspect. These questions are revisited later when we discuss the meaning and place of 'theory' in social research.

There are many other valuable ideas in the history of social research where it is unclear whether they are inferences from the research data, guiding a priori hypotheses, imaginative insights, or creative models for viewing the social world. One is Gardner's idea of multiple intelligences (Gardner, 1993), which argues that intelligence has many different facets. Gardner went further than other psychologists by claiming that there is not a single thing called intelligence, but a set of as many as eight distinct sets of abilities (multiple intelligences). Guilford's (1967) model of the human intellect, which distinguishes between 'divergent' and 'convergent' thinking is another example. It is not clear whether these models of the human mind are based on speculation or on evidence – and this is true of other theories in social science.

The purpose of this brief history, with its limited range of examples, has been to show that none of the major issues discussed in this book are new. The following debates or questions all have a past and will all have a future:

- the relation to, and impact of, research on practice;
- the difference between research in an experimental or a laboratory setting and investigations of naturally occurring situations;
- the range of foundation disciplines which have and have not related (and should or should not relate) to social

research: philosophy, biology, history, sociology, psychology, anthropology;
- the importance of ethics in conducting research and analysing the data;
- the nature and role of theory in research and the mystery of where theories come from (we know they come from people, but how?).

Finally, there are two recurring key questions: *who* is doing the research ... and who *is paying for it?*

Changing (and Recurring) Definitions of Social Research

One of the recurring themes in the history of research involving human beings, which surfaces in past attempts to define it, has been the belief that it should attempt to mirror or mimic so-called scientific method. Thus, Gay (1981) defined social research as: 'The formal systematic application of the scientific method to the study of social problems' (Gay, 1981, p. 6).

Nisbet and Entwistle (1970) had earlier commented that social research should be restricted to 'areas which involve quantitative or scientific methods of investigation'. In the same textbook they argued that the key to social research is to 'design a situation which will produce relevant evidence to prove or disprove a hypothesis'.

A later definition by Ary *et al.* (1985) follows similar lines: 'When the scientific method is applied to the study of social problems, social research is the result'.

These extracts from different sources are sufficient to illustrate three fundamental issues in attempts to define social research which were prevalent throughout the last century.

Firstly, there has been a persistent view that there is something called 'the scientific method' which 'scientists' follow and which should be adopted by social research. In the last quarter of the twentieth century there has been a lorry load of publications which show that this belief bears no resemblance to real science (Kuhn, 1970, Medawar, 1963 and 1979, Woolgar, 1988 are just a few starting points; more recently, see Rowbottom and

Aiston, 2006). There is no *one* scientific method – there are as many methods as there are sciences and scientists.

Secondly, it follows that the view of science and therefore social research as being always totally hypothesis driven has no foundation. Some scientific research may be driven by hypotheses, but some is not.

Finally, one important mistake has been to confuse the terms 'quantitative' and 'scientific', as if the two were synonymous. Quantitative data can (and in our view often *should*) be involved in social research without thereby inviting the accusation that it is blindly trying to mimic the sciences. Social research should not attempt to mimic some outmoded view of scientific method – but that does not prevent it from using quantitative data where appropriate. To reject the quantitative while (quite rightly) denying that social research should uncritically mirror the so-called scientific method would be to throw the baby out with the bath water.

Social research should take a scientific approach whenever the research problem calls for it. Whenever the research is concerned with explanation (third-person perspective), prediction or control (producing and monitoring outcomes that are believed to be desirable, for example, measuring the effectiveness of an educational intervention), then a hypothesis-testing approach borrowed from the sciences is the only way. And much of social science is concerned with explaining, predicting and controlling social and psychological phenomena. But if our investigation is concerned with initial exploration of as yet unknown territory, or with understanding social phenomena (first-person perspective, i.e. perspective of the people involved) then a scientific (sometimes called 'positivist') approach is constraining and inappropriate.

One theme taken up in many of the more recent definitions and discussions of social research, which seems blindingly obvious now, is that research should involve practitioners, not only at the receiving end (as users or consumers) but in the research process itself. The writing of Lawrence Stenhouse is probably the most notable on this theme, with his concept of the 'teacher-as-researcher'. Stenhouse (1984) defined educational research as:

systematic activity that is directed towards providing knowledge, or adding to the understanding of existing knowledge which is of relevance for improving the effectiveness of education.

We come back to Stenhouse later, but the word 'systematic' is interesting here. In 1986, Best and Kahn defined social research as:

> The systematic and *objective* analysis and recording of controlled observations that may lead to the development of generalisations, principles, or theories, resulting in prediction and possibly ultimate control of events.
>
> (Best and Kahn, 1986 p.22)

Another author to use the word 'systematic' was Mouly, in 1978:

> Research is best conceived as the process of arriving at dependable solutions to problems through the planned and systematic collection, analysis, and interpretation of data. It is the most important tool for advancing knowledge, for promoting progress, and for enabling man to relate more effectively to his environment, to accomplish his purposes and to resolve his conflicts.
>
> (Mouly, 1978, cited in Cohen and Manion, 1994, p. 40)

Both definitions are notable for their optimism – the beliefs, for example, that social research might result in the 'ultimate control of events' or could enable man (*sic*) to 'resolve his conflicts'. This language may seem rather overoptimistic, but what are the alternatives? Attempts at control based on hunches, inner conviction, faith? Relinquishing all control? The term 'objective' used by Best and Kahn (1986) is also extremely problematic – the belief in objectivity in research is also discussed later.

There have been varied attempts at defining social research. Themes have recurred and resurfaced. The notion that social research should be 'scientific' is perhaps most common, although none of its proponents have attempted to define the word or spell out the meaning of its partner, 'scientific method'.

The notion of objectivity has also persisted, again largely undefined. Another theme is that social research should attempt to generate a body of knowledge and theory. Finally, social research has often been seen as the process of producing solutions to problems, i.e. as a problem-solving activity, aiming to provide dependable solutions to the problems of society.

Attempting a Definition

As with most attempts at a watertight definition, those striving to define social research usually find it (like an elephant) much easier to recognize than to define. One of the most widely quoted versions is Stenhouse's (1975) view of research as 'systematic enquiry made public'. Bassey (1990) elaborates on this by defining research as: 'systematic, critical and self-critical inquiry which aims to contribute to the advancement of knowledge' (p. 35). The adjective 'critical' implies that the data collected and samples used in the research are closely scrutinized by the researcher. 'Self-critical' implies, similarly, that researchers are critical of their own decisions, the methods they choose to use, their own analysis and interpretation, and the presentation of their findings.

So, we support the view that social research is inquiry that is critical, self-critical and systematic, that is, rational. But we would also add the word empirical. Not all research is empirical in a strict sense, and certainly not 'empiricist', but all research should be grounded in and constrained by empirical data.

And Finally ... Why are there So Many Books on Method and Methodology in the Social Sciences but So Few in the So-Called 'Natural Sciences'?

One answer is that, in the study of people, research cannot capture the whole story with just one method. Thus some factors might be observable, such as a person's behaviour. But so many characteristics are latent or hidden. They cannot be observed but must be inferred from other things, e.g. a test, an interview, a person's story, a focus group. Thus in studying human beings we are generally not interested in behaviour per se, but what lies 'underneath' it: the human mind in its various attributes (intelligence, mood, attitude, and motivation), group dynamics, societal forces, culture and so on. That 'underneath' constitutes a realm of latent, or hidden, variables, which cannot be observed directly, but only inferred from observable behaviour. How that should be done is never straightforward. Further still, the very existence of those latent constructs is often a matter of heated controversy (think of the Marxist construct of base and superstructure, or the Freudian concept of personality as a dynamic interplay between Id, Ego and Superego).

For example, a study of depression could involve observation, a questionnaire and life history interviews or, at the other extreme, even an investigation of the chemistry of the brain. The necessity for a range of methods leads to debate over which methods are most 'appropriate' (in some circles, which methods are 'better'). This is a debate that looks likely to remain live and contested.

Another answer is that researchers working in the natural sciences appear to simply 'just get on with it' without really questioning their methods or whether what they are seeking is 'the truth' or (more instrumentally) the best theory. This may be because they are dealing with observables and (in most cases) with variables that can be identified and controlled. It may also be due to the fact that scientists as a community seem to spend little time reflecting on the so-called 'scientific method' (although there are numerous books, dating back for decades, on the philosophy and sociology of science). One of the famous scientists of the past, Sir Peter Medawar, once described the scientific method as a 'mixture of guesswork and checkwork' (Medawar, 1979). He also recounted his experiences with fellow scientists who, when asked what the scientific method is, went very coy and cloudy-eyed.

Perhaps the answer is that there is no such thing as 'the scientific method' although there may be many methods that could be deemed to be 'scientific'. In this book, we examine the traditional meaning of 'scientific' and ask whether any twenty-first-century science could possibly live up to those standards in a complex, postmodern world. But if we question these old hallmarks, by which standards should social research be judged? Again, we offer our own discussion of these questions.

Further Reading

See Baker, M. (1994), 'Media coverage of education'. *British Journal of Educational Studies*, 42(3), 286–97, for an interesting account of the way that the press have handled current issues in education.

Gardner's accounts of multiple intelligences can be found in Gardner, H. (1983) *Frames of Mind: The Theory of Multiple Intelligences*. New York: Basic Books; and Gardner, H. (1993) *Intelligence Reframed: Multiple Intelligences for the 21st Century*. New York: Basic Books. Is Gardner's idea a theory, a model, a metaphor, a useful idea or simply wild speculation about the human brain? For an interesting critique see White, J. (1998) *Do Howard Gardner's Multiple Intelligences Add Up?* London: Institute of Education.

For a 'balanced' account of Cyril Burt's work, see Joynson, R. B. (1989) *The Burt Affair*. New York: Routledge.

Rowbottom, D. P. and Aiston, S. J. (2006) 'The myth of "scientific method" in contemporary educational research'. *Journal of Philosophy of Education*, 40(2), 137–56.

Vignette One

Left-handed women run twice the risk of breast cancer

Headlines of this ilk featured in many of the papers in September 2005. The media reported a study carried out in Utrecht which investigated 12,000 women, born between 1932 and 1941, and claimed to show that left-handed women were over twice (2.41 times to be exact) as likely to develop breast cancer before the menopause as right-handed ones. The relationship held even after other factors connected to breast cancer in past studies (such as body weight, smoking habits, family history and socio-economic status) were taken into account. The authors explained the results by proposing that higher levels of sex hormones (oestrogen) in the womb induce left-handedness and also increase the risk of breast cancer later on in life.

The study was reported in the *British Medical Journal* and in fairness this should be read in full before one can offer a reasonable evaluation of it (we have not done that). But for this vignette, we simply raise a few pertinent questions that might be asked of this study as reported in the media – and indeed, of any similar headline news.

1. How was 'handedness' defined and operationalized? Strange as it may seem, this is not a straightforward matter. Many label as 'left-handed' a person who writes with her left hand? But what if the same people eat with their right hand? Such inconsistencies in hand preferences are very common, indeed they are the norm (Bishop, 1990). It may be more accurate, therefore, to think of handedness as a continuum of preference (from fully consistent right-handedness to fully consistent left-handedness). This consistency can then be measured by self-report (e.g. filling in a questionnaire about hand preference on a number or activities) or by observation. Thus, classifying someone as left- or right-handed depends crucially on how handedness is defined and measured (Bishop, 1990).

2. How credible is the reported finding? A large sample size means that the finding should not be dismissed out of hand: there may be a genuine correlation between the handedness and the risk of breast cancer. Yet large sample size does not, by itself, prove anything: the correlation may be spurious, an artefact of some unrecognized methodological flaw in sample selection or data collection. Replication is the only way to deal with the doubts. No new finding (and especially strange finding!) should be taken as proven until it is demonstrated independently by several research teams.

3. How plausible is the proposed explanation? It appears that the authors proposed a *causal mechanism*, which links pre-natal levels of oestrogen with left-handedness of one hand, and increased risk of breast cancer on the other. Yet this is surely just a hypothesis: pre-natal levels of oestrogen were not

measured in the study. To evaluate the plausibility of this hypothesis, we must rely on the *principle of connectivity* (Stanovich, 2000). A hypothetical causal explanation is plausible only insofar as it is consistent with the existing body of knowledge (in this case, our knowledge about the action of oestrogen on a foetus) that comes from prior research.

3. How *high* is the reported risk? A greater than two-fold increase in the incidence of breast cancer sounds serious, but its seriousness depends entirely on the *baseline rate* of that condition. If breast cancer affects around 12 in 100 women at some point during their lifetimes (a lifetime risk figure reported for the US: National Cancer Institute, 2007) then a 2.41 increase in risk would mean an additional 17 cases per 100 left-handed women – a substantial increase. But if breast cancer was rarer (one case per 100 women, say), then the same 2.41 times increase would translate into just one or two extra cases per 100 women. It is therefore important to report not just relative increase in risk, but also an absolute increase (the number of extra cases per 100 people) – yet this was not generally done in media reports.

4. What is the *relative importance* of left-handedness as a factor? How does it compare in importance with other factors such as smoking or diet?

We realise that most newspaper coverage of complex issues is inevitably oversimplified and even simplistic, but the purpose of this vignette has been to put forward questions that can be posed for research of this kind, which always seems to attract the headlines.

References

Bishop, D. (1990) *Handedness and Developmental Disorders*. Hove, Hillsdale: LEA Publishers.

National Cancer Institute (2007) Cancer starts fact sheets: cancer of the breast. www.cancer.gov, 22 January, 2007.

2 Approaches to Social Research

There are many different approaches, types, or paradigms in social research with labels implying opposite poles such as: positivist/interpretive; interventionist/non-interventionist; experimental/naturalistic; case-study/survey and qualitative/quantitative. One thing that may add confusion is the use of words such as approach, style, philosophy, method, methodology and paradigm as if they were synonymous. We will try to clarify the use of these terms in this and subsequent chapters.

In actual research, however, there may well be a complementary mixture or overlap of styles or approaches, e.g. survey and case study work; collection of qualitative and quantitative data. In addition to these supposed contrasts we often hear the terms 'action research' and 'practitioner research' used to describe a project or even a paradigm. In this chapter we introduce some of the many terms used in discussing approaches to, and philosophies of, social research.

Contrasting Philosophies: Qualitative and Quantitative

One of the most common 'contrasts' presented in social research is the distinction between quantitative and qualitative as if they were two separate paradigms (frameworks) and never the twain will meet. The table below shows some of the contrasting descriptions attributed to each label.

Table 2.1 is, of course, a gross oversimplification of reality. Quantitative methods are not always theory-laden or hypothesis-driven and certainly never (because they are employed by people) value-free. Similarly, qualitative research can never be complete fiction – it must depend on some intersubjective (if

Table 2.1 Contrasting Research 'Philosophies'

	Quantitative, 'hard scientific', 'positivistic'	Qualitative
View of the world	Reality 'just is', it is observer independent. Facts and values are independent.	Reality is subjective, socially constructed. Facts and values are inextricably linked.
View of the researcher	Researcher should be neutral, objective. Ensuring objectivity is crucial.	Researcher is always involved; he/she is a part of the situation. Reflectivity is crucial.
Researcher's status	Researcher as an expert: higher status and privileged point of view.	Democratic (involves informants and stakeholders); equal status of researcher and all participants.
Model of science	'Hard sciences' (physics, biology) are 'the gold standard' for social sciences. Analytical tendency: individual variables are identified, and the relationships between them are studied. Reductionism and descriptive parsimony (Ockham's razor).	Social sciences are an autonomous discipline. Holistic approach: complex social phenomena perceived as irreducible.
Aim	Explaining, predicting, controlling social phenomena.	Understanding social phenomena.
Perspective	3rd person (search for objective, generalizable knowledge).	1st person (search for personal knowledge).
Emphasis	Nomothetic (focus on formulating general laws).	Ideographic (focus on describing individual cases).
Participant selection	Ideally random (though opportunistic selection often done in practice).	Opportunistic, purposive.
Nature of data	Numerical	Non-numerical (narratives or images).
Data analysis	Hypothesis-driven. Relies on statistical techniques.	Inductive Interpretative
Writing	Anonymous, passive tone, impersonal style.	Personal, collaborative writing, account, story.
Specific methods associated with the approach	• Experiments (including single-case experiments); • quasi-experiments; • correlational studies; • structured observations; • structured interviews; questionnaires and surveys.	• case-studies; • participant observation; • interviews: path and structure partially determined by participants; • Ethnographic research; • Action research (could be classified as a specific 'method' or a more general 'approach').

not objective) reality. The two approaches can complement each other. Background statistics, or just a few figures from available records, can set the scene for an in-depth qualitative study. When it comes to data collection most methods in social research will yield both qualitative *and* quantitative data (discussed further in, for example, Layder, 1993, p. 112). Interviews can produce quantitative data; questionnaires can collect qualitative data, e.g. in open-response questions; case studies can involve systematic, semi-quantitative observations.

This book is based on the premise that qualitative and quantitative methods are complementary. The choice of the method should always be dictated by the nature of the problem. When a researcher's primary concern is with explaining and predicting, then a choice of quantitatively oriented methods may follow. If, however, he/she wants to understand the experiences of an individual (or a community) from a first-person perspective, a qualitative approach must be taken.

To give a specific example: if my job is to predict whether a convicted criminal is likely to reoffend (and decide, on that basis, whether his custodial sentence is justified), then it is natural to choose a quantitative approach (building statistical/ actuarial prediction models); indeed this is the only approach that works (Swets, Dawes and Mohanan, 2000). If, on the other hand, I want to know *what it is like* to be an offender (or a victim of crime), then choosing qualitative methodologies is a natural way forward. We can also use an analogy: if we read a report on a football (or cricket, netball or hockey) match, we seek both qualitative (descriptive) and quantitative (numerical) information. The reporter can wax lyrical about what a great game it was, who played well, how the crowd reacted, who eventually triumphed, and whether the referee survived the ordeal. But we also require the following:

CHELSEA 2   **BOLTON 1**

(Scorers: Lampard, 18 minutes, Drogba, 20 minutes)   (Campo, 4)

Sent off: Nolan, 32 minutes

Attendance: 35,343

A crude analogy: but the qualitative data can give the

richness and the colour – the quantitative data can provide a structure. The quantitative data can give the 'facts'; the qualitative data can give people's views and perspectives.

'Naturalistic' and 'Experimental' Approaches to Research

Experimental research is often contrasted with the *naturalistic approach*, although in practice the distinction is not always clear cut and is often a matter of degree rather than kind. The main features of a naturalistic approach to research are:

1 *Setting*: Research is carried out in the natural setting or context, e.g. workplace, home, street, football ground, classroom, playground.
2 *Primary data-gathering instrument*: The researcher.
3 *Background knowledge*: Personal, tacit, intuitive knowledge is a valuable addition to other types of knowledge.
4 *Methods*: Qualitative rather than quantitative methods will be used but not exclusively.
5 *Sampling*: Purposive sampling is likely to be preferred over representative or random sampling.
6 *Design*: The research design tends to unfold/emerge as the study progresses and data is collected.
7 *Theory*: Theory tends to emerge from (be grounded in) the data, as opposed to being based on an initial hypothesis, which the research sets out to support (it can never be verified) or on the other hand to falsify.

Thus naturalistic research is conducted in a natural context as opposed to a controlled or clinical setting.

The *experimental approach* is in direct contrast. In the traditional experimental study a control group is set up with features supposedly identical in all relevant respects (a difficult goal to achieve) to an experimental group. Things are 'done' or given to the experimental group but not the control group, e.g. they are taught with an item of new technology; they use a different teaching or learning approach; as a fictional example (we hope) the experimental group is injected on a daily basis with a wonder drug which makes them learn more efficiently while the control group are given sugar lumps.

If an experimental study is a genuinely randomized and controlled trial (RCT for short) then it has been said by some authors (see, for example, Torgerson's 2003 summary of the literature in this area and her discussion of Systematic Reviews) to be the 'gold standard' in education and medical research. To meet this 'standard', the two groups would have to be truly randomized i.e. the groups would have to be selected by a genuinely randomized mechanism such as a random number table. In this way, participants are then truly randomly assigned to either the experimental group or the control group. Random allocation to groups should avoid any of the possible selection bias, which might arise if other methods of allocation are used.

Torgerson (2003, p. 50) points out that, in reviewing the literature on an area, it is often difficult to determine whether a study is truly an RCT or not. The notion of an RCT is important to certain advocates of systematic reviewing in education, who maintain the strict and highly restrictive criterion that only RCTs should be included in a rigorous, systematic review. This criterion is not as tightly adhered to by many advocates of systematic reviewing.

Problems With the Experimental Approach
Although the experimental approach and the ideal exemplar of it, the RCT, may have enormous value in exploring 'what works' in both education and medicine, there are certain issues that must at least be guarded against:

Practical issues: the creation of genuinely randomized groups is often very (difficult) in practice. It can require a large amount of funding to achieve good sample sizes and from that lead to properly randomized control and experiment groups. Without a decent-sized sample, researchers often have to resort to selecting and allocating groups in some other way, e.g. by matching like with like, and this can lead to selection bias. Equally, any intervention (whether it be a drug or a new style of teaching) needs to be given full time to work and to have an impact. This requires adequate time and in turn may need proper funding. There is a great danger for a researcher, who may have great belief or even faith in an intervention, to rush the 'experiment' and attempt to find an effect or an impact where there really is none.

The placebo effect: this is a well-documented effect in medicine, in which the placebo (i.e. the drug or medicine designed and expected to have no effect) actually makes a difference.

The Hawthorne effect: this is a similar effect in some ways, with its history in social science rather than medicine. It can be defined as any *initial* improvement in performance following any newly introduced change – this is an effect or problem which researchers need to be wary of if making an intervention, e.g. introducing new teaching methods to assess their impact. The name is based on a 1924 study of productivity at the Hawthorne factory in Chicago. Two carefully matched groups (experimental and control) were isolated from other factory workers. Factors in the working conditions of the experimental group were varied, e.g. illumination, humidity, temperature, rest periods. No matter what changes were made, including negative ones such as reduced illumination or shorter rest periods, their productivity showed an upward trend. Just as surprisingly, although no changes were made to the conditions of the control group, their output increased steadily.

Ethical issues: educational (and medical) interventions can sometimes be accused of being unethical if they treat one group more favourably than another, e.g. if one group is given a new laptop computer while the other is not.

A final comment on the experimental approach is that it can explore what works, i.e. it can test efficacy or effectiveness, but does not really look at the process of why something works or the causal factors behind it – critics say that it treats the process as a black box.

In summary, although the experimental approach and the 'gold standard' within it (the RCT) are often upheld as the best way of conducting social science research, they do have their problems and critics. Equally, however, a naturalistic approach can be messy, complex and open to criticism.

Practitioner Research and 'Action' Research

One idea which has received wide recognition in social research is the notion of 'practitioner research'. This is research conducted by a practitioner/professional in any field (be they a doctor, nurse, policeman, solicitor, or teacher) into their own practice. Terms and notions expressing a similar idea or research philosophy are 'the reflective practitioner' (Schon, 1983) and 'the teacher-as-researcher' (Stenhouse, 1975). Practitioner research has a number of advantages, some of which relate to the earlier summary of naturalistic research, e.g. being able to carry out research in a 'natural setting' such as one's own workplace or classroom. It may also pose certain problems. Table 2.2 sums up the potential benefits and difficulties of practitioner research.

Table 2.2 Practitioner/Insider Research: Potential Advantages and Possible Problems

Potential Advantages	Possible Problems
Prior knowledge and experience of the setting/context (insider knowledge).	Preconceptions, prejudices.
Improved insight into the situation and people involved.	Not as 'open-minded' as an 'outsider' researcher.
Easier access.	Lack of time (if working inside the organization) and distractions/ constraints due to 'being known'.
Better personal relationships, e.g. with teachers, pupils.	'Prophet in own country' difficulty when reporting or feeding back.
Practitioner insight may help with the design, ethics and reporting of the research.	Researcher's status in the organization, e.g. a school.
Familiarity.	Familiarity!

A notion linked to practitioner research is the now well-established concept of 'action research'. In one of the classics in this field it is defined as:

a form of self-reflective enquiry undertaken by participants (teachers, students or principals for example) in social (including educational) situations in order to improve the rationality and justice of (a) their own social or educational practices (b) their understanding of these practices, and (c) the situations and institutions in which these practices are carried out.

(Carr and Kemmis, 1986)

This is obviously linked to the idea of practitioner research in that it may well involve a teacher studying, researching into, or intervening in his or her own practice, setting or system. But the key aim of action research is to bring about critical awareness, improvement, and change in a practice, setting or system. It therefore involves reflection, planning and action as key elements.

People sometimes ask us the question: 'Is what I'm doing action research?' The answer probably lies most clearly in the *intention* behind the research. If the research is conducted with a view to *changing* or improving a situation e.g. a policy, a curriculum, a management system, then it probably merits the label of action research. But for some advocates of action research this description would probably be too broad and include too much. A less inclusive definition would be to say that action research involves intervening in a situation and later evaluating that intervention. This would be part of a cycle: identify the issue or problem → research it → suggest action → implement action → evaluate → revisit the issue/problem.

Research of a contrasting kind (though it would be derogatory to call it 'non-action' research) would have the purpose of studying, exploring or illuminating a situation – it might not be driven by the intention to change it. Such research would therefore not *intervene* in the situation (except that every researcher or observer has an effect on the situation being studied), and would probably not manufacture or create a situation, i.e. it would explore naturally occurring events or situations.

Models and Representations of Research Approaches

Each discussion of research approaches/styles/paradigms/ methodologies seems to attempt its own diagram to show the process of research, and many are (in our view) too complicated to be of value.

The research process has often been depicted as a linear, logical sequence starting with the formulation of aims, then planning, collecting, analysing and interpreting data, and ending with conclusions and writing up. One example of the 'ideal' research sequence is shown in Figure 2.1.

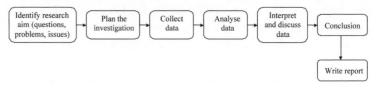

Figure 2.1 Linear/Traditional/Idealized Approach to Research

As Medawar (1963) famously pointed out, this after-the-event portrayal is a fraud, and many others since have admitted that it does not happen like this. Medawar often called scientific research a mixture of 'guesswork and checkwork'. A more realistic approach (see Figure 2.2) is to admit that the process is cyclical or iterative in that people go back and replan/refocus their research, collect and analyse their data and realize that they need more, or different, data; start to write up and realize they are addressing the wrong questions; find that the targets or samples they have set themselves are too low/high, and so on. Even the cyclical version in Figure 2.2 is a cleaned up and idealized version of what really happens.

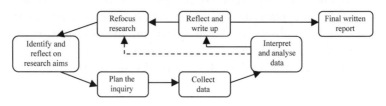

Figure 2.2 Cyclical/Realistic Approach to Research

Another diagram is sometimes used to depict the nature of action research. The essence of the process seems to be a spiral of cycles involving: planning, acting, observing/evaluating, reflecting, re-planning, and so on. Our own attempt to present this as a diagram is shown in Figure 2.3.

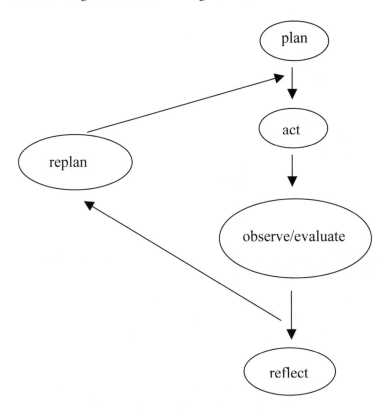

Figure 2.3 The Action Research Spiral

Finally, the spiral shown below is a depiction of the process of quantitative research which is sometimes used to show the cyclical nature of this research approach:

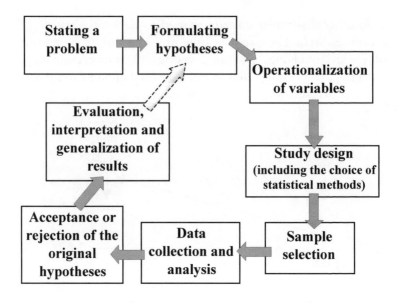

Figure 2.4 The Quantitative Research Spiral

And Finally ... a Framework for Describing the Research Process

No model can capture the process of carrying out research perfectly (all models are by definition simplifications of reality). But having considered a range of models and representations of the 'research process' we arrived at the framework shown in Table 2.3. This was inspired by a page in Denzin and Lincoln (1998, p. 25), where they set out five 'phases' in the research process. We have chosen the metaphor of 'layers' in our table, as a reminder that the process is not a linear, time-bound sequence – rather, the layers overlap and interweave in any research endeavour. Even the idea of layers does not capture the complexity – but it's the best image we could come up with!

In addition, three considerations will always infiltrate (or permeate, to use Denzin and Lincoln's word) the entire research process from initial planning through to eventual dissemination and writing up. These factors are: the values of the researcher; the requirement of being ethical (this will involve not only the researcher's personal values but also 'external'

Table 2.3 Research Process Framework

Layer 1: The researcher	Who is he/she (biography)? Where does he/she work? What is his/her relationship with participants?
Layer 2: Philosophies, paradigms, ontologies, hidden assumptions	• What is worth looking at? • Does objective truth exist? • What is the place of theory in research making?
Layer 3: Methodologies, approaches	Experiments (e.g. RCTs) Quasi-experiments Correlational studies Biographical studies Action research Ethnographic studies
Layer 4: Methods	Observation Interview Psychometric testing Document/artefact analysis
Layer 5: Analysis/interpretation	Statistical approaches Discourse analysis
Layer 6: Presentation/ dissemination	Primary research reports Literature reviews (including quantitative literature reviews) Posters Conference presentations Blogs Online discussion fora

codes of conduct and formal ethical guidelines); and finally the social, temporal and political context of the research.

We have used this table as a framework for the contents of this book. Thus Chapter 3 considers methodology and the role of theory; Chapter 4 discusses the researcher's role and responsibility. In later chapters we discuss specific methods and also approaches to analysing data, both qualitative and quantitative. In Chapter 9, we present and explore a variety of ways of presenting and reporting research – modes of presentation which are determined by a range of factors ranging from the researchers' own values and strengths to the economic and political context of the research, including the sordid but ubiquitous questions: 'who is paying for it?' and 'who is publishing it?'

Further Reading

Denzin, N. and Lincoln, Y. S. (eds) (1988) *Collecting and Interpreting Qualitative Materials*. London: Sage.

Robson, C. (1993) *Real World Research: A Resource for Social Scientists and Practitioner-Researchers*. Oxford: Basil Blackwell.

Torgerson, C. (2003) *Systematic Reviews*, London: Continuum.

Websites

http://en.wikipedia.org/wiki/Randomized_controlled_trial

Vignette Two

THE POWER OF PRAYER: COULD IT MAKE THINGS WORSE?

In April 2006, several newspapers reported a major study carried out in the USA to see if prayer really can help people. The study (Benson *et al.*, 2006) lasted a decade and was funded to the tune of 2.4 million US dollars. A total of 1802 patients at six US hospitals – all requiring heart bypass surgery – were involved. The patients were randomly assigned into one of three groups:

- 597 patients were told that they may or may not be prayed for, and they were not prayed for;
- 604 patients were told that they may or may not be prayed for, and they were prayed for;
- 601 were told they would be prayed for, and were prayed for.

Importantly, of all the patients, 65 per cent were reported to believe in the power of prayer.

Three congregations were given the job of praying that the patients would have a successful operation followed by a speedy recovery with no complications. One of the prayer groups was Protestant, the other two Catholic. The groups were given the names of the patients. Prayers started the night before the surgery and continued for 14 days.

The research team monitored patients' progress during 30 days following the surgery, taking note of any post-surgery complications. In the two groups who were uncertain about receiving prayer, complications occurred in 52 per cent of patients who were prayed for and 51 per cent of patients who were not. This difference was not statistically significant. Thus, prayer itself appeared to have no effect whatsoever on recovery from heart surgery. The third group (who were prayed for and knew it) suffered more complications (59 per cent) than the other two – a slight but statistically significant difference. The authors stated that they can offer 'no clear explanations for the observed excess of complications' in patients who were certain they were prayed for – though some of them ventured with some speculations (e.g. the role of 'performance anxiety') when interviewed about the study.

Our aim here is simply to raise several pertinent questions that might be asked of this study, which could be equally applied to other research:

- What conclusions are the researchers here justified in making?
  - Is 14 days long enough for prayer to make a difference? Is 30 days long enough to detect its impact? In general terms, how long should any intervention be used for, and its effects monitored for, in order to give it a 'fair crack of the whip'?
  - Is 'the amount of prayer received' a quantity that can be scientifically controlled? After all, all participants, no matter what group they were assigned to, could pray for themselves and be prayed for by their relatives and friends – and, indeed, by numerous religious communities across the world who pray for *everyone* in need.

- Is the prayer of different individuals (and different religious communities) equally effective?
- More generally, could – and should – an experimental study be used to assess the 'impact' of a phenomenon such as prayer, which (by its very nature) deals with the supernatural? Is it not something beyond the realms of science?
- Is such research ethical?
  - 'God moves in mysterious ways' according to many believers – does this make a study of this kind (or indeed any study designed to test the power of prayer) totally inappropriate, or indeed objectionable in the eyes of some people? Could it be seen as being 'anti-God' i.e. putting God to the test or 'checking up on Him'?
  - Is it ethical to pray for some people but not for others?
- Is such research useful?
  - Would a research study of this kind ever change people's actions? Would it stop people from praying? We doubt it – there are far more effective forces at play in determining how people behave than the results of research studies. Some of our practices and actions may be evidence-based, but beliefs can be far more potent than evidence, whether we like it or not.
  - The resources that we can spend researching the ways to improve recovery from coronary bypass surgery are limited (even in the USA!). Was spending $2.4 million to check whether prayer makes a difference a sensible choice?

References

Benson H., Dusek, J.A., Sherwood, J.B., Lam, P., Bethea, C.F., Carpenter, W., Levitsky, S. (2006) 'Study of the Therapeutic Effects of Intercessory Prayer (STEP) in cardiac bypass patients: a multicenter randomized trial of uncertainty and certainty of receiving intercessory prayer'. *American Heart Journal* 151(4), 934–42.

3 Considering the Quality of Research: Methodology, Theory and Location

Methodology: What's it All About?

Methodology is defined by the Shorter Oxford English Dictionary as the 'science of method' or more historically as 'treatise on method'. Our own interpretation of methodology is: the activity or business of choosing, reflecting upon, evaluating and justifying the methods you use. Indeed, the latter is an essential feature of any research report or thesis – i.e. justifying the decisions that have been made on methods. No one can assess or judge the value of a piece of research without knowing its methodology. Thus, the aim of methodology is:

> to describe and analyse methods, throwing light on their limitations and resources, clarifying their suppositions and consequences, relating their potentialities to the twilight zone at the frontiers of knowledge.
>
> (Kaplan, 1973, p.10.)

Although most of this book discusses methods, it should not be forgotten that methodology, i.e. reflection on those methods, is a vital part of any research project, small or large. Table 3.1 summarizes some of the key aspects of methodology in social research.

Table 3.1 Methodology: Questions to Consider

- How was the study designed?
- Was the design appropriate?
- Why were particular methods of data collection used, and not others? Could, or should, other methods have been used? Why?
- How could the sample have been better?
- What was the quality of the data?
- Why were the data analysed in the way they were? Could, or should, other methods have been used? Why?
- Can one 'generalize' from the data (extrapolate the findings to different situations)?
- How did the researcher affect the data collected?

Integrating Methods: Triangulation

Even in a small-scale study, a mixture of methods can often be adopted. Schatzman and Strauss (1973) refer to such an approach as 'methodological pragmatism':

> The field researcher is a methodological pragmatist. He sees any method of inquiry as a system of strategies and operations designed – at any time – for getting answers to certain questions about events which interest him.
>
> (Schatzman and Strauss, 1973, p. 7)

Such a view therefore implies that qualitative and quantitative methods can exist side by side in an enquiry:

> there is no fundamental clash between the purposes and capacities of qualitative and quantitative methods or data.
>
> (Glaser and Strauss, 1967, p. 17)

The concept of using a multi-method approach in collecting data, information or evidence (these terms are discussed later) can be called 'triangulation'. Cohen and Manion (1994) define triangulation as 'the use of two or more methods of data collection in the study of some aspect of human behaviour' (p. 254). The origin of the term lies in the use by navigators, surveyors, astronomers, artillerymen and others involved in physical measurement, of several locational markers to pinpoint a certain position or objective. In research, triangular techniques can be used to 'map out, or explain more fully, the richness and complexity of human behaviour by studying it from more than one standpoint and in so doing by making use of both quantitative and qualitative data' (Cohen and Manion, 1994, p. 233).

A typology of triangulation has been suggested by Denzin (1970) who lists the principal types of triangulation which might be used in research. The types can be summarized briefly as follows:

1. **Data Triangulation** which is subdivided into:
   (a) Time triangulation: the researcher attempts to consider the influence of time using cross-sectional and longitudinal research designs. Cross-sectional designs exclude any considerations of time, by definition.
   (b) Space triangulation: researchers engage in some form of comparative study, e.g. of different regions, different countries.
   (c) Person triangulation at the following levels of analysis:
      (i)   the individual level;
      (ii) the interactive level among groups;
      (iii) the collective level.
2. **Investigator Triangulation:** more than one person examines the same situation.
3. **Theory Triangulation:** alternative or competing theories are used in any one situation.
4. **Methodological Triangulation**, which involves 'within method' triangulation, that is, the same method used on different occasions, and 'between method' triangulation, where different methods are used in relation to the same object of study.

(after Denzin, 1970)

This book relates mainly to research involving methodological triangulation of the latter kind, i.e. where a variety of methods are used to study the same issue. However, another important kind of triangulation can be used when analysing and reporting on individuals' views and attitudes gleaned from surveys. Triangulation can be achieved by checking with the individuals that the researcher's interpretation matches and accurately reflects the respondents' views and attitudes.

More quantitatively oriented researchers (e.g. Stanovich, 2000) often prefer to talk about 'converging evidence' rather than triangulation. The two concepts are closely related, however. A particular claim (a theory, a hypothesis, a clinical diagnosis, etc.) can be said to be well supported if it is consistent with a large body of evidence that comes from a variety of sources (methods, researchers, etc.) and rules out alternative explanations. The main criteria of converging evidence for a scientific theory, based on Stanovich, can be found below:

- come from different populations;
- come from different researchers (working independently of each other);
- differ in methodology (study design, methods of data collection, etc.);
- provide case for falsification (they are consistent with just one theoretical account among many competing ones);
- gradually elaborate/refine the theory.

The concept of converging evidence emphasizes the continuity of 'scientific' enquiry. A well-supported claim is not a matter of a single, definite 'proof', but depends on the confluence of many separate studies, most of which must reach the same conclusion (albeit they come from different 'directions').

The Importance of 'Theory' in Achieving Quality in Social Research

There is nothing so practical as a good theory.

(Lewin, 1952, p. 169)

One of the perennial debates in social research over the years has concerned the status, the purpose and the function of theory. The matter is complicated, of course, by lack of agreement over what theory actually is. The issue is complex but it is an important one for anyone involved in social research. The discussion of 'theory' is more than a theoretical matter – students, writers and researchers are often accused of lacking a theoretical framework or a 'theory base' to their work.

Practical outcomes of this accusation could be the non-award of a higher degree by thesis, the rejection by a referee of an article submitted for publication, or the refusal of a funding body to hand over thousands of pounds. In short, being accused of lacking a theoretical base or even worse of being 'atheoretical' can be practically very serious.

What is 'Theory'?

Like most problematic words, 'theory' does not lend itself to easy definition – and worse, we cannot (unlike the proverbial undefinable elephant) always recognize one when we see one. The Oxford English Dictionary shows that the word originates from the ancient Greek idea of a *theōros*, a person who acts as a spectator or an envoy, perhaps sent on behalf of a state to consult an oracle. More recently, the word theory was taken to mean a mental view or a conception; or a system of ideas used or explanation of a group of facts or phenomena (dated 1638 in the Oxford English Dictionary).

In the physical sciences, the distinction between phenomena/events (i.e. things which happen), laws and theories is relatively clear. A *law* is a statement telling us *what* happens in terms of a general pattern or rule. If a metal rod is heated it expands; if pressure is exerted on a gas in a container, its volume decreases (Boyle's Law); every action has an equal and opposite reaction (Newton's Third Law). Laws are simply statements of patterns or connections. For this reason they are less tentative and more long-lasting than theories. The law 'When a gas is heated it expands' (Charles' Law) will be true in two centuries from now. But the theories used to encompass or support laws are more tentative.

Theories are used to explain *why* specific events and patterns of events occur as they do. As such, they are explanations constructed by human beings and therefore subject to improvement, refinement and sometimes rejection – i.e. they are tentative.

Take a concrete example. If some air is trapped in a tin can and heated, its pressure increases. This event or phenomenon is one instance of a general law which says that 'Gases trapped in a container and heated will increase in pressure' (the Pressure Law). But *why* does this happen? The current theory (the Particle Theory of Matter) tells us that everything (including a gas) is made up of tiny little bits called particles which jig around all the time, get faster and faster when heated, and bang against the wall of their container, harder and harder. This theory is good enough to explain why heating gases makes them expand if they are allowed to, or just increases their pressure if they are trapped. It is just a theory, but it is a very good one and has its roots in the time of Democritus, a couple of millennia ago.

But Democritus' idea that matter is made up of tiny, indivisible particles like billiard balls is just not good enough to explain other events and phenomena, e.g. electricity, radioactivity. These phenomena required new theories at the end of the nineteenth century and the beginning of the last. The atomic model of that era portrayed Democritus' 'atoms' as being 'rather like' the Solar system with a nucleus in the middle and electrons orbiting round the outside. This model or theory lasted well and still works in explaining many events. But it has since been superseded by the quantum theory of matter and the introduction of new subatomic particles such as quarks and leptons to explain new observed phenomena. Similarly, the theories of Newton, which work perfectly well in everyday life, have been complemented by Einstein's theory of relativity which is broader and capable of explaining at a more 'universal' level.

So what has this to do with social research? Firstly, theories are used to explain *why* things happen. They are tentative, but not *that* tentative (Newton was born over 300 years ago and his theories still have widespread applicability and practical value, e.g. building bridges; getting to the Moon and back). Secondly, theories are a way of *seeing things*. They often involve models or metaphors which help us to visualize or understand events, e.g. the atom is 'rather like' the solar system. Thirdly, the existence of an established theory (certainly in science but more debatably in social research) can shape or determine the way we subsequently 'see' things. In short, observation in science is often *theory-laden*. The theory determines the observation. In social research we return to this debate later – does theory determine observation and data collection, or does theory 'emerge' from our observations or data? Finally, it needs to be noted that an established theory can *predict* as well as explain, i.e. theories may be predictive as well as explanatory. The particle theory of matter can be used not only to explain what happens to matter, e.g. phenomena like melting or boiling, but also what *will* happen in new situations (e.g. if impurities are added, how will boiling be affected?).

Theories in Social Research

The role of theory in social research, just like the physical sciences, is to help us to understand events and to see them in a new or a different way. A theory may be a metaphor, a model or a framework for understanding or making sense of social events. Other elements in social research which are sometimes (often unjustifiably) given the name 'theory' are little more than generalizations, alleged patterns, ideas or even simply labels.

Our own view is that a theory in social research is only worthy of the name if it helps us to *explain* phenomena and thereby aid our understanding of it. It provides a new way of 'seeing' things. A theory may also have *predictive* power as well as explanatory value, although this may be expecting too much in social research.

Metaphors and models often fulfil at least the first criterion. A model is basically a simplification of reality – it simplifies and aids our understanding by concentrating on certain features of a phenomenon while ignoring others. An example of a model from learning theory is Vygotsky's idea of a 'zone of proximal development': this is a model which talks about a 'zone' between what a learner already knows or can do and what the learner can potentially do, with help from a teacher. A metaphor in learning is Bruner's notion of 'scaffolding' – this is the idea that a student's learning can be 'brought on' or built up by using support or scaffolding to move the learner to a new level. It is a useful metaphor for teachers at all levels, provided it is used with care and not taken too far!

Metaphors are like bridges (the word 'metaphor' literally

means 'carry over' or 'carry across') which link the unknown or the unfamiliar to the known or familiar. While it is possible to build a theory totally devoid of metaphors (i.e. expressed totally in the formal language of science, or, indeed, language of mathematics) this does not happen often – at least not in social sciences. Scientists use metaphors to capture complex relationships between phenomena that would otherwise be difficult to explain. The metaphors are a double-edged sword, however: when used well, they penetrate to the heart of the problem, when used sloppily, they offer only an apparent explanation (does the Freudian-derived concept of 'anal personality' really explain anything?).

Models are similar in that they provide highly simplified representations of very complex events or realities. A classic case is the world-renowned map of the London Underground – a simplification or idealization of a messy, complicated system. But the model or map we use serves its purpose. Similarly, models of teaching, education or the learning process are simplifications of reality. But – like metaphors – they help in making complex situations clearer, more intelligible and therefore better understood. Piaget's model of stages of development is one example. It is a simplification of reality, especially if taken too literally (and wrongly) as a series of discrete, concrete steps with definite ages attached to them. But it has great value in explaining conceptual progress and children's development.

Another example is the Big Five personality model: human personality can be described in terms of five, largely independent traits/dimensions: Neuroticism, Extroversion, Agreeableness, Conscientiousness and Openness to Experience. Certainly a gross oversimplification, but an aid to thinking and understanding.

Models are often presented in visual form (diagrams, flow-charts, etc.) (e.g. Bohr's model of atomic structure is invariably explained with an aid of a drawing). The preponderance of metaphors and (visually aided) models gives an interesting insight into the nature of human mind. While precision of theory is best served by formal description (ideally, in the language of mathematics) such descriptions are often hard to understand. A good image (or a metaphor) can be worth a thousand words, and aid understanding.

One final point in ending this subsection concerns the use of *labels* which have emerged in social research. For example, Shulman (1987) has identified and labelled different categories of 'teacher knowledge' which teachers draw upon in their practical teaching. These are often labelled (though Shulman's actual categorization is more refined) as 'subject knowledge' (SK) and 'pedagogical content knowledge' (PCK). The latter includes teachers' knowledge of explaining, putting things across, pedagogy, breaking down complex ideas into simpler steps, and so on. Generally, it relates to the art, craft and wisdom of teaching. Now Shulman's ideas have great application in considering initial teacher education, mentoring, professional development and other areas. But are they theories? Our own view is that they do help us to understand the above areas and underlying the labels are valuable conceptualizations or categorizations. They have some explanatory value and perhaps even predictive power. A similar discussion could be held over Schon's ideas of the 'reflective practitioner' and the 'stable state' (Schon, 1983 and 1971), Willis's notion of 'the lads'; the label 'vocationalism' (applied by many authors to the growing links between schooling and industry/employment in the 1980s); or the notion of the 'hidden curriculum'. Perhaps, in the end, it is a semantic debate over whether they are theories or not – so we will use this as an excuse to cut a very long debate short!

When Does Theory Come In: A Priori (Before) ... or A Posteriori (After)?

The key question for those engaged in, or about to embark on, social research is not *whether* theory should make its entry but *when*. One of the recent criticisms of social research is that new research is not always based on previous work, i.e. it is 'non-cumulative'. It is argued that, in turn, this has led to the failure of social research to create a sound, reliable body of knowledge which can inform practitioners and ultimately improve education (as, allegedly, medical research has done with medical practice). Whether or not these criticisms are justified is discussed later. The point here is: how can social research become 'cumulative'? Should theory be brought in prior to the research in order to guide it and make observation theory-laden, i.e. a priori? Or should theory 'emerge' from data collection and observation and be developed from it i.e. inductively, a posteriori?

On the one hand, Anderson urges that:

> in your study and prior knowledge you should attempt to identify appropriate theoretical and conceptual frameworks which bare [sic] relation to your problem.
>
> (Anderson, 1998, p. 47)

He counsels researchers to ground their research in antecedent work which has 'generated contemporary constructs guiding subsequent investigation', i.e. data collection will be theory-guided or theory-laden to use the term from science. In other words, data are collected in order to verify explicit hypotheses that are derived from the theory the researcher adopts. The cumulative nature of science is quite obvious in this approach: some theories survive (partly because they are consistent with the data), others perish, and those that survive are used to generate new hypotheses.

An apparently opposite approach is to generate theory (inductively) from the data. Theory 'emerges' as the data collection progresses and is firmly 'grounded' in it, and derived from it, i.e. a posteriori. This approach is often called 'grounded theory' (after Glaser and Strauss, 1967; for a recent, detailed critique see Thomas and James, 2006).

So the crucial questions are: should categories, patterns or theories be generated from the data, or should they be imposed upon it? How can research be 'cumulative' if it does not use previously determined categories? Do researchers have to recreate theory every time they collect and analyse data?

These are complex and important questions. But the simple answer is: it depends totally on the nature of the research, its purpose and the area being investigated. In some fields there are ample theories, sufficiently well developed that it would be wrong not to use them in shaping research design and data collection. In others, there may be a shortage of suitable theory, or it may be extremely tentative, thus implying a different approach. Similarly with the purpose of a research project – a key aim of a project may be to *replicate* previous research in order to lend support to a theory, or perhaps to attempt to refine it. In others, the aim may be to develop new, tentative theories which (perhaps) subsequent researchers might build on.

Two Contentious Terms: Validity and Reliability

These are two terms which have been widely used in discussing the quality of research, not least in social research. They also tend to be commonly abused, partly (in our view) because they are difficult to define and hard to gain an intuitive understanding of. For example, the terms are often (especially in conversation) used to signal *approval*. Thus people (in meetings, say) may comment: 'That's a valid point', meaning no more than that they agree with it. Similarly, people (including the media) may describe a piece of research as 'reliable', meaning that they approve of it and/or trust the person or team who conducted it.

The two words do have technical meanings however; we will attempt to define them and also give a loose intuitive meaning for them here.

Validity

Validity refers to the degree to which a method, a test or a research tool actually measures what it is supposed to measure. For example, in the old debate on IQ tests the main issue was whether the tests actually did measure what they claimed to measure, i.e. intelligence. Does a person's ability to do an IQ test measure their intelligence, or something else (attention, motivation, complacency, factual knowledge, etc.)?

Validity tends to be related to the notion of 'truth': a measurement is valid according to the degree to which the measuring instrument or procedure matches its label. For example, if a test allegedly measuring intelligence is ridiculously long, e.g. over 3 hours, it may in fact be measuring a person's attention span, perseverance, obedience or compliance.

There are some important points here which apply across the whole of social research.

Firstly, no method is 100 per cent valid, in the sense of measuring one, and only one variable. Performance on any task, however simple (such as pressing the button as soon as you hear the sound) is always influenced by a multitude of hidden variables. Establishing validity means identifying the main variable (or variables) which the task really measures (speed of information processing, in our example), knowing full well that other variables (motivation, anxiety, attention, etc.) also impact on performance. Establishing validity should be a matter of empirical study, not just theoretical task analysis.

Secondly, any discussion of validity rests squarely on the foundation of how the characteristic being measured is defined. If you define 'intelligence' to mean academic intelligence (verbal and problem-solving aptitudes necessary to succeed at scholastic tasks) then commonly used IQ tests are certainly highly valid. If, however 'practical intelligence' is meant as the ability to solve problems arising at work or at home (especially interpersonal problems) then the validity of the IQ tests is rather weak (Carroll, 1997; Sternberg, 1998; for further discussion see Chapter 8). In other words, any assessment of validity depends heavily on the definition or meaning of the term underlying it – and many of the terms in social sciences are extremely problematic: numeracy, literacy, racism, nationalism, empathy, and so on

In Part 3 of this book we stress and discuss the importance of validity even more. The demand of validity encapsulates all requirements put on science: a study that is (internally and externally) valid, can be said to be a good scientific study.

In practice, researchers work in a kind of 'community' – within this community they use certain criteria and practices to judge the validity of their own (and others') work. These will include: sharing, communication, inter-subjectivity and mutual control, cumulativity (mentioned earlier) and connectivity (new theories must respect established theories, laws and observations; i.e. be consistent with them). Their external manifestation is the peer-review process.

Reliability

We can take a more cheerful view of reliability. This is a judgement of the extent to which a test, a method or a tool gives consistent results across a range of settings, and if used by a range of researchers. Words associated with reliability are: repeatability, consistency, replicability; the idea of 'replicability' concerns the extent to which a piece of research can be copied or replicated in order to give the same results in a different context or with different researchers.

Le Compte and Preissle, more pessimistically, define reliability and then claim that no researcher studying the social world can achieve total reliability. They describe it as:

> the extent to which studies can be replicated. It assumes that a researcher using the same methods can obtain the same results as those of a prior study. This poses an impossible task for any researcher studying naturalistic behaviour as unique phenomena.
>
> (Le Compte and Preissle, 1984, p. 332)

We would concur with this view – but the consolation is that current philosophers and sociologists of science are increasingly sceptical about the possibility of total reliability and replicability in modern scientific research (see, for example, Collins, 1985 and Woolgar, 1988 as early examples of this scepticism).

Also, although reliability is conceptually related to replicability it is *not* the case that, in order to establish the reliability of a research procedure, a study has to be replicated. A number of procedures (e.g. inter-rater, parallel test, split-half and internal consistency reliabilities) have been developed to measure reliability without the need to replicate the study. These procedures are relatively uncontentious. Reliability is certainly not as complex and contentious as validity. Whereas validity is always multifaceted, and establishing validity (or lack thereof) can only be a result of a large-scale research programme, reliability can essentially be expressed as a single number, and some tricky conceptual issues (e.g. defining the latent trait being measured) do not arise. Reliability has been convincingly demonstrated for many methods used in psychology and education, e.g. some IQ tests (whatever they measure) are test-retest reliable over a period of 60 years.

As for total reliability, no one has ever required this – the question is: is the instrument reliable enough to answer my question? So, what constitutes 'good' reliability is relative to the problem being posed.

As for an intuitive 'feel' for reliability and validity, imagine a situation in which a group of people set out to measure the depth of an empty swimming pool with an elastic, stretchy tape measure. They do not realise that the swimming pool has a deep end and a shallow end. They each take measurements at different points along the pool believing that this is the average depth – so their measurements are invalid (they are not mea-suring what they think they are measuring). In addition, some measurers stretch the measuring tape more than others – the elasticated ruler is unreliable. The researchers are unreliable in that they cannot all be relied upon to hold the rubbery ruler at exactly the same tension (understandably).

Another way of imagining the two terms is to think of bathroom scales. They may be reliable if they consistently tell you that you are 3 kilos above your 'true weight'. They are then reliable but certainly not valid.

Achieving Quality by Locating Research in 'What's Been Done Before'

Before discussing particular methods (in Parts 2 and 3), it is worth commenting on the initial importance of finding out what is already 'known' in an area of research, what's been done before, and (just as importantly) how it's been done. This is an aspect of research which many of us, including physical scientists at times, are apt to neglect. One of the dangers of such neglect is the old cliché of reinventing the wheel.

There are many methods of finding what is already known, e.g.

- Start by reading a textbook or a review paper that gives a broad overview of the area we are interested in, and then following selected references.

- Start from a seminal or much-cited paper and go from there. Each paper will have references at the end which will lead to other references, and so on. This method can be called 'snowball searching'. The problem is that the process is rather like a chain reaction and the list of publications one 'should' read grows exponentially.
- Ask the experts in the field (e.g. one's own supervisor) for a list of key authors or references.
- Use an online search engine (e.g. Google Scholar) to research the problem.

These simple search techniques are invaluable and generally sufficient to get a broad overview of the problem. However, serious research requires more systematic bibliographic search. This became much easier with the arrival of electronic citation indexes, providing abstracts and key bibliographic details of most peer-reviewed scientific publications. Although by no means exhaustive,* they are by far the most comprehensive sources of scientific information there are. Arguably the largest citation index is Web of Science; a social scientist will also make use of ERIC (Education Resources Information Center) and PsychInfo (indexing literature in psychology and related disciplines).

The general rule is that any study should be located in the context of what has been done before. The researcher's job is not just to mould their own brick but to slot it into the wall of existing understanding in that field.

One valuable source that we would like to emphasize is 'other people'. Researchers at all levels can sometimes use people who may be experts in the field. If you cannot arrange to see them, then write, telephone or email them asking for help and advice. It is surprising how willing experts in a field are to give up time and energy to someone who is, or will be, working in the same field.

Ultimately, only the researcher can decide which references to follow up, which ones to skim or which to examine closely,

---

* Indexing of non-English language publications is very patchy, for example.

and which publications to weave into the eventual report, thesis, article or book. The process has to stop somewhere. But the lines and boundaries can only be drawn by the researcher – and the drawing of these lines has to be justified in writing up.

Reading and Judging Other People's Research

One of the difficult knacks of reviewing the literature is knowing when to stop and where to draw the boundaries. An equally difficult skill is to be able to judge – critically but fairly – the research reported by others. We tread on dangerous ground if we examine too negatively the work of others – ancient slogans about not throwing stones if we live in glass houses spring to mind. But there are certain areas, and within them certain criteria, which can be applied when critically examining research reports. We suggest ten, though there are probably more:

1. *The title*: is it descriptive, i.e. does it accurately reflect what is in the article? Is it attractive? (see Woods, 1999, p. 28: the title should be 'informative', 'accurate', 'succinct and clear', 'designed to awaken interest').

2. *The abstract*: does it tell you: why the research was done and why it's important; how it was done, with whom, with what; and what were the key findings? Does it provide a map for the reader?

3. *The literature review*: does it give an overview of the range of literature related to the research? Is it new or creative in suggesting other, alternative areas of literature which might be 'laterally applied' to this area? Does it explain where and why boundaries were drawn?

4. *Theoretical framework*: does it start from a theoretical framework which might help to inform it or structure it? Does it shed light on any existing theories or models? Does it lead (inductively) to new theories or models?

5. *The aims of the research*: is it addressing a significant problem or issue? Are its aims and purposes clear? Is it reasonably well focused?

6. *Methodology*: is it adequately described, so that the reader

could replicate the study, should they wish? Do the methods chosen match the purposes/aims? Why were these methods chosen and not others? Did they prove to be appropriate and productive?

7. *Sampling*: is the sample described in sufficient detail? On what grounds was the sample chosen, e.g. why these schools/colleges; why these classes, why these documents or reports?

8. *Data analysis*: is the way of analysing the data appropriate for the problem? Is it described in sufficient detail?

9. *Evaluation, self-evaluation and reflexivity*: is the research evaluated, both for 'content' and method/methodology, i.e. is it a *reflective* account? Do the researchers evaluate their own role, their own position, and their effects on what is being researched, i.e. are positionality and reflexivity included?

10. *Drawing out conclusions and implications*: have the data been 'milked' for all they are worth? Are the conclusions related back to the literature review – are the two woven together? Do the researchers stick their necks out too far ... or not far enough?

11. *Presentation*: is it clearly written and well structured? Is it turgid and verbose? Could Ockham's Razor have been applied in places? Does it have at least some storyline?

These points together make a hard act to live up to – we do realize that they are counselling perfection and that they do not all apply to every piece of published research. But they can be a useful checklist in examining and reading research in a critical way. The requirement to be 'critical' and reflective is part of the researcher's responsibility, which we turn to in Chapter 4.

Further Reading

For a recent critique of grounded theory see: Thomas, G. and James, D. (2006) 'Re-inventing grounded theory: some questions about theory, ground and discovery'. *British Educational Research Journal* 32(6), 767–95.

For a more radical critique of theory itself see: Carr, W. (2006) 'Education without theory'. *British Journal of Educational Studies* 54(2), 136–59.

See also Clarke, A. (2005) *Situational Analysis: Grounded Theory after the Post-Modern Turn* London: Sage.

4 The Researcher's Role and Responsibility

The Researcher and the Researched

In social research the researcher himself, or herself, is the key 'instrument'. This is now generally accepted, even if it was contested in the earlier history of social research. Even in the biological and physical sciences it is now more widely accepted that the researcher plays a key role. Thus, Medawar (1963) talked of the 'myth of objectivity' in the sciences. Polanyi (1967) talked of the importance of 'mutual control' among scientists in regulating their work, i.e. inter-subjectivity rather than objectivity. The physicist Heisenberg had, 40 years earlier, developed his Uncertainty Principle, which stated (roughly) that we cannot determine the exact position *and* momentum of a particle. This, effectively, brought to an end a belief in a perfectly predictable universe and subsequent developments such as Chaos Theory put further nails in the coffin (Gleick, 1988). At the atomic or subatomic level the measuring instrument seriously affects or disturbs what is being measured. The Researcher affects the Researched. A similar rule applies in social research; a rule we might call the 'Social Uncertainty Principle': the researcher influences, disturbs and affects what is being researched in the social world, just as the physicist does in the physical universe.

Minimizing the Researcher Effect?

One option might be to ignore this effect or perhaps to attempt to diminish it. The latter has been done in examples of 'covert research' from the field of sociology. Hockey (1991), for example, in his research on 'squaddies', spent a lengthy period with young soldiers in training camps and on the streets of

Northern Ireland. He was able to pass as one of them due to his previous experience as a soldier. Similarly, Holdaway (1985) spent four years 'inside' the police force, and researched their practices while working as a policeman. Fielding (1981) took an even more risky role as a member of the National Front while carrying out research into the behaviour of its members.

These are all examples of covert research. In a later section, we consider whether covert research of this kind can be ethical.

Less extreme and less deceptive strategies have been adopted by researchers who attempt to become accepted by a group, but who do not deceive them totally. This has been done by dressing in a similar manner or behaving in a similar way to the group in order to gain acceptance and establish a rapport. Such an approach might be part of a research tradition known as ethnography, derived to a large extent from anthropology (roughly speaking, the in-depth study of a society, group, tribe or organization which involves getting 'inside them': for examples, see Woods 1985, 1986, 1993).

Reflecting on the Researcher Effect: Reflexivity and Reflectivity

An alternative is to acknowledge the effect of the researcher and accept the impossibility of a completely neutral stance. Reflecting on this bias is part of the business of *reflexivity*. Being 'reflexive' is part of a more general approach to research – being 'reflective'. The former is a subset of the latter.

Being reflective involves thinking critically about the research process; how it was done and why, and how it could have been improved. Reflection is an important part at every stage, i.e. in formulating questions, deciding on methods, thinking about sampling, deciding on presentation and so on. Most writers on research (at least in the social sciences) would agree on its importance and many would argue that these reflections and evaluations should be put into print in reporting the research and going public (see, for example, Greenbank, 2003 and Carr, 2000 on the necessity of 'partisanship').

But an important part, or subset, of reflectivity is the notion of reflexivity. This involves reflecting on the self, the researcher, and the person who did it, the me or the I. The 'x' in the word reflexivity denotes the self, the person who did the research, the subject. In Hammersley and Atkinson's terms (1983, p. 234), reflexivity requires 'explicit recognition of the fact that the social researcher, and the research act itself, are part and parcel of the social world under investigation'. Another author (Bonnett, 1993, p. 165) has referred to it as 'auto-critique'. Thus being reflective is an important part of being reflective, but they are not the same thing.

The extent to which reflexive accounts should be included in writing up and publishing research is open to debate. Thus Hammersley and Atkinson argue that it 'is no good being reflexive in the course of planning and executing a piece of research if one is only to abandon that reflexivity when it comes to writing about it' (1983, p. 209).

But how much of this 'auto–critique' or self-analysis should social researchers engage in ... or indulge in? Troyna (1994) was highly sceptical of the 'confessional tone' of many research biographies, which have become almost obligatory in some areas of social research. He accused some authors of suffering from 'delusions of grandeur'. More seriously, he argued that excessive use of reflexivity or research biography could diminish the status of qualitative research in the eyes of its critics in populist circles such as the newspapers and other media.

Our own view is that reflectivity and the more specific reflexivity are vital (but different) parts of the research process and should not be confused. Reflection is part of evaluation and forms an important component of any rational enquiry, including empirical research. Being reflexive is equally important but does not merit an excessively long, confessional, autobiographic account which includes unnecessary details. A statement of the researcher's position (positionality, as it is often called) can be brief and should include *relevant* information only. Personal information such as gender or age may be important for readers of the research, but other details (such as shoe size, to take a silly example) are not. To take a more realistic example of a personal characteristic that is relevant in some contexts but not in others: a researcher's own religious beliefs and affiliations would be of vital importance in ethnographic studies of new religious movements, but may not be relevant in studying children's educational achievement.

Questioning and Exploring Positions

One of the roles of any social researcher is to examine and question the positions or assumptions which are often taken for granted:

1. The first task, as discussed above, is to question any assumptions about yourself: your own values, ideas, knowledge, motivation and prejudices. For example, what's my own position in relation to this research? What are my relevant past experiences and prior knowledge? Am I carrying a bias, a prejudice, or insider information which will affect my role as researcher?

2. The second task is to examine the assumptions taken for granted by institutions, such as schools, colleges or employers. (For example, national curricula in many countries carry tacit assumptions that all children should acquire prescribed knowledge or skills at approximately the same time; another occurs when employers may assume that quality of work is a simple concept that can be measured easily using one or two performance indices.) What are their subcultures and underlying values? Does the rhetoric of their public documents or mission statements, e.g. in a brochure or prospectus, match the hidden values, ideas, ethos and assumptions? An outsider may sometimes be better placed to question and examine these than an insider. Similarly, the assumptions and tacit ideas or values in one institution can often be exposed and challenged by comparing it with another.

3. Finally, the researcher's role is to examine and question the *language* used in discussing their field. This might be the *spoken* language of practitioners or policy-makers during interviews (or in ethnography, overheard conversations); or it might be the *written* language of documents such as White Papers, prospectuses, mission statements, legislation or minutes of meetings. Both the style or tone and the actual words need to be questioned.

In summary, the role of the researcher is often said to be to 'make the familiar strange'. It needs to be noted, however, that the postulate of questioning tacit assumptions is sometimes construed as an obligation to *reject* those assumptions. This is a misunderstanding. A researcher may question a certain assumption implicit in the field (e.g. 'there must be one best method of teaching children to read') and reach the conclusion that this assumption is essentially true (e.g. 'phonics is such a method': e.g. Chall, 1967).

Another way in which the role of the researcher may be minimized lies in maximizing the role of inter-subjectivity in the research process. A variety of specific methods can be used. For example, the way in which certain observations or statements are classified can be verified using the consensus method (often referred to under the technical name of 'expert judges' procedure'). In certain contexts, participants themselves may contribute to the analysis and interpretation of results, correcting researchers' biases (an approach adopted extensively in the *life story* method of narrative analysis (Atkinson, 1998)).

The ultimate 'checks and balances' of researchers' subjectivity are also provided by the peer-review process (see later in the book). Although certainly inter-subjective rather than objective, the peer-review process is more systematic and rigorous than most forms of public scrutiny. This makes scientific debates a rather special form of public discourse – many would say a unique and privileged one (Stanovich, 2000).

The Researcher's Role in Planning and Designing Research

The Process of Social Research

The starting point for a research project may be a question, or questions, that the researcher would like to address. It may be an idea or a hypothesis to be tested. A slightly less focused start might be an issue to be explored or, more ambitiously, a problem to be solved.

The research problem (synonymous with aim or question) identifies what the researcher does not know, and is interested in studying. It may be presented in the interrogative (question) form (e.g. 'what is the effect of wealth on happiness?'). A *hypothesis*, on the other hand, is the *answer* to the research question, which a researcher believes to be true before he analyses his data. It must be stated in the affirmative form (e.g. 'Happiness increases in line with wealth').

While it is possible (at least in principle) to carry out research without having specific hypotheses in mind, there can be no research without an underlying purpose, problem or question.

Stating or formulating your purposes under one (or perhaps more) of these categories can help at all stages of a research enquiry, especially at the outset, i.e:

- What question(s) are you asking/addressing?
- What hypothesis are you testing?
- What problem(s) are you trying to solve/alleviate?

If you can formulate the questions you wish to ask, it then helps to decide whether they are:

- 'what, which or where' questions;
- 'how' questions; or
- 'why' questions.

'What, which or where' questions often involve descriptive research, sometimes a fairly straightforward collection of information. For example, what computer programs are most commonly used in Year 6 of primary education? Which children in a certain school have parents who participate in the daily reading scheme? Where are the multimedia stations in secondary schools located? In developmental psychology we might explore the 'ages and stages' of development of children (e.g. average age when crawling and walking start); in economics, the distribution of income in the UK population; in sociology, the distribution of religious affiliations in the UK. These kinds of question might form the aim of a research project, i.e. simply finding out the names, numbers or extent of something; or they might lead on to more exploratory or explanatory research, i.e. finding out how a scheme or programme is working or is being used, or why teachers/parents/ students behave in certain ways or use certain methods/ resources more than others.

The 'why and how' questions (i.e. exploratory and explanatory) are usually the more interesting but invariably the most complex and intractable. A search for 'how' certainly implies a 'hunt' for some sort of mechanism; the search for 'why' implies looking for a reason. Both seem to be searches for different types of causal explanations. Finding causal explanations (cause-effect relationships) can be acknowledged as the very core of science, part of any process really worthy of the label of 'science'. Though, naturally, there are complications. We may have to acknowledge a chasm between *explaining* (neutral, 3rd-person, nomothetic accounts of cause and effect) and *understanding* (1st-person, ideographic accounts).

Framing research questions should always be the first step in the research process. It should always be a case of questions first, methods later. For example, it makes no sense to decide: 'I am going to use questionnaires/interviews/observations' before clarifying the questions which you wish to address or shed light upon. As discussed earlier, they may be what, which, where, how or why questions. The former may imply a straightforward collection of information, perhaps a survey approach. But the latter, i.e. the how and why questions which seek *explanations* will demand more in-depth exploratory approaches.

Difficult Decisions for the Researcher

Another way of portraying what really happens in social research is shown in Figure 4.1. This shows the difficult decisions that have to be made in real research. They cannot always be made in the ideal order. For example, we may plan to interview a certain sample of people, e.g. politicians, employers, students, only to find that we cannot gain access to them, e.g. they are unwilling, too busy, too sensitive or just fed up with 'being researched'. This may, in turn, force us back to reconsider our methods and even our original research questions. All the decisions are intertwined and connected by arrows going both ways. Even constraints on the way the research must be presented, e.g. in the form of a report, book or thesis which is written *and* in the public domain, can impinge upon decisions about who to involve in the research and which methods to use.

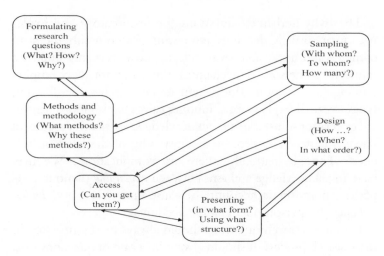

Figure 4.1 Difficult and Interconnected Decisions in Social Research

Figure 4.1 is an attempt to represent the difficult and inter-connected decisions which go into the *actual* design of a social research project, as opposed to the idealized version we showed in Chapter 2.

In summary, social research is a messy business and it would be wrong to pretend otherwise in a report, article, thesis or a book. One of the most common activities in real research is compromise. We compromise over time spent, distance tra-velled, methods used, samples chosen, literature reviewed, words written and money spent.

Ethics: The Researcher's Responsibilities

Ethics in Social Research

Ethics are important in the physical sciences (which investigate inanimate objects); but they figure even more prominently in the biological sciences where plants and animals are the objects of study. This factor is multiplied in social research, where people are studying people.

Morals underpin ethics, but the two terms are not quite synonymous. Morality and morals are to do with our beliefs about what is right and wrong, while ethics can be defined as a systematic reflection on morality, an attempt to clarify and codify what is right and what is wrong. Ethics are *postulates* regarding what people *ought* to do. An ethic is concerned with the way people act or behave. The term 'ethics' usually refers to the moral principles or guidelines for conduct, which are held by a group or even a profession (though there is no logical reason why individuals should not have their own ethical code). Our own view is that the main criterion for social research is that it should be ethical. Hence it is worth not only devoting some space to it here but, more importantly, for every researcher to place it foremost in the planning, conduct and presentation of his/her research. Ethical considerations override all others.

A social research project could be unethical in four aspects:

1. The *design* or *planning* of the research.
    Example: Testing hypotheses about cause and effect requires experimental design: the random assignment of participants to groups which are then treated differently. There is nothing unethical about such design per se. Indeed, such *randomized controlled trials* are the only way to directly investigate potential benefits of new treatments (e.g. new drugs or teaching methods). However, the design that deprives some participants of goods they would normally enjoy (standard medical care, recreation time, privacy) or, worse still, *exposes them to some known risks*, is likely to be unethical.

2. The *methods* and *procedures* employed.
    Examples: Failure to obtain informed consent from participants is nearly always unethical; so is deception or manipulation to gain access (e.g. requesting a 10-minute interview that lasts half an hour). Lack of respect and putting participants in situations that are likely to make them feel inadequate are other examples. Although some argue that, in certain research contexts, failure to obtain consent, deception and even harsh treatment are ethically justified, such situations are rare indeed (see below).

3. The *analysis* of the data.
    Examples: Needless to say, fabricating data is unethical, but so is ignoring or 'filtering out' results that do not 'fit'

the researcher's cherished hypothesis. A very common transgression is adopting the method of data analysis that 'glosses over' unwanted or cumbersome complexities and limitations of the data (e.g. a decision not to control for a known confounding variable).

4. The *presentation* or reporting of the research.
   Examples: Revealing personal information about participants without their consent, or describing them using derogatory or biased language. Presenting conclusions that are inconsistent with the results, or go beyond the results (i.e. presenting hypotheses as facts). Last but not least, a decision *not to publish* a piece of research because its results were inconsistent with the researcher's cherished hypothesis is a frequently overlooked ethical transgression (resulting in so called *file-drawer problem*).

Thus social research might be unethical in its design, its methods, its data analysis or its presentation. Incidentally, research in the sciences could equally well be unethical in any of these areas, despite the myth that it is value-free.

Ethical Dilemmas

Research ethics resembles research methodology in that their core postulates are clear and easy to grasp, but their applications are complex and fraught with dilemmas and uncertainties. The researchers often disagree as to what constitutes the best method of studying a different problem, equally often they disagree with respect to ethics. What conduct is *likely* to be unethical is rather uncontroversial (see Table 4.1), but is it *always* so? Obtaining informed consent is a sound postulate, but is it really necessary when carrying out observational research in public places? Deceiving participants as to the researcher's identity and intentions is generally wrong, but may be it is justified in some cases (e.g. studying extremist political movements)? Harsh, degrading or humiliating treatment is generally wrong, but maybe it is justified when the participants are debriefed following their experience, and are likely to gain valuable insights into their own functioning – and the findings are of considerable value to society?

Table 4.1 Ethically Problematic Research Situations

1. Research without participants' prior knowledge, permission and informed consent. Participants are unaware of what they are letting themselves in for and where the findings might be published.
2. Asking people to do anything unsafe, or forcing them to do something.
3. Withholding relevant information about the nature and purpose of the research.
4. Deceiving the participants.
5. Invading participants' privacy or taking too much of their time.
6. Withholding benefits from some participants (e.g. in a control group), or imposing disadvantages upon others (e.g. in a control or experimental group).
7. Lack of consideration, respect and honesty.
8. Breaching confidentiality and anonymity, especially in publication.

In resolving these dilemmas, individual researchers should not trust their own ethical intuitions too much. After all, their perception is likely to be biased by their interest in developing their own research (and careers). Inter-subjectivity (in the form of open debate with colleagues, as well as written professional codes of conduct), is necessary.

Responsibilities and Codes of Conduct

Responsibilities in social research could fall into several areas: responsibilities to the participants, to a profession being studied, to the research community and (in funded research) to the sponsoring body or council. This range of responsibilities, especially in funded research, which may be driven and pressurized by an outside body, may sometimes be difficult to reconcile and balance. Our own view is that there is no room for 'moral relativism' in doing social research, i.e. there are certain rules which should not be broken. The area of ethics (unlike, in the views of some, methodology) can never be a domain where 'anything goes' (Feyeraband, 1993). For this reason we have put forward our own set of guidelines in Table 4.2 which we feel should be adhered to.

To design a study ethically, you must consider it from the point of view of your participants. It helps to ask: 'Would I like

Table 4.2 Principles to Follow in Ethical Research

Conscientiousness

- The interests of research participants (their emotional, personal, psychological and physical wellbeing) should be safeguarded. No research project should be undertaken which may cause harm to a participant or his/her family.
- Research should not affect or interfere with any other treatment that the participant would otherwise receive.
- Participants should not be referred to in derogatory or stigmatizing ways (e.g. using 'people/children with autism' rather than 'autistics').
- When describing participants, make sure that your description is carefully researched and properly referenced in a professional, responsible way. It should not be based on casual or anecdotal information.
- Be scrupulous in your dealings with research participants – be polite, organized and reasonable in your demands.

Consent

- Participants (or authorized relatives/carers) should give written, informed consent prior to taking part in the project. This means that they should be made aware (usually by way of an information sheet) of the requirements of their participation in layman's terms (what exactly will happen and how long it will take) and have the chance to ask questions.
- In the case of research in schools, both teachers' and parents/guardians' consents are usually obtained.

Confidentiality

- Confidentiality and anonymity of participants, their families, and any data collected must be maintained at all times.

Coercion

- Participants must be recruited in a way that does not subject them to any pressure to participate.
- Participants need to be explicitly informed at the onset of the study that they have the right to withdraw at any point. Participants who withdraw from studies should not be made to feel as though they have disappointed the researcher or upset his/her study in any way.

this to be done to me?' or 'How would I feel if this was done to me?' All that is said above can be derived from the core ethical imperative: 'I must never treat a person merely as a means to some other end'.

It is also worth remembering that unethical research is likely to be illegal as well. For example, serious breaches of confidentiality are an offence under the Data Protection Act.

Ethics Review Committees

In recent years, most professional bodies and all universities formalized the process of ethical consideration by requesting that all research involving human participants is approved by a formal ethics committee. Researchers often bemoan the excessive paperwork involved in this process – but no one should criticize being requested to reflect on the ethics of his or her work. It is now almost certain that anyone carrying out social research within an organization (private or public) will be subject to detailed ethical review procedures, laid down and monitored by an ethics review committee. This process will involve the researcher going through a rigorous set of questions, likely to include:

- What procedures, methods, measurements and tools will be used?
- What amount of time will be required for participants in the study?
- What methods will be used for obtaining informed written consent?
- How will participants' anonymity and confidentiality be protected?
- How will participants be fully informed about the study including that they may withdraw from it at any time?
- Where will data be stored and how will results be published?
- Are there any possible physical or psychological risks and how will these be addressed?

The Researcher's Role in Sampling: An Issue of Choice and Compromise for the Researcher

Samples and Populations

A *sample* is a small part of anything which is intended to stand for, or represent, the whole. Thus we can smell a sample of perfume, drink a sample from a glass of wine or sample a small piece of fudge before we buy the whole bar. In each case, we are not interested in the sample per se, but in the whole thing. We use samples because we believe that they represent the whole thing – that is, the *population*, as it is formally called. In social sciences, a population usually means a set of people, but it need not be so – a set of behaviours (e.g. all murders committed in the UK in 2005) or cultural artefacts (e.g. all documents written on a certain topic, all words of the English language) can also constitute a population.

Sampling inevitably poses a challenge: can I be reasonably sure that my sample is representative of the population? These questions cannot be answered unless a more basic one is answered first: what is my population? If my 'population' is a single bottle of wine then it is safe to assume that a single sip represents it well. However, we could not safely extrapolate that that sip represents the entire vintage (*all* bottles of wine from the same producer and same year). The same applies to social research: when we choose a sample (which we must), e.g. a class of Year 8 children, then we can (perhaps) treat it as representative of every Year 8 pupil in that school. It would be problematic, however, to assume it represents all Year 8 pupils in that city, or in the UK, and preposterous to claim it represents every pupil of that age band in Europe, or the northern hemisphere, or the world.

The first challenge of good sampling, then, is to decide what my population of interest is. Only then can the next two questions about sampling be answered adequately: how should I select my sample, and how large does it need to be?

Probability and Non-Probability Sampling

Probability sampling includes various types of drawing by chance. The main types of probability sampling are listed in Table 4.3.

Probability sampling is most suited for larger populations and for studies where the researcher is interested in the *typical* trends and patterns occurring in those populations (and not in the *exceptions* to those patterns). Probability sampling is used most often in the context of quantitative research. The main

Table 4.3 Some Types of Probability Sampling

- *Simple random sampling.* A prespecified number of individuals is selected at random from the target population. Each individual from that population has an equal chance of being included. Simple random sampling is most appropriate for relatively small and homogeneous populations. It requires using tables of random numbers, random number generators – or tossing a coin!
- *Systematic sampling.* Participants are selected at fixed 'intervals' (e.g. every seventh or every twentieth person). This is a methodologically less ideal but simpler variant of simple random sampling.
- *Stratified sampling* involves dividing the whole population into relatively homogeneous subpopulations (strata), which are then sampled randomly. The size of the random is usually chosen to reflect the proportion of each stratum in the total population. For example, a household expenditure survey may stratify the whole UK population into high, medium and low socio-economic status strata, and then select a sample of 1,000, 4,000 and 5,000 participants from each stratum, respectively, to the fact that high, medium and low socio-economic status people represent 10 per cent, 40 per cent and 50 per cent of UK society, respectively.* Stratified sampling is most appropriate for large-scale studies of highly heterogeneous populations.
- *Cluster sampling* is appropriate whenever the population can be divided into 'natural' groups (clusters), and each cluster can be seen as a scaled-down version of the whole population (e.g. a town being divided into individual households). A researcher would first randomly select a subset of clusters and then investigate all participants within that cluster (e.g. randomly select 10 per cent of households in a town and then interview each person within those households). Cluster sampling massively reduces the effort necessary to access participants (especially the travel time).
- *Stage sampling.* An extension of cluster sampling appropriate when the target population has a multi-level ('nested') structure (e.g. students, who are 'nested' within classes which are nested within schools which are nested within counties, etc.). A researcher would carry out a random sampling at each level, gradually 'zooming in' on the final sample. For example, sampling participants for an educational study may involve a random selection of a few counties, then a few schools within each of those counties, then a few classes within each of those schools and then, finally, some students within each of those classes.

---

* These proportions are fictitious. For information on true socio-economic structure of the British society, see Rose and Pevalin (2005) and Hall (2006).

advantage of random sampling lies in the fact that the probability of a sample being *unrepresentative* of the population can be
calculated precisely using statistical techniques, and taken into
account when interpreting the results. All so-called statistical
tests of significance (Chapter 7) assume probability sampling. If
they are used with non-probability samples, the validity of their
results cannot be assumed. Non-probability sampling includes
methods of participant selection that do not rely on chance
draw, but on researcher's judgement. Its main types are listed in
Table 4.4.

Table 4.4 Some Types of Non-Probability 'Purposive' Sampling

- Convenience: Accessible, easy-to-contact, well-known (to the
  researcher) people or settings are selected.
- Opportunistic: Selecting people or settings that present themselves
  during fieldwork.
- Typical: Selecting people or setting that the researcher believes to be
  most typical for the target population.
- Maximum variation: Deliberately selecting people or settings that
  represent the greatest differences or extremes in the target population.
- Atypical: Cases clearly outside the norm are chosen deliberately, e.g.
  exceptional events or people.
- Criterion: A more generic label for samples chosen according to
  predetermined criteria.
- Snowball: One case suggests another who suggests another (also called
  'ancestry' or 'recommendation' sampling).
- Critical: Choosing special cases, e.g. those with a reputation for 'good
  practice' in a certain field.
- Guided (directed): An informant, a knowledgeable guide or an
  'expert' in a field suggests particular settings, and may even help with
  access.

Non-probability sampling is generally associated with qualitative research methods. It is most valuable in studying cases
that are exceptional in the population of interest. Non-
probability sampling techniques are often inevitable in studying
very small, or very hard to access populations (e.g. people
suffering from a rare disorder, or prisoners).

It should be pointed out that probability and non-probability
sampling   may   sometimes   be   combined,   e.g.   a   group,

organization or other unit may be selected for its convenience or its special features and then random samples may be taken within it.

Sampling always involves a *compromise* between the desire to make the sample representative and the practical constraints of time, money and access opportunities. Making such compromises is an inevitable (if frustrating) part of being a social science researcher. Social research is always the art of the practical or the 'art of the possible' (Medawar, 1979). For example, a PhD student interested in surveying educational achievement of teenagers with Down syndrome may initially hope to carry out a nationwide study involving stage sampling of 1,000 participants, only to discover that a combination of convenience and opportunistic method is the only realistic option, and the sample can be no larger than 150 if the study is to be finished before funding runs out. And even if a sample is large and well selected, it is still not fully representative of the whole population. This is equally true of probabilistic and non-probabilistic sampling.

The key responsibility for the researcher is to describe, clearly and candidly, all relevant characteristics of the samples studied, including all limitations of the sampling process the researcher is aware of. Transparency is the key. Sadly, this basic methodological responsibility or requirement is often not met. A large proportion of published research output is useless for future generations of researchers and practitioners (e.g. policymakers) because of inadequate description of sampling, which makes it impossible to establish in what contexts (if any) the findings apply.

The Researcher's Role in Gaining Access

The Problem of Access

Whatever plans we might make in social research, they are almost certain to be compromised – or in some cases completely scuppered – by the problem of gaining access to what we want. This might involve access to people, to places, to organizations or to documents. Let's start with some extreme examples: in the UK many of us would like to interview the

Prime Minister and a range of his minions in various departments; some researchers might like to interview a range of
'captains of industry' to ascertain their views on current topics;
one might like to interview a range of convicted criminals in
high-security prisons to probe their social backgrounds;
someone might even wish to interview or observe the President
of the United States.

In every one of these extreme cases, access is likely to be
impossible and would therefore force the unrealistic researcher
to return to their drawing-board. But there are far less fantastic
examples where access may well be a problem: for example,
interviewing all the pupils who have been excluded from a
given school in, say, the last three years; interviewing all the
head teachers from a cluster of schools; observing the lectures,
or the lessons, of every lecturer, or teacher, in a given
department; interviewing a random sample of parents and/or
observing them in their own home.

In all conceivable cases, unrestricted access and a 100 per cent
success rate are likely to be difficult if not impossible to achieve,
often for purely practical reasons (and sometimes for ethical or
safety reasons). The business of access can therefore seriously
affect the design, planning, sampling and carrying out of social
research. Social research is always the art of the practical or the
'art of the possible' (Medawar, 1979). But we have to do
something, and a compromise is always involved. This is why
opportunistic or convenience sampling feature so commonly in
social research.

Guidelines in Gaining Access

Access is difficult; it requires time, effort and perseverance. But
there are certain guidelines which can be followed in
improving it. These may help to avoid upsetting people and
falling foul of any of the ethical issues discussed already.

1. First, remember that a researcher may be viewed in a
   selection of different ways:
   As an academic whose feet are 'off the ground', as a
   suspicious stranger, as a knight to the rescue, as a friend
   or confidante, as a trusted colleague, as an expert, or as a

puppet or instrument of the funding body, principal or the managing director. Attitudes towards the researcher are likely to vary from suspicion, mistrust or cynicism, to awe, trust or friendship. It is to be hoped that any negative viewpoints and attitudes at the outset would give way to positive attitudes and dispositions towards the end of the research.

2. Secondly, the important first task is to establish individual contacts who can act as a link, i.e. names with direct phone numbers or email addresses. These 'contact points' will help with the next task which is to ascertain which people, or 'gatekeepers', and channels need to be gone through in order to gain permission and consent. This involves understanding the structure and hierarchies in an organization. Insider knowledge needs to be tapped in order to follow the correct protocol and to not leave anyone out (especially those who might take offence).

3. This links to the next task which is to make clear to all concerned the extent of the study, the demands it will make, the reasons for doing it and the likely forms of publication. This will involve telling people exactly what will be expected of them (e.g. a 30-minute interview, being a member of a focus group, and filling in a two-page questionnaire) and telling them what you plan to do with it. This applies to informants of any age or status.

4. Fourthly, the researcher needs to become aware, as early as possible, of any sensitive or controversial issues which might arise – for an individual or for an organization. As mentioned in the first point, subjects of research may feel threatened or intimidated by a newcomer, a researcher, or even by an insider adopting the role of researcher.

These are just a few of the points needing consideration in gaining access. They are partly a matter of common sense and a good general approach is to establish yourself as a credible person doing a 'worthy project' (Woods, 1986, p. 23). Dress and behaviour will also be important in gaining access. No less important is the problem of establishing rapport and credibility in interviewing.

A final concern in gaining access is to establish contact with a key informant, i.e. someone who can provide the information required either to maintain a sampling strategy or to allow the development of theoretical sampling.

The important general point is that it would be foolish to pretend that a project could be designed and planned, or sampling established, before access had actually been arranged; hence the portrayal of 'messy decisions' shown earlier (Figure 4.1) and the unrealistic idea that a research project proceeds along a straightforward linear pathway.

In Summary: Metaphors for the Researcher

A researcher has a wide range of roles and responsibilities in conducting social research. The main responsibilities, perhaps, are to conduct the research ethically and reflectively. This involves researchers in pondering upon their role in conducting research. Various metaphors for the researcher can be, and have been, put forward. Researchers might see themselves as: an active participant; an observer from a distance; a market researcher; a 'rambler' through an unknown terrain; a detective; a hunter–gatherer; an experimentalist; a gardener; an under-cover police officer; or an investigative journalist.

In carrying out an enquiry, a researcher may play a role which relates to one, or more, of these metaphors. It is worth stressing that the way researchers see themselves may be totally different to the way they are perceived by other people involved in the research (especially when children are involved!). Whatever the researcher's self-perception or image in the eyes of the participants, he or she must be aware of, and be able to reflect upon, the key roles and responsibilities which we have outlined in this chapter.

Further Reading

One of the best introductions to the ideas behind chaos theory is still Gleick, J. (1988) *Chaos: Making a New Science*. London: Heinemann.
Greenbank, P. (2003) 'The role of values in educational research: the case for reflexivity'. *British Educational Research Journal* 29(6), 791–801.

You can obtain further information on ethical standards of conducting research from relevant bodies such as:

- British Psychological Society (BPS): www.bps.org.uk. Select Practitioners, then Ethics, Rules, Charter, Code of Conduct, then The Society Code of Conduct – Ethical Principles for Conducting Research with Human Participants.
- The Department of Health (DoH): www.dh.gov.uk/Home/fs/en. Select Research and Development and then Research Governance or COREC.
- The Medical Research Council (MRC): www.mrc.ac.uk. Select Ethics & Research Governance.
- The British Educational Research Association: http://www.bera.ac.uk/publications/guides.php.

Vignette Three: Ethical Dilemmas of Social Science Research

In most cases it is fairly straightforward to decide whether an experiment or a research study is ethical or not: for example, if the participants were deceived or were forced into being involved. But in some cases there may be disagreement between two sets of opinions or two groups. One example, is the conflict between those who believe that any tests involving animals are morally wrong, compared with the 'pro-testers', who argue that testing certain products e.g. life-saving drugs, with animals is morally justified if sick people can be saved or the 'human condition' in general is made better as a result of using animals in research. In social research, it can be argued that studies in which it is impossible or undesirable to gain participants' consent, e.g. observing people in public places such as parks, streets or sports matches, can still be ethical.

One classic experiment is described below – could this be defended in any way?

The Case of Stanley Milgram's Obedience Experiment

How much pain will one person inflict upon another, simply to be obedient to someone in authority (in this case, the scientist in the white coat)?

This was the question posed by Stanley Milgram, who decided to conduct an experiment as part of his PhD at Yale University in 1961. The time context was the aftermath of the Holocaust and the trial of Adolf Eichmann for his part in the Nazi war crimes of the Second World War. Were Eichmann and his numerous Nazi collaborators in the Holocaust crimes just following orders and therefore not really 'accomplices'?

In the initial study Milgram (1963) advertised for individuals to help in an experiment on memory and learning, for the sum of $4.50 per hour. They arrived and met the experimenter in a white coat, who told them that they would be participating in a study on the role of punishment in learning – some would be teachers and some learners. They were then tricked into believing a genuine lot was drawn to decide who would be a learner and who a teacher. In reality, all the paid participants became teachers – the 'learners' were in fact all actors.

Next, the 'learner' was taken to a room and strapped to a chair, with an electrode in their arm. The teacher was told of this and put in an adjoining room, sitting next to the white-coated experimenter. The teacher was instructed to read a list of two word pairs and ask the 'learner' to read them back. If correct, the learner moved to the next pair – if incorrect, the teacher used a special machine to give the learner an electric shock, starting at 15 volts.

With each wrong answer the shock was increased by 15 volts. The teacher was told this and that the maximum shock available was 450 volts. So the teacher believed that he or she is administering a shock – in reality, the actor next door was never harmed in any way. The teacher heard an ascending range of prerecorded sounds, rising as high as screams of pain, each time a shock was given. After a number of increases, the actor banged on the wall and pretended to complain.

Many of the 'teachers' objected when they reached 135 volts; at this level they began to ask about the purpose of the experiment. The experimenter asked them to continue, at different levels of assertiveness, the highest being 'you have no choice, you must continue'.

Before the trials, Milgram asked his psychologist peers for their prediction. They all believed that only very few (around 1 per cent) teacher-volunteers, who happened to be sadists, would give the highest, 450 voltage.

In fact, in the first trial, as many as 27 out of 40 'teachers' (67 per cent) gave the highest shock, even though they were very uncomfortable in doing this. Everyone did pause and question what they were doing, but no one flatly refused to stop before the 300 volt level. Males were just as obedient as females, although the women 'teachers' were said to be more nervous.

Subsequently, Milgram carried out several versions of his experiment, later described in a book (Milgram, 1974a; see also Milgram, 1974b). It was also replicated several times by other researchers across the world, with roughly similar results (Blass, 1999).

The findings are no doubt amazing and overturned conventional wisdom that only the most sadistic monsters among us would inflict such cruelty in order to be obedient. It is clear that they gave us a powerful insight into the mechanisms of authority-sanctioned violence, from the Holocaust to Abu-Ghraib prison. Yet it is equally clear that the study poses an ethical conundrum. Today, it would almost certainly not receive approval from a research ethics committee (there were few such committees in Milgram's days). Yet many would argue that it should. How can we decide? And who is to decide?

We list but a few more specific ethical questions that can be asked here:

- It is clear that the participants suffered during the study. Were they actually harmed by the study?

Milgram argued the opposite was, in fact, the case. Following the study, he debriefed his participants about its nature and purpose. When he surveyed them some time later, 92 per cent responded, of which 84 per cent stated that they were 'glad' or 'very glad' to have participated, and 15 per cent were neutral. In at least one case, the participation turned out to be a life-changing experience, contributing to a decision to become a conscientious objector during the Vietnam War (Wikipedia, 2007).

Others, however, argued that Milgram's debriefing was not thorough enough, and many participants failed to grasp the true meaning of the experiment.

Thus, the general question remains: Under what circumstances (if any) can certain distress be justified by uncertain hope of personal insight or development?

- What are the ethical limits of deception? Most would agree that some deceiving of participants is justifiable, providing no methodological alternative exists and a full debriefing is offered following the study. But how far can this deception go?
- Could the importance of the findings outweigh our (moral or emotional) qualms about the conduct? In other words, when, if ever, do the ends justify the means?
- Could studies such as Milgram's be justified according to the principles of utilitarian ethics (Bentham and Mill), i.e. they eventually lead to the greatest happiness of the greatest number?
- Who should have the authority to decide on all this? The researcher? But, naturally, he or she has a vested interest in the project going ahead, and so may not be objective. Ethics committees? But they may be too conservative, as they defend not only ethical principles, but legal interests of the institutions they represent.

References and Further Sources.

Blass, T. (1999) 'The Milgram paradigm after 35 years: some things we now know about obedience to authority'. *Journal of Applied Social Psychology* 25, 955–78.

Milgram, S. (1963) 'Behavioral study of obedience'. *Journal of Abnormal and Social Psychology* 67, 371–8. Reproduced at *http:// www.radford. edu/~jaspelme/gradsoc/obedience/Migram_Obedience.pdf* (retrieved 29 January, 2007)

Milgram, S. (1974a) *Obedience to Authority; An Experimental View.* London: HarperCollins.

Milgram, S. (1974b) 'The perils of obedience'. *Harper's Magazine.* Reproduced at *http://home.swbell.net/revscat/perilsOfObedience. html* (retrieved 29 January, 2007).

'The Milgram Experiment: A lesson in depravity, peer pressure and the power of authority'. Retrieved 29 January, 2007 from *http:// www.new-life.net/milgram.htm.*

Milgram's experiment (2007) in *Wikipedia, The Free Encyclopedia.* Retrieved 29 January, 2007 from *http://en.wikipedia.org/wiki/ Milgram_experiment.*

Zimbardo, P. G. (2007) 'The Stanford Prison Experiment. A Simulation Study of the Psychology of Imprisonment Conducted at Stanford University'. Retrieved 29 January, 2007, http:// www.prisonexp.org/. This is a detailed account of another social psychology experiment which brings in similar ethical issues.

Part 2: Qualitative Approaches: their Value and their Limits

5 Some Qualitative Methods Considered

In this chapter we consider some of the commonly used non-quantitative methods and approaches used in social research: interviewing, focus groups and observation, as commonly used methods; and the case-study approach, which may involve the use of several methods.

If we look at the range of methods available to practitioners in social research we can divide them crudely into those acting as primary sources of data and those acting as secondary sources. This crude distinction is shown in the tree diagram in Figure 5.1 Primary sources would include observation, interviews, questionnaires, focus groups and so on. The secondary sources we will put together and call 'documents' (these are discussed in Chapter 6).

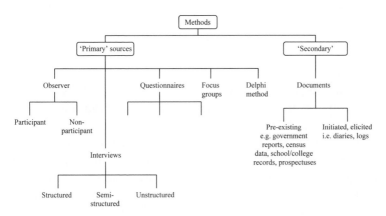

Figure 5.1 A Way of Crudely Classifying Methods in Social Research

Observation

The nature of observation has been widely discussed in social research. A variety of observational techniques that exist can be classified along two dimensions: the degree of the involvement with 'the observed', and the degree of structure. With respect to the involvement, a useful framework for considering observation in different settings is drawn up in Hammersley and Atkinson (1983, p. 93) and has been adapted into the continuum shown in Figure 5.2.

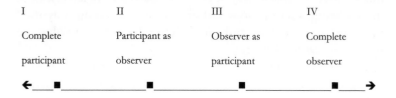

Figure 5.2 A Spectrum of Observation

Different kinds of observation from this spectrum may be possible to achieve in different situations. This will depend on a number of variables. For example, a teacher researching her own practice in a school will be very much a participant but will need to become an observer in a sense. Equally, in a long-term study of an organization, an observer may start as a complete observer but gradually become more and more of a participant. Participant observation requires time, acceptance, carefully negotiated access, and tact – problems all discussed at length by commentators on ethnographic method from Glaser and Strauss (1967) to Woods (1986).

The role of 'complete participant' has often occurred where the researcher's activities are wholly concealed from the group being studied – this has happened in studies of a Glasgow gang (Patrick, 1973), the police force (Holdaway, 1985) and studies of the army, alcoholics and a mental hospital mentioned in Hammersley and Atkinson (1983).

Another issue in observation is the degree of structure which can be used: conceivably, observation could be totally open-ended and unstructured, i.e. the observer simply goes in to observe the natural setting. Arguably, this is impossible to achieve, as every researcher has some prior concepts or frameworks through which we observe and understand the world. At the other extreme, observation in the past has been used which is totally structured and predetermined, sometimes called 'systematic'. Observers are trained in observation techniques, using a shared schedule, and instructed in exactly what to look for and how often. For example, frequencies of certain events or interactions in the observed situation have been recorded over set time periods, e.g. four seconds, in order to analyse quantitatively. Of course, semi-structured observation lies somewhere along the continuum between these two poles.

Interviewing

Why Interview?

Interviews are often said to 'reach the parts which other methods cannot reach'. Observation, for example, can allow us to study people's behaviour in 'strange' situations (such as meetings, play areas, clinics or classrooms). Studying documents (such as a brochure, a website or a prospectus) can allow a researcher to see the way an organization portrays itself in print. But interviewing allows a researcher to investigate and prompt things that we cannot observe. We can probe an interviewee's thoughts, values, prejudices, perceptions, views, feelings and perspectives. We can also elicit their version or their account of situations which they may have lived or taught through: his or her story.

Types and Styles of Interviewing

There are several different approaches to interviewing, therefore different ways of designing and structuring interviews and, in turn, different techniques for conducting them.

Some early authors have described interviews as 'a conversation with a purpose' (Webb and Webb, 1932), and this is a useful way of viewing them. However, a researcher's style and approach to interviewing will largely depend on the purpose of the research. We might consider various metaphors for the interviewer:

- a sponge
- a sounding board
- a prober
- a listener
- a counsellor
- a recorder ('tabula rasa')
- a challenger
- a prompter
- a sharer

They all need to be kept in mind and a flexible researcher may need to adopt different roles for different purposes, for different situations and with different interviewees. Interviewers will need to reveal something about themselves (and their motives and purposes) but should never treat the interview as their platform rather than the interviewee's.

Deciding on the Key Informants

The term 'key informant' is used to describe the person who may be the key figure in a piece of qualitative research. If only one person is to be interviewed in an organization, e.g. a school, college or company, then it is vitally important to attempt to identify the key informant, e.g. the principal, the director, the personnel manager. Le Compte and Goertz (in Fetterman 1984) describe key informants as:

> individuals who possess special knowledge, status or communication skills and who are willing to share that knowledge with the researcher. (Fetterman 1984, p.34)

Key informants may be subject to bias but this needs to be recognized:

> of course there may be forms of bias within our key informants. The usual safeguards apply to them, but it also helps to have various kinds of informants. The more they constitute a cross-section of the population in question, the easier we might feel about the danger of bias. (Woods, 1986, p. 86)

Degrees of Structure in Interviewing

One of the issues which has featured most prominently in discussions of interviewing concerns the degree of structure in an interview. A distinction is often made between three degrees of structure in interviewing:

1. Firstly, in a structured situation the interview may be little more than a 'face-to-face questionnaire' (Parsons, 1984, p. 80). No deviation is made from either the wording or the order of a set list of questions. If properly administered such structure can be of value when a large number of interviewers and interviewees are involved e.g. in market research. The interview may then provide quantitative as well as quantitative data.

2. At the other extreme, an unstructured interview will vary from one interview and one interviewer to the next. There is no set list of questions or rigid order.

3. A compromise can be reached between the two positions which will overcome the problems inherent in the latter approach but avoid the inflexibility of the former. The compromise, although it can take various forms, can be referred to as the semi-structured interview. This general approach is often the most valuable. The approach will involve some kind of interview guide or checklist. The guidelines may involve a checklist of issues to be covered, or even a checklist of questions. Degrees of structure will vary enormously within the framework, depending on the expertise of the interviewers and their interaction with the interviewees. In some styles of interviewing the structure and path of the interview will be dictated as much by the respondent as by the questioner.

Table 5.1 below gives a summary of the three degrees of structure in interviewing.

Designing an Interview

A common approach in interviewing is to start by formulating a set of key questions which the researcher wishes to follow in an interview. The next stage is to start to classify and categorize

Table 5.1 Styles of Interviewing

Unstructured	Semi-structured	Structured
some 'control' on both sides	more control by interviewer	most control by interviewer
very flexible	flexible	less flexible
guided by the interviewee, direction unpredictable	not completely pre-determined	guided by researcher's pre-determined agenda, more predictable
may be difficult to analyse, often analysed by theme and emerging categories	may be analysed in a thematic way or using more quantitative approaches	may provide easier framework for analysis, may be analysed using numerical coding and statistical analysis

these ideas or questions. Maykut and Morehouse (1994, p. 84) call these 'categories of inquiry'. These are put into groups or clusters and then a selection is made before transferring the categories of inquiry onto a new sheet of paper. This forms the interview guide.

For some researchers, this may be enough to take out into the field. But for many the next step is to convert it into an interview schedule. This involves, firstly, turning all the ideas or areas of inquiry into meaningful questions for the target interviewees. It involves careful use of language, e.g. avoidance of jargon and careful phrasing. The questions need to make sense and be unambiguous.

The knack of developing a good interview schedule is to sequence it with the easy, closed questions early on and the more difficult open questions requiring a good deal of thought and introspection towards the end. Start simple and build up to a crescendo!

In order to complete Stage 4 well, it is necessary to try out or 'pilot' an interview, as you would with a questionnaire.

Table 5.2 Forming Interview Guides and Interview Schedules

STAGE 1	BRAINSTORMING: jumbled, unjudged list of ideas, questions, areas of interest.

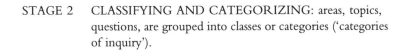

STAGE 2	CLASSIFYING AND CATEGORIZING: areas, topics, questions, are grouped into classes or categories ('categories of inquiry').

STAGE 3	INTERVIEW GUIDE: selection and judgement on which areas/questions will actually be explored.

STAGE 4	INTERVIEW SCHEDULE: phrasing of all questions into meaningful language, e.g. for certain groups of people; removing ambiguity; careful sequencing of questions; identifying and ordering closed and open questions.

Factors Affecting the Quality of Interview Data

A large number of factors, many of which are related to the execution of an interview and mentioned above, will affect the quality of the data collected. Firstly, as mentioned earlier, the interaction between interviewer and interviewee is crucial. If 'social involvement' is too high then bias may result. However, sufficient rapport should be established between the parties (enhanced by some social interaction) in order to allow any ambiguity or lack of clarity to be cleared up.

Ambiguity in questions is a major source of error, as is lack of agreement over the meanings of the terms being used (see Table 5.3). Another factor affecting quality is the use of leading questions or excessive prompting during interviewing. There is a famous example from the (purely fictitious) entry exam to the Leningrad Academy: 'Who is your personal hero and why is it Lenin?'

The recording of interviews may involve notetaking, more detailed record keeping, tape-recording or, in some cases,

Table 5.3 Five Types of Questions to Avoid

1. Double-barrelled questions: avoid double-barrelled questions!
   Example: 'Have you ever experienced severe stress and what did you do to cope with it?'
   Ask one question at a time. Do not combine questions and expect an answer.
2. Two-in-one questions.
   Do not combine opposite positions in one question.
   Example: 'What are the advantages and disadvantages of working in an independent school?'
   Separate out the parts.
3. Restrictive questions.
   Avoid questions which inherently eliminate some options.
   Example: 'Do you think that female company directors are as good as male directors?'
   This question eliminates the possibility that women might be better.
4. Avoid 'double-question' questions.
   Example: 'Do you ever feel irritated and depressed by your students?'
   The respondent might be irritated but not depressed, or vice versa, or both, or neither.
5. Leading questions.
   Do not precede questions with a position statement.
   In this type of question, the interviewer states a view or summarizes a position and then asks for a response. This could lead the respondent in a given direction.
6. Loaded questions.
   Avoid questions which are emotionally charged and use loaded words.
   Example: 'Would you favour or oppose murder by agreeing with a woman's free choice concerning abortion?'
   (adapted from Anderson, 1990)

photographic or video records. Notes and tape-recordings can be used together in interviewing to improve accuracy and quality of data/evidence. However, some informants may not wish their views to be recorded on tape, particularly if they are forthright (or even unprintable) or if they are at odds with other informants. The use of an aid such as a tape recorder should, therefore, always be negotiated with a special eye on the issue of data privacy or anonymity. On the other hand the use of a tape recorder (particularly of the high-quality, purpose-made variety) is often seen as a compliment by the person being interviewed. Table 5.4 gives a summary of the relative merits of tape recording versus notetaking in interviewing. Our own view is that it is generally best to record interviews on tape (if given the interviewee's permission) if only so that researchers can analyse and reflect initially upon their own interviewing style and technique.

Table 5.4 Tape-recording Versus Notetaking

Advantages	Disadvantages
Tape-recording	
Preserves actual natural language i.e. a verbatim account.	Can generate enormous amounts of data.
Can be flattering for interviewee.	Time-consuming to transcribe.
'Objective' record.	Context not recorded.
Interviewer's contribution is also recorded and can be reflected upon.	Presence of machine can be off-putting, e.g. create anxiety.
Allows interviewer to concentrate, to maintain eye contact and to observe body language.	Core issues may be masked by irrelevancies.
Notetaking	
Central issues/facts recorded.	Recorder bias.
Economical.	Can be distracting for the interviewee.
Off-record statements not recorded.	Encoding may interfere with interview.
	Status of data may be questioned (difficult to verify).

Focus Groups and Group Interviewing

Group Interviewing

It should not be taken for granted that interviewing is best done in one-to-one, interviewer to interviewee situations. Group interviews in which an interviewer talks with (say) three or four people together can often have advantages. The interviewees may feel safer, more secure and at ease if they are with their peers (this may be especially true of infants, or even teenagers or teachers). They are also more likely to relax, 'warm up' and jog each other's memories and thoughts. On the other hand, group interviewing has potential disadvantages: the maverick voice or the long monologue; dominant individuals who may mono-polize the interview or invisibly 'threaten' the others by their presence; the reduction in time devoted to each individual; the person who is afraid to speak in a group. These disadvantages need skilful management, even control, if they are to be avoided. Seating also needs to be carefully arranged to allow proper eye contact and, of course, the strategic location of a microphone/recorder if the session is to be taped. (Incidentally, a group interview requires a higher-quality recording system than a one-to-one situation).

One other strategy which can be valuable and enjoyable is for two researchers to jointly interview a group of people. This may seem labour-intensive but it has many benefits: an extra perspective on the interviewer 'side', leading perhaps to fuller and richer questioning; the chance for interviewees to interact with two people (e.g. a male and a female interviewer) thus doubling the chance of empathy; if one interviewer becomes tired, inattentive or loses concentration for a short time the other can take over; two people listening and recording can share their perspectives afterwards; one person may pick things up (e.g. body language, group interactions, tone of voice) which the other has missed (with a structured, scheduled interview an interviewing pair are less likely to miss items); one person can listen, record or even take a breather while the other questions and manages the group, and vice versa. In short, two interviewers working together can have several advantages and may help to improve the quality of the data.

Focus Groups

This is a very similar method which can enrich and comple-ment both survey research, and a case study. Focus groups are often seen as best for giving insights of an exploratory or pre-liminary kind (Krueger, 1994). But they can also be a standalone, self-contained way of collecting data for a research project, i.e. as a primary method (Morgan, 1988, p. 10).

A focus group is rather more than a group interview. A focus group is a small group made up of perhaps six to ten individuals with certain common features or characteristics, with whom a discussion can be focused onto a given issue or topic. It is often a homogeneous group of people. Groups might meet perhaps three or four times or have as many as a dozen meetings. A group session may last from 45 minutes to two hours.

The focus group sets up a situation where the synergy of the group, the interaction of its members, can add to the depth or insight of either an interview or a survey. Quite simply, members of the group, brought together in a suitable, conducive environment, can stimulate or 'spark each other off'.

Morgan (1988, pp. 9–10) gives three short examples of uses of focus groups:

i) In a seminar room, a group of returning students, all in their forties, are discussing the role of stress in causing heart attacks. There is consensus around the table that stress is indeed important, but what matters even more is how one deals with this stress.

ii) In a rural village in Thailand, two groups, one of young men and one of young women, discuss the number of children they want to have and how this has changed since their parents' day.

iii) In a church meeting room, a group of young widows compare their experiences. One woman complains that other people wanted to stop her grieving in six months but that really it takes much longer. Another agrees, and says that in some ways the second year is harder than the first.

Conducting a Focus Group

The focus group needs to be carefully planned and chosen with the objectives of the research in mind. Some agenda needs to be set, although (as with interviews) degrees of structure can vary. The group requires a skilled moderator or leader and a convivial setting. Group members need to be at ease, and seated so that all of the group can make eye contact with each other.

Data can be collected with a good quality tape-recorder, given the group's permission (a recorder with a poor microphone may be good enough for one-to-one interviews but will not pick up all the voices of a group). Some researchers advocate the use of video-recording but this can be off-putting. Detailed notes will also be needed. Ideally, a written account of the meeting(s) should be fed back to group members for comment. Table 5.5 below gives a summary of some of the main points to remember when planning and carrying out focus-group work.

Although they have been most commonly used in private sector market research in the last 30 years, focus groups do have

Table 5.5 A Checklist for Conducting Focus Group Interviews

1. Planning,
   Contact participants by phone one to two weeks before the session.
   Send each participant a letter of invitation
   Slightly over-recruit the number of participants.
2. Asking the Questions,
   Design the schedule so that questions flow in a logical sequence.
   Make key questions focus on the critical issues of concern. Consider probe or follow-up questions. Limit the use of 'why' questions.
   Use 'think back' questions as needed.
   Provide a summary of the discussion and invite comments.
3. Logistics,
   The room should be satisfactory (size, tables, comfort, etc.).
   Arrive early to make necessary changes. Background noise should not interfere with the tape-recording. Place a good microphone on the table. Bring extra tapes, batteries, etc.
4. Moderator Skills
   Be well rested and alert for the focus group session. Ask questions with minimal reference to notes. Be careful to avoid head nodding. Avoid comments that signal approval, such as 'Excellent', 'Great', 'Wonderful'. Avoid giving personal opinions.
5. Immediately after the Session
   Prepare a brief written summary of key points as soon as possible.
   Check to see if the tape-recorder captured the comments.

Source: Adapted from Krueger, 1994, pp. 122–3.

a value in other qualitative research and, indeed, were born in 1930s social science work (Rice, 1931). Some feel that they may now experience a revival in social science (Krueger, 1994). Our own view is that focus groups can be a valuable tool, efficient for collecting data and sometimes giving insights in addition to one-to-one interviews. (For a fuller account see Anderson, 1990, pp. 241–8, Krueger, 1994.)

Limitations of Interview and Focus Group Data

Undoubtedly, interview and focus group data are the richest source of knowledge about people's understanding of themselves, and the life around them. The problems may arise, however, if the researcher accepts those personal narratives as a prima facie explanation of why people behave the way they do, or a reliable account of what happened. Decades of research in clinical and social psychology have taught us that our ability to predict our own actions, and understand their psychological causes, is rather limited. What we do is often at odds with our declared (and earnestly believed) motivations. While Freud may have been wrong about the causes of our behaviour he was certainly right in claiming that we are largely unaware of them – or, as Francis Crick succinctly put it, 'We are deceived at every level by our introspection' (Crick, 1979). Our personal narratives are shaped by our desire to maintain high self-esteem, make sense of (often random) events and reduce the cognitive dissonance between conflicting pieces of information. Even the recall of factual information can be highly selective and inaccurate, especially if the information is emotionally charged. This is widely acknowledged in the context of criminal investigation (witness testimony), but not always in the context of social science research. Interview data should be taken for what they are – personal narratives – not explanations or factual records.

Case Study

A good definition of 'case study' was offered by Bogdan and Biklen (1982, p. 58): 'A case study is a detailed examination of one setting, or one single subject, or one single depository of documents, or one particular event'.

Table 5.6 gives a summary of what might count as a case study.

Table 5.6 What Might Count as a 'Case Study'?

1. An account of one individual or one group:
    Example: Armstrong (1980): a diary of one primary classroom.
    Diamond & Sigmunson (1997): a case of a genitally mutilated boy raised as a girl.
    Chagnon (1968): an anthropological study of a South American tribe.
2. An account of two or more individuals:
    Examples: Edwards (1994): The Scars of Dyslexia (8 boys).
    Turkle (1984): The Second Self (a large number of computer users/'hackers').
3. A study of one organization:
    Example: Ball (1981): Beachside Comprehensive.
    Lacey (1970): Hightown Grammar.
    Walford and Miller (1991): City Technology College.
4. A study of two or more organizations, e.g. schools, employers:
    Example: Wright (1992): on four primary schools.
    Wellington, J.J. (1989): on five employers.
5. An account of one or more groups, e.g. a family, or a community:
    Example: Whyte (1943): Street Corner Society.
6. A study of specific events or relationships:
    Example: Woods (1993): on 'critical events'.
    Tripp (1993): on 'critical incidents'.
    Sherif *et al.* (1961): a naturalistic experiment of intergroup cooperation and competition in pre-adolescent boys.

A case study of an organization may well involve a true mixture of methods: observation, focus groups, discussion, interviewing, visits to different sites, and the study of written records and documentation. Together, data from these sources allow a 'picture' to be built up of the case being studied. Table 5.7 gives a summary of the various sources of data which might go towards a case study record.

Table 5.7 Data Collection in Case Study – a Summary of Commonly Used Techniques

---

1. Observation.
   (a) Participant observation: the researcher is more than a passive observer and participates in the events being studied.
   (b) Systematic observation: use of standardized observation instrument.
   (c) Simple observation: passive unobtrusive observation (e.g. of facial expression; language use; behaviour).
2. Interview.
   (a) Structured interview: set of predetermined questions in a set order.
   (b) Focused/semi-structured interview: interview schedule specifying key areas but order of questions not fixed.
   (c) Open-ended interview: no prespecified schedule or order of questions; little direction from interviewer.
3. Use of documents and records.
   Includes a wide range of written or recorded materials, e.g. minutes of meetings, written records, statistics, diaries, brochures, reports.
4 A wide range of other techniques including: questionnaires; standardized tests (e.g. of intelligence, personality or attainment); scales (e.g. of attitude); repertory grids; life histories.

Advantages and Disadvantages of Case Study

Case study research has a large number of attractions and advantages, in addition to the fact that it can be enjoyable to do. Case studies can be illuminating and insightful; if well written, they can be attention holding and exude a strong sense of reality; they are often accessible and engaging for readers; no wonder they are sometimes best-sellers (e.g. Chagnon, 1968). Case studies derived from research can be of great value in teaching and learning; case studies can lead into subsequent quantitative research by pointing to issues which can or should be investigated over a wider range; they can also follow on from a broader survey or quantitative approach by exploring a phenomenon in greater depth, in a more exploratory, explanation-seeking fashion.

Table 5.8 sums up some of the main alleged strengths, and the alleged weaknesses, of case study research. The next section looks at the problems felt by many to be inherent in the case study approach.

Table 5.8 Case Study: Strengths and Weaknesses

STRENGTHS	WEAKNESSES
Case studies should be...........	Case studies may not be..........
illustrative	generalizable
illuminating/insightful	representative
disseminable, accessible	typical
attention holding	replicable
strong on reality/vivid	repeatable
of value in teaching	

The Old Chestnut of 'Generalizability'

The problem of generalizing from a study of one case was summed up by Bogdan and Biklen (1982):

> Purposely choosing the unusual or just falling into a study leaves the question of generalisability up in the air. Where does the setting fit in the spectrum of human events? The question is not answered by the selection itself, but has to be explored as part of the study. The researcher has to determine what it is he or she is studying: that is, of what is this a case? (Bogdan and Biklen, 1982, p.66)

There have been several interesting responses to this issue, some of them quite ebullient. We consider a few of them below:

- Wolcott (1995, p. 17) is perhaps the most 'bullish' in responding by posing a question and giving an answer: 'What can we learn from studying only one of anything?' The answer: 'All we can'. He later elaborates on this by arguing that 'each case study is unique, but not so unique that we cannot learn from it and apply its lessons more generally' (p. 175).
- A similar point was made over 50 years ago by Kluckhohn and Murray (1948, p. 35) in, despite the gendered

language, a memorable quote: 'Every man is in certain respects, like all men, like some men, like no other man'.

- Walker (1980, p. 34) expressed the same view by saying: 'an instance is likely to be as typical and as atypical as any other'.
- Yin (1994) takes a different tack in his book by advocating the use of multiple case studies, over an extended period at different sites. These multiple cases can then, cumulatively, be used to produce generalizations.

Whatever stance we take on the issue of generalizability, there seems to be one important general point. In examining case studies part of the onus rests upon the reader. The validity of a study needs to be assessed and judged by the reader, given his or her experience, knowledge and wisdom, i.e. the value or 'truth' of case study research is a function of the reader as much as the researcher. People reading case studies can often relate to them, even if they cannot always generalize from them. This ability to relate to a case and learn from it is perhaps more important than being able to generalize from it.

Questionnaires

The concern of many participants in, and perhaps readers of, research involving solely in-depth interviews and case studies is that of representativeness. One way of allaying such fears has been to add the use of a survey, most commonly involving the use of a questionnaire, to give a wider picture or an overview. This section discusses briefly the use of questionnaires, their drawbacks and their 'rapid' way of obtaining 'information'.

It is often said that surveys can provide answers to the questions What? Where? When? and How?, but it is not so easy to find out Why? The main emphasis with a survey questionnaire tends to be on 'fact finding'. However, survey results can be used to test a hypothesis or add weight to a theory. In addition, it is often forgotten that some of the data collected in a survey can be 'qualitative' in nature, e.g. people's views or perceptions of an issue. This data may contribute to the development of theory as much as interview or observational data.

Walker (1985a, p. 91) summed up both the pros and cons of a questionnaire:

> The questionnaire is like interviewing-by-numbers, and like painting-by-numbers it suffers some of the same problems of mass production and lack of interpretative opportunity. On the other hand it offers considerable advantages in administration – it presents an even stimulus, potentially to large numbers of people simultaneously, and provides the investigator with a relatively easy accumulation of data.

Response Rates

The best-laid plans for designing a sample and carrying out a survey with a questionnaire can be ruined either by a low or an unrepresentative response rate. One stratum of a carefully stratified sample may respond at a far greater rate than another and this will bias results A response rate can be improved by care in design, presentation and distribution.

Table 5.9 suggests six ways of maximizing response rate in survey research.

Table 5.9 Ways of Maximizing Response Rate to a Questionnaire

- Target the respondent by name.
- Give clear instructions and the usual assurances, e.g. anonymity.
- Go for brevity and clarity.
- Warn the respondent in advance of the questionnaire.
- Include a stamped addressed envelope if using 'snail mail'.
- Give polite reminders (after a suitable time) by letter and by phone.

(And don't take it personally if your response rate is low; it won't be the first time.)

Methods of Distribution: Email or Snail Mail?

Traditionally, the method used for carrying out a large-scale survey has involved the conventional postal system to distribute questionnaires, give polite reminders and receive responses. However, the advent of electronic networks has opened up new possibilities which are not always fully exploited in research surveys. Electronic distribution can potentially be more efficient and far quicker in distributing and 'collecting' a questionnaire than by conventional post. The possibility of sending a polite reminder by electronic mail is also present. Large numbers of electronic questionnaires can be distributed – the questionnaire can then be printed out at the receiving end for completion and return by conventional methods, or completed on screen and relayed back over the network.

What are the advantages and disadvantages in using email or other online tools as a way of collecting data?

- For example, it can save money and time, it can give easy access to worldwide samples (Selwyn and Robson, 2002), it can ease the burden of transcribing from paper or audiotape, it can eliminate transcription bias and error, and it can provide rapid response rates (Mann and Stewart, 2000).

- On the other hand, response rates are not always as high (or as rapid) as paper-based surveys: Mann and Stewart (2000, p. 68) report studies where the email response has been only slightly better than half of a paper-based response.

- Another interesting issue concerns the language used by respondents to email surveys or 'interviews'. In some ways it is a mixture, somewhere between spoken and written language (rather like text messaging). This can lead to some discussion on how to transcribe the text from an email response into a report or a thesis; and also the extent to which the language in the responses should be changed, filtered or improved (again discussed by Mann and Stewart, 2000, p. 189).

Questionnaire Design and Construction

Perhaps the most important point for a questionnaire is that it should begin with straightforward, closed questions, leaving the open-ended, 'matter of opinion' questions to the end. As Neuman (1994, p. 237) put it, 'one should sequence questions to minimize the discomfort and confusion of respondents'. If a questionnaire is broken down into sections, topics or themes, then each section/area of enquiry should follow this pattern, i.e. closed, matter-of-fact questions to begin, followed by the open-ended questions requiring opinions, feelings and valued judgements at the end. These can be time-consuming and difficult to answer – and hard to analyse – so it is best to avoid too many. But they will yield fascinating qualitative data. Phrasing questions in both interviews and questionnaires is a difficult art, as we saw earlier.

Secondly, the questionnaire should be targeted at a particular, named person within a group or organization. If a range of information is required then a person in a position to co-ordinate and collate that information should be chosen. A third simple but important point concerns presentation. Your would-be respondent is likely to receive a fair quantity of unsolicited mail, much of which is filed in the wastepaper bin. If a questionnaire is not attractively and clearly presented, and brief, it may well be ignored.

If it is one part of a research project, the design of a questionnaire should be influenced by other methods within that project, e.g. an interview schedule, information gathered or issues raised by a case study. This is an important feature of triangulation. Thus questions which were particularly successful during an interview (including open-ended questions) can be followed up with greater numbers of subjects. Prior interviewing will also help with the wording of questions which should of course be clear and unambiguous.

A questionnaire, and the questions within it, can be developed from prior research methods, but the use of a pilot is still essential. The printed word raises problems unforeseen in spoken, human contact. A pilot questionnaire is therefore an essential stage in design and construction. You should not underestimate the amount of time and drafting required to produce a good questionnaire. Testing it on colleagues, friends and family at every stage is one good way to ensure comprehensibility.

Finally, a consideration of the analysis of responses must also be a feature of questionnaire design. How is the data collected to be analysed? Will the questionnaire gather masses of

Table 5.10 Some Guidelines on Questionnaire Design and Layout

---

- Write a brief covering letter explaining the purpose of the questionnaire and containing full assurances of confidentiality.
- Give clear instructions on how to fill it in.
- Present it attractively with a clear layout, obvious structure and adequate space for open-ended responses.
- Make the typeface legible and the English readable.
- Don't go over the top with different typefaces, fonts, headings, bold, italics, colour, etc.
- Sequence questions carefully, starting with the easier, closed questions leading up to more thought-provoking, introspective open questions.
- Provide an 'Open Forum' at the end, allowing space for the respondent to say anything they wish to, i.e. a platform or a dais.
- Say 'thank you' at the end.
- Always try it out before distributing to your sample, i.e. pilot the questions.

---

information which cannot be categorized or presented in a final report? While drafting the questionnaire you should keep in mind the analysis of the data, and if, for example, you are going to use a computer package such as SPSS, this should influence design of items to ensure ease of data analysis and recording.

Further Reading

Fuller discussion on the issue of online versus postal questionnaires can be found in:

Mann, C. and Stewart, C. (2000) *Internet Communication and Qualitative Research*. London: Sage.

Selwyn, N. and Robson, K. (2002) 'Using e-mail as a research tool'. *Social Research Update* 21, University of Surrey.

A great deal has been written on the actual design of questionnaires. Valuable summaries for practitioners are provided in Youngman (1986), Cohen and Manion (1994) or Fink (1995), all listed in the references at the end of this book.

6 Dealing with Qualitative Data

The Challenge...

There are several important features of qualitative research:

1. It is usually an exploratory activity.
2. Data are usually collected in a real-life, natural setting and are therefore often rich, complex, descriptive and extensive.
3. The human being or beings involved are the main research 'instrument'.
4. The design of a study emerges or evolves 'as you go along' – sometimes leading to a broadening or blurring of focus, at other times leading to a narrowing or sharpening of focus.
5. The typical methods used are observation, interview, collection of documents and sometimes photography or video-recording.

These features of qualitative research lead to one major consequence: qualitative research produces large amounts of data! The data are lengthy and, by definition, verbose, i.e. mostly in the form of words. This is why, with many researchers using largely qualitative methods, panic commonly sets in: 'I can't see the wood for the trees'; 'What am I going to do with all these data?'

This chapter offers some ideas and further reading on qualitative data analysis, including documentary analysis. It starts from the premise that there is no one, single, correct way of doing it. But there are general principles and guidelines which can be followed in doing it systematically and reflectively.

Stages in Data Analysis

The activity of analysing qualitative data is often messy and complicated. To put it crudely, it involves taking all the data in, digesting them, taking them apart, then putting them back together again – sometimes leaving lots of bits lying around unused at the end and sometimes returning to collect more. We suggest the following stages:

1. *Immersion*

   This involves getting an overall sense or feel for the data, e.g. listening to tapes or reading and rereading transcripts. It involves notetaking, active reading, highlighting or annotating transcripts. This is the stage of 'immersing oneself' in the data – which can often give rise to a drowning or sinking feeling to carry the metaphor further!

2. *Reflecting*

   The next stage is often to 'stand back' from the data or, literally, to 'sleep on it'. This is, allegedly, the way in which the nineteenth-century chemist Kekule discovered the structure of Benzene. He struggled in his lab for months to put forward a model or theory which would explain its properties and structure. Then one tired night he fell asleep in front of his hearth and dreamt of snakes curled up around a campfire. Each snake had its tail in another's mouth, completing a stable, cosy and complete ring. Kekule woke up and, before breakfast, had postulated the theory of the Benzene ring, a major breakthrough in organic chemistry. This story may take liberties with the truth and Kekule's sleepy insight did follow months of painstaking research (as Pasteur once said, 'Chance favours the prepared mind'). But it does show the importance of standing back from data which a researcher may be very close to. A similar example would be the (seemingly serendipitous) discovery of antibacterial properties of penicillin by Alexander Fleming.

3. *Taking Apart/Analysing Data*

   The word 'analyse' literally means to break down into

components, or to divide a whole into its parts. This is the stage which is, strictly speaking, the analysis phase. The activity of taking apart or analysing the data can involve:

(a) Carving it up into manageable 'units' or chunks, e.g. sections of an interview transcript. This can be done by literally using scissors and paste on a photocopy of the transcript, or electronically using computer software.

(b) Selecting or filtering out units which can be used: this process inevitably depends on the researcher's 'judgement', a term which carries many connotations.

(c) Categorizing or coding units, i.e. beginning to create categories, patterns or recurring themes which can gradually be used to 'make sense' of the data.

(d) Attempting to subsume subsequent units of data under these provisional categories, or, if units do not fit, then developing new categories in which they can find a home.

By this stage the process of taking apart or dividing up the data is well underway. The next phase, of putting it back together again, is beginning as the categories develop.

4. *Recombining/Synthesizing Data*

As Delamont (1992) described it, this phase consists of searching for patterns, themes and regularities in the data or units of data; it also involves looking for contrasts, paradoxes and irregularities. As the categories emerge they can be applied in assimilating new data – or they can be adapted to accommodate other material. The next stage is to examine and refine the categories themselves. Researchers can look for *similar* categories which could then perhaps be merged to form one new one. Conversely, one category might be developing into a large, amorphous class encompassing far too much. It then becomes too big and too unwieldy. The category needs to be divided into two or even three smaller groups.

This examination of the categories themselves is an

activity of *continuous refinement*. Early categories are adapted, merged, subdivided or simply omitted: new categories are developed. New patterns and relationships are discovered (discussed in more detail in Maykut and Morehouse, 1994, pp. 134–6 and, more generally, in Le Compte and Goertz, 1981).

The 'carving up', or analysis stage literally involves cutting the data up and taking them out of their context, i.e. *decontextualizing* the data. The recombining, or synthesis, stage involves *recontextualizing*; finding them a new home.

The next stage is to integrate the data so that they 'hang together' and also to locate one's own data in existing work, i.e. other people's data. This is important at this stage – we are not suggesting that researchers working through Phases 1–3 should deliberately refrain from reading the existing literature on the topic of their interest, to keep their minds 'uncontaminated'. The relationship between reading existing research (which inevitably structures one's own enquiry) and data analysis is vital at every stage.

5. *Relating and Locating Your Data*
    A researcher's inquiry, to use a common analogy, is just another brick in the wall. The next stage is therefore to position this brick and relate it to the existing structure. This important activity can only be done, of course, from a position of knowing and understanding existing research, i.e. from the base of a strong literature review.

    The process of locating and relating again involves the use of constant comparison and contrast. This can be used in examining the following areas: categories, methods and themes.

    (a) How do your *categories* compare or contrast with others in the literature?
    (b) What are the strengths and weaknesses of your data and your methods? How do they compare or contrast with the strengths and weaknesses in the methodology of other studies?
    (c) What theories/frameworks/models have been

applied in, or developed from, other inquiries? To what extent can they be applied in yours?

The business of locating and relating your data to other people's research is an important part of reflecting upon it and making sense of it. Having reflected back on it, in some research projects one might see the need to actually return for more data. In some projects this is practical and realistic, i.e. given time and resources. In others, this may not be possible.

6. *Knowing when to stop*

Whatever the circumstances, we have to stop somewhere. Knowing when to stop collecting data is difficult, but most experienced researchers talk of reaching a kind of 'saturation point'. After a certain number of, say, interviews or case studies, perspectives and issues begin to recur and reappear. Interviewees begin to repeat important points; case studies begin to exhibit recurring themes and patterns. This can be very comforting for a researcher and can begin to create some confidence in generalizability. It is a nice feeling; a kind of redundancy in the data eventually develops and the researcher knows that future data collection will be subject to the law of diminishing returns. Categories and themes have begun to develop in the researcher's mind and subsequent data collection serves only to support and reinforce them.

7. *Presenting Qualitative Data*

The final, and arguably the most important stage in any research project is to present the data as fairly, clearly, coherently and attractively as possible. Justice needs to be done, and to be seen to be done. In qualitative research, this is where verbatim quotes can come into their own. They can give a research publication (be it a book, thesis, article or a newspaper summary) a reality and vividness which quantitative data cannot.

The problem, of course, is one of how to select these verbatim accounts ('voices') and how many to use, given the usual constraints on every platform for publication. Should we select only the snappy, glib statements, i.e. the 'sound bites'? On the other hand, should we also use the

longer, heartfelt accounts or anecdotes that are sometimes yielded in the best interviews? Should we only
look for quotable 'gems' which will enrich and enliven
our own perhaps more boring written work, or should
we try to be fair to all our informants, and include all
voices, however mundane they seem?

One thing is certain: difficult choices have to be made.
An in-depth interview for 30–40 minutes can be transformed into as much as 12 pages of transcript. Thus the
25 interviewees needed to reach Douglas's (1985)
saturation point will produce 300 pages of print. At 250
words per page the interview data alone would amount
to about 75,000 words (the size of many PhD theses). It
is often possible to 'archive' voices for future research or
more extensive publication in the future – but of course,
there are issues of consent, security and confidentiality
around storing or archiving data.

There are no straightforward answers. Verbatim
quotes can be used to illustrate and reinforce key themes
or perspectives, but it is impossible to represent every
'voice'. The more general issue of writing up research,
structuring and presenting work, and attempting to reach
different audiences is discussed in a later chapter.

The next section goes on to look in more detail at specific
ways of analysing qualitative data from different sources.

Exactly How Do We Analyse Data: a priori or a posteriori Categories?

The main general issue is this: are categories for analysis brought
to the data or are they derived from it? Quite simply, there can
be three possibilities here:

1. The categories used to analyse the data are pre-
   established, i.e. a priori. This can occur if they are
   derived from the literature, e.g. from a previous research
   study in this area. Those pre-existing, a priori categories
   which have been used in previous research are then
   applied to one's own, new data. This can occur, for

example, in research attempting to replicate earlier work. The use of a priori categories also occurs if a researcher or a research team decides on categories *before* data collection begins, for other reasons. For example, they may have been told (in funded research) to explore certain themes or issues, or to investigate certain questions. In another situation, a researcher or research team may put forward certain hypotheses which then guide data collection and data analysis.

2. The categories used to analyse data are not pre-established but are derived from the data themselves, i.e. a posteriori. Categories are then said to 'emerge' from the data by some sort of process of induction. Frankfort-Nachmias and Nachmias (1992, p. 323) describe this 'extraction' as 'inductive coding'.

   The 'emergence' of categories from newly collected data often occurs in a project and this can be one of the more satisfying aspects of doing research. But we should never pretend that they somehow magically or mysteriously do this independently of the researcher, like Excalibur rising from the lake. This pretence would be naive realism or empiricism at its worst. No, the 'emergence' of categories from data depends entirely on the researcher. This is part of the 'research act' (Denzin 1970). In social sciences, as in the physical sciences, theories do not come from observations or experiences; they come from people.

3. The third possibility is that some categories are pre-established while others are derived from the data, i.e. a mixture of a priori and a posteriori. This is probably the most common and, in our view, the most rational approach to analysing qualitative data. In our experience it almost always happens whether people admit it or not. Existing categories, derived from past research and previous literature, can be brought to the data and used to make sense of it. But frequently there will be new data which require new thought and new categorization (even in a replicative study). Pre-existing categories may not be enough to exhaust all the data and it can feel very

unsatisfactory to develop a 'sweeper' category ('miscellaneous') in an attempt to be exhaustive. This is where creativity is required in analysing data and developing new categories in an attempt to consider and do justice to it all. New data can also show that pre-existing categories are not mutually exclusive, i.e. they overlap and data could easily fit into more than one.

In summary, new research can help to refine and clarify existing categories – it can also help to develop new categories, frameworks and theories.

Practical Approaches to Analysing Data

There are all sorts of practical questions when it comes to the nitty-gritty of analysing qualitative data: do we use a highlighting pen to seek and mark key words or should we use a computer? Should we photocopy our interview transcripts, cut them up into units then paste them together into themes/categories, or is it best to use a computer package do this for us? Here are some of the possible tactics:

1. *Returning to Research Questions*
    One valuable tactic when faced with a large volume of data is to return to the original research questions which were used to guide and plan the research. When data have been divided up into manageable units (either by scissors on a photocopy or 'cut and paste' on a computer file) each 'unit' can be matched to a research question. By matching units to questions, piece by piece, the data gradually shed light on or illuminate those questions. This matching of items of data to individual questions can also provide a structure for writing up and presenting research.

2. *Looking at Language*
    Qualitative data most commonly consist of words, e.g. interview transcripts, documents. One strategy for analysing them is to examine the language itself. This can involve:
    - looking for buzzwords;

- looking for other commonly used words and phrases by, say, an informant or an interviewee, or in documents;
- searching for and examining commonly used metaphors, such as 'level playing field' (in discussing competitors) and 'shifting the goalposts' (in discussing managers and policy-makers). Such metaphors have become so embedded in our language that they are now 'metaphors we live by' (Lakoff and Johnson, 1980).

3. *Searching for Patterns and Themes*

This has already been discussed in the section on stages in analysing data. The method of constant comparison and contrast is well documented in the literature on research methods and, in our experience, is largely very practical and effective. As Delamont (1992) reminds people in social research, we should search for irregularities, paradoxes and contrasts as much as patterns, themes and regularities.

4. *Manual or Computer Labour?*

As we said earlier, data can be sorted and analysed manually, e.g. by physically cutting up materials, doing a 'scissors-and-paste' job, or sorting material into files and folders. But computers can also be used, with appropriate software, to analyse, sort and code data. Indeed, one of the interesting debates over the analysis of qualitative data is over whether it should be done manually or by using a suitable computer program, e.g. N-VIVO, Ethnograph, NUDIS, ATLAS Ti. Computer programs can certainly help in the process (see Tesch 1990), but they cannot replace the researcher's own analysis, lateral thinking, intuition and craftsmanship. It is difficult to say when or if one technique is 'better' than another. Perhaps the answer is that it depends on the preference of the researcher or the research team.

Analysing Documentary Data: 'Documentary Research'

Why Analyse Documents in Social Research?

The analysis of documentary sources has a number of advantages in any research project:

- documents can provide an important historical perspective on any area being studied;
- documents provide an excellent source of additional data, e.g. as a complement to quantitative data, interviews or observation;
- documentary research can be extremely efficient, cost-effective and productive.

It forms an excellent means of triangulation, helping to increase the trustworthiness, reliability and validity of research (especially as most documents are publicly accessible).

Types of Document in Social Research

A list, in no particular order, of documents which can act as valuable sources in social research might include:

Letters	Media coverage
Annual reports	Circulars
Minutes of meetings	Bulletins
Curriculum documents	Life histories
Web pages	Newsletters
Photographs	Leaflets
Blogs (web logs)	Accounts
Audiotapes of meetings or group discussions	Videotape/film
	Government papers
Email discussions	Oral histories
Email correspondence	Policy documents
	Memoirs/autobiographies

The list could include many more: some on paper, some distributed and presented electronically, some on tape or disk. The word 'document' would normally be stretched to include a range of media and modes of presentation.

The use and analysis of documents might be the main focus

of a piece of research, i.e. the documents are the subject of systematic research in their own right. On the other hand, the study of documents might be done in conjunction with other methods of research, involving primary sources. For example, the collection and analysis of a range of documents will often be done in a case study in conjunction with interviews, observations or questionnaires.

Documents available for research can vary according to their 'degree of access'. Table 6.1 shows the range from closed or restricted access to openly published documents and, at the extreme, documents which are not only public but also freely distributed to all.

Table 6.1 Degrees of Access and Examples of Different Types of Documents

Degree of access	Description
Closed	Available only to a limited number of insiders, e.g. personal diaries, learning logs, letters.
Restricted	Available only by gaining special permission or having access granted.
Archived	Access via a special place of storage, or archive, e.g. very old documents; privately owned papers.
Published 1	Available in libraries, bookshops or on the internet but at a price, e.g. intentionally published diaries, newspapers, White Papers.
Published 2	Available free on application or via the internet, e.g. some Government documents, curriculum statements, prospectuses, blogs.
Published 3	Freely distributed to every household or organization, e.g. health education leaflets, propaganda, pressure group publications.

Equally, documents can range according to their authorship. This can vary from a private individual to a private group, an organization such as a school, an official private group or to an official, 'public' organization such as a government department. In the case of some documents, establishing the actual authorship may be difficult, and may be a matter of considerable controversy (see, e.g., the infamous claim that 'Iraq's military forces are able to use biological and chemical weapons ... within 45 minutes of a decision to do so' (UK Government 2002, p. 173).

The nature of a document being analysed will have important implications for the nature of the analysis, the ethical concerns and the eventual writing up of the research. For example, certain documents, e.g. personal diaries or learning logs, will need to be treated sensitively and confidentially. At the other extreme, public documents such as White Papers or National Curriculum statements might be treated as 'fair game' for harsh critical analysis. This, in turn, will guide the ethics of the writing up of any analysis.

Thus documents can be of value at different stages of research and can be 'brought in' to the research process for different purposes: to open up and explore a field; to complement other research approaches and methods; and to conclude or consolidate research, including the enrichment of the final process of writing up and publishing. The actual business of assessing and analysing documents is discussed in the next section.

Searching for 'Meaning' in Documentary Analysis

This section starts from the premise, put forward several decades ago, that a text or document does not have a single, objective, inner, essential meaning. Its meaning depends on the intentions of the author(s) and the perspectives of the reader. To search for a single, objective, essential meaning is to search for a chimera. Texts and documents must be studied and analysed as 'socially situated products' (Scott, 1990, p. 34).

Searching for meaning, therefore, is not some kind of hunt for, or pursuit of, a single inner meaning or essence. It is a matter of interpretation. Documents have multiple meanings. Documentary research starts from the premise that no document should be accepted at face value, but equally that no amount of analysis will discover or decode a hidden, essentialist meaning.

One simple, but useful, distinction is that between *literal* understanding and *interpretative* understanding of a text or document. The former involves the understanding of the literal or surface meaning of the words, terms and phrases – this might be called their denotation. The latter involves a deeper understanding and interpretation of the document – its *connotation*. The activity of exploring and 'decoding' the underlying, hidden meaning of a text is part of the discipline of *semiotics* (the study of signs and symbols), which is part of the more general activity of interpretation in social research, known as *hermeneutics*.

Enough of the jargon: what does this mean when it comes to the practical activity of analysing documents in social research? It means that the literal reading of a document must be accompanied by an examination of the document's context, authorship, intended audiences, intentions and purposes, vested interests, genre, style and tone, presentation and appearance.

Another way of putting it, in more 'postmodernist' language, is suggested by Usher and Edwards (1994) and Usher (1996). They suggest four aspects of documents which require interrogation and interpretation:

1. Con-text, e.g. the author's own position.
2. Pre-text – that which exists before the text.
3. Sub-text – that which is beneath the text.
4. Inter-text – the relation of this text to other texts.

Table 6.2 suggests eight different areas for interpretation and analysis with a list of questions within each area. Not all of these questions will apply to every document of course, but it does provide a useful checklist.

These points can be used as a framework for exploring and analysing documents of any kind (further discussion is provided by McCulloch, 2004).

This section of the chapter has considered how a range of documentary sources might be analysed in order to enrich a piece of social research. Some of these sources are *pre-existing;* others are *initiated*, elicited and sometimes sponsored by the researcher, i.e. the research diary. As with all methods in social research, the business of collecting and analysing documentary data is accompanied by the usual issues of access, ethics and researcher effect, previously discussed. But, as we have tried to show, the use of documentary sources has many advantages in any social research project.

Table 6.2 Questions Which Might be Posed in Analysing Documents

- *Authorship*: who wrote it? Who are they? What is their position and their bias?
- *Audience*: who was it written for? Why them? What assumptions does it make, including assumptions about its audience?
- *Production*: where was it produced and when? By whom? What were the social, political and cultural conditions in which it was produced?
- *Presentation, appearance, image*: how is it presented, e.g. colour or black and white; glossy paper; highly illustrated? What 'image' does it portray?
- *Intentions*: why was it written? With what purpose in mind?
- *Style, function, and genre*: in what style is it written? How direct is the language? Is it written to inform, to persuade, to convince, to sell, to cajole, to provoke? How clever is the language?
- *Content*: which words, terms or buzzwords are commonly used? Can additional insights be gained by counting their frequency? What rhetoric is used? Are values conveyed, explicitly or implicitly? What metaphors and analogies does it contain?
- *Context/frame of reference*: when was it written? What came before it and after it? How does it relate to previous documents and later ones?

And Finally. . . .

Part 2 of this book has examined a variety of methods which might be used in a study and how the data from these methods might be analysed. The intricacies of those methods and the care and reflection which should be taken in their use have been discussed in each case. We have tried to illustrate that different methods can be compatible with each other – different methods can provide different insights and answer different questions.

This notion of a 'triangulation of methods' was illustrated some time ago by Faulkner in proposing his notion of a 'Triad':

The strategic strengths and advantages of multi-method inquiry stand on three legs that I have called a Triad. Each leg represents a unique mode of data collection: one from interviews with both informants and respondents; the second from observation of people at work; and the third from documents, records and archives of the organization or industry in question. Each leg presents the researcher with a different vantage point. While it may be useful to focus extensive time and energy on one mode, the advantages of moving sequentially across all three are formidable. (Faulkner 1982, pp. 80–1)

The principle of triangulation can be extended beyond Faulkner's formulation. Any combination of methods (two, three, or several), whether qualitative or quantitative, strengthens the reliability and validity of the study, providing these methods are complementary ways of 'getting at' (operationalizing) the same variable or entity being studied.

Similarly, Woods argued that triangulation can provide both strength and accuracy:

Triangles possess enormous strength. Among other things, they make the basic frames of bicycles, gates and house roofs. Triangulation enables extraordinary precision over phenomenal distances in astronomy. Similarly, in social scientific research, the use of three or more different methods or bearings to explore an issue greatly increases the chances of accuracy. (Woods, 1986, p. 87)

Of course, this only applies if they really do explore the same issue.

Further Reading

For a wide range of chapters on dealing with qualitative data see Denzin, N.K. and Lincoln, Y.S. (eds) (1998) *Collecting and Interpreting Qualitative Materials*. London: Sage.

For an excellent discussion of the use and analysis of documents see McCulloch, G. (2004) *Documentary Research in Education, History and the Social Sciences*, London: Routledge.

See also a seminal text from the 1940s: Allport, G. (1947) *The Use of Personal Documents in the Psychological Sciences*. New York: Social Science Research Council.

Part 3 Quantitative Approaches: Their value and their Limits

7 Dealing With Quantitative Data

In Chapter 1 we discussed the key attributes of quantitative research. Here comes a quick reminder:

- Quantitative research relies on *measuring* variables – or, at the very least, on *counting* of objects or events. That is, the data are *numbers* (or are converted into numbers before their analysis begins).
- Quantitative research is about hypothesis testing, and theory testing. That is, the predictions are stated explicitly, and then confronted with the data.
- Quantitative research relies heavily on *algorithms*: sequences of clearly defined procedures which, when applied, always produce a desired end result. This does not mean that each quantitative research study is just one big algorithm (like a long division or a computer program) – far from it. The results of various algorithms have to be integrated and evaluated by the researcher, in order to arrive at the conclusion about the truth of the initial hypothesis. The researcher's *heuristics* (hunches and rules of thumb) play a key role there. Nevertheless, various algorithms are employed widely as tools.
- Quantitative research is nomothetic in its focus – it strives to formulate general laws that apply to whole populations of objects, events or people.

Among various algorithms deployed by quantitative researchers, statistical procedures are undoubtedly the most important ones. It is to *statistics* that we now turn our attention.

Why Statistics?

This question has been asked by generations of social science students, taking (usually against their will), an introductory course in statistics. A quick answer may be: 'Because stats allow you to get rid of the noise'.

The numerical data that social science deals with are usually very 'noisy' – that is, they are contaminated by a considerable amount of random error. This error comes from two sources. *Measurement error* is the result of imprecision of our measurement instruments and procedures – that is, their imperfect reliability. We discuss this issue further in Chapter 8. *Sampling error* arises whenever we want to use findings from the samples we studied and extrapolate them onto the whole populations from which these samples came (e.g. when we use the results of the exit poll to ascertain the results of the election). Statistical algorithms allow you to remove that noise, thus to see the underlying patterns of relationship between variables more clearly. Putting it differently, statistical procedures help the researchers acknowledge that all research conclusions are only *probabilistic* and provisional. The nature of many statistical procedures is paradoxical: they do not tell us whether our conclusions are right, but how likely they are to be *wrong*.

The use of statistics is by no means limited to social sciences. It is also a tool of biology and some branches of physics (particle physics, cosmology) – disciplines that, like social sciences, have to deal with a considerable degree of measurement or sampling error. In fact, some statistical procedures now routinely associated with social sciences (e.g. analysis of variance) were originally invented in the context of agricultural research (experiments on improving crop yields; Fisher, 1978). Professions that also rely on measurements but do not use statistical procedures routinely (e.g. land surveyors or engineers) can afford to do so only because their measurement and sampling procedures produce negligible error.

Descriptive versus Inferential Statistics

The first task of a researcher analysing numerical data is to describe and present them clearly. *Descriptive statistics* procedures used to accomplish this deal only with the properties of the samples that the researcher actually studied. Once sample description is done, a truly interesting job begins: the sample data are examined to see what valid conclusions they can offer about the properties of the population from which that sample was drawn. This is accomplished through *inferential statistics* procedures. It is thanks to them that the job of 'taming random noise' described above is actually done (see Table 7.1).

Table 7.1 Descriptive versus Inferential Statistics

Descriptive Statistics	Inferential Statistics
Aim	
• Examining the data from a sample you studied.	• Going beyond the sample data you have.
• Presenting them in a compressed form, getting their 'gist'.	• Using the known characteristics of the sample (*sample statistics*) to draw conclusions about the unknown characteristics of the whole population (*population parameters*) from which the sample came.
• Extracting the overall pattern of the data (their *frequency distribution*).	
Commonly Used Tools	
• Measures of central tendency (mean, median, mode) and dispersion (range, interquartile range, variance, standard deviation).	• Statistical tests of significance (null hypothesis significance testing).
	• Confidence intervals.
• Descriptive tables and figures (e.g. pie charts, histograms, boxplots, scatterplots).	• Parameter estimation and model fitting techniques.
	• Bayesian analysis.

The main aim of descriptive statistics is to present the results in a comprehensive, clear and succinct way. While this is relatively straightforward, incomplete and potentially misleading (not to mention the intentionally dishonest) data descriptions do occur fairly often. To address this problem, some professional organizations have issued guidelines regarding comprehensive and effective presentation of descriptive statistics (e.g. American Psychological Association, 2001). They tend to be rather general, however. Fortunately there is no shortage of very specific and practical help books (e.g Huff, 1991; Jones, 2006; Nicol *et al.*, 1999 and 2003). We also offer some tips on effective (and honest) data description (see Chapter 9).

Inferential statistics are no doubt more complex than the descriptive ones, so, inevitably, more often misapplied and misinterpreted. Thus, we devote the remaining part of this chapter to explaining the key aspects of inferential statistics, and clarifying some of the most common misunderstandings that surround them.

Statistical Hypothesis Testing

Consider the following two hypotheses:

Hypothesis 1: The more hours a day children spend watching TV, the greater their chance of becoming obese.

Hypothesis 2: Single men live shorter than those in stable relationships.

Both hypotheses are statements about whole populations: all children who have access to TV, and all men. They apply to individual members of the population, of course (e.g. Marcin Szczerbinski, a bachelor, living in Sheffield, UK), yet essentially they are statements about the population as a whole.

The only way to fully test hypotheses about populations would be to investigate each and every member of a given population. Since this is usually impossible (even if we narrow down our specification of population considerably, e.g. to include only all school-age UK children, or only all retired men living in London), the only viable option is to select and study a fraction of the population (a sample) and then try to extrapolate the conclusions onto the whole population. To achieve this, we need to translate our general hypothesis about populations into specific questions involving inferences, e.g.:

HYPOTHESIS		QUESTION
The more hours a day children spend watching TV, the greater their chances of becoming obese.	⇒	Given the relationship between daily TV watching and obesity we observed in a sample of 500 UK children, how likely is this hypothesis to be true?
Single men live shorter than those in stable relationships.	⇒	Given the mortality rate observed in a sample of 1000 retired men (some single, some married or co-habiting) living in London, how likely is this hypothesis to be true?

It is the kind of questions illustrated above that statistical hypothesis testing deals with.

The most popular approach to statistical hypothesis testing is the *null hypothesis significance testing* (thereafter NHST). It was developed at the beginning of the twentieth century and reached its maturity in the work of the British statistician and geneticist Ronald Fisher (1890–1962), whose books *Statistical Methods for Research Workers* (1925) and *The Design of Experiments* (1935) became classic references. Important modifications of Fisher's approach were suggested by his contemporaries Jerzy Neuman and Egon Pearson; these were widely adopted (hence the term 'Neuman-Pearson theory of hypothesis testing' that is often used). The approach gradually grew in popularity, so much so that today it is hard to find a quantitative research paper that would not report at least one null hypothesis significance test. Although often criticized or even rejected by some as logically flawed (e.g. Cohen, 1994), NHST remains the most commonly used approach to hypothesis evaluation in social sciences.* It is also very popular in biology and medicine.

---

* See Nickerson (2000) for an in-depth overview of the controversies surrounding NHST. Another interesting source is the polemic between Cohen (1994) and Hagen (1997) and the debate that followed it (*American Psychologist* 53, 796–803).

The process of NHST is presented in detail in every text-book on statistics, and on numerous webpages. Therefore, it would make little sense to write another extensive presentation of this type. Instead, we offer a non-technical précis, which is meant to aid the reader's understanding of standard textbook material. This précis is not intended for statisticians (who would probably be appalled by its simplistic nature) but for learners unfamiliar with, or confused by, standard textbook material.

Null Hypothesis Significance Testing: A Step-by-Step Guide

1. **Formulating the research (alternative) hypothesis**
   This is the hypothesis you ultimately want to test. It claims the existence of some type of a *population effect*: a difference or an association. It can take one of three general forms:
   - Hypothesis about differences between groups, e.g. *Women are better at multitasking than men.*
   - Hypothesis about difference between tasks or conditions, e.g.
     For English native speakers, it is easier to learn German than Chinese.
   - Hypothesis about association between variables, e.g. *The higher the children's productive vocabulary (measured at 4), the greater their reading comprehension (measured at 11).*

2. **Formulating the null hypothesis**
   The null hypothesis is the logical alternative to your research hypothesis. It states that the population effect postulated in the research hypothesis actually does not exist, e.g.:

Research Hypothesis	Null Hypothesis
Women are better at multitasking $\Rightarrow$ *than men.*	Men and women are no different in terms of their multitasking ability.
For English native speakers, it is $\Rightarrow$ *easier to learn German than Chinese.*	For English native speakers, German is just as easy (or hard) to learn as Chinese.

| *The higher the children's productive vocabulary at 4, the better their reading comprehension at 11.* | $\Rightarrow$ There is no relationship between children's productive vocabulary at 4 and their reading comprehension at 11. |

Typically the null hypothesis predicts that the population effect measured equals zero, e.g.:

'There is no difference between population A and B' = the difference between these populations is zero.

'There is no association between variables X and Y' = the coefficient of correlation between these variables has a value of zero.

However, sometimes the null hypothesis predicts different values, e.g.:

'The mean IQ of UK university students is no different from the mean IQ of the rest of the population' = mean IQ of university students is 100 (i.e. identical to the mean IQ of the whole UK population).

'7-year-old children are unable to perform this multiple choice reasoning test' = proportion of correct answers they will give is going to be 25 per cent (i.e. as expected by chance on a 1 out of 4 multiple choice test).

Formulation of the null hypothesis is usually an implicit step of the NHST process: unlike the research hypothesis, the null hypothesis is typically not spelled out in a research report.

At this point, we come upon the main paradox of the NHST process. Although we are interested in testing the truth or falsity of the research hypothesis, we are not actually testing it – not directly, anyway. Instead we ask *whether the data we collected could possibly be accounted for by the null hypothesis*. It is only when our data appear very unlikely in the light of the null hypothesis that we decide to reject it and adopt the alternative (research) hypothesis as a more plausible explanation for the data. In other words, we check whether the null hypothesis can be *falsified* by the data. If it can, we reject it and adopt its logical alternative – the research hypothesis.

People are often puzzled by this roundabout approach to the hypothesis testing. Surely the research hypothesis could be tested directly? The main reason why this would be difficult is that the research hypothesis is typically not specific enough. Take the research hypothesis:

Women are better at multitasking than men.

The hypothesis specifies the *existence* of an effect (average performance is different in male and female populations), and its *direction* (the average is higher in the female population), but not its *magnitude*. This could be 2, 3, 30, 34.6789 point difference on a multitasking test we used – or indeed, any other average difference favouring women. So, we have no specific expected value to test. In contrast, if you test the null hypothesis, a specific value is always given: in our example it is zero (i.e. no difference between men and women). This expected value becomes a starting point for the subsequent probability calculations (see below).

3. **Selecting a sample from the target population, collecting the data, obtaining descriptive statistics**
   The process of NHST assumes that a sample being tested is drawn by chance from the target population – that is, some kind of probability sampling is used (see Chapter 4). Probability samples may not reflect the whole population well because of *random sampling error*, but it is precisely this error that the NHST is set to control. If, on the other hand, we select our sample by non-random means we run a risk of *systematic error*, which is hard to control statistically. Researchers frequently use NHST with non-random, 'purposive' samples, since probability sampling is often difficult or even unfeasible (see Chapter 4). They should remember, however, that this makes their conclusions harder to generalize: it becomes unclear what constitutes the population to which the findings actually apply.

4. **Choosing the appropriate statistical test of significance**
   Null hypothesis significance testing is carried out using a large number of *statistical tests of significance* (or *significance*

tests for short). Each significance test is tailored to a specific class of research problems. Choosing the appropriate test depends on a few factors, including:

- The nature of the research question; in particular whether it concerns differences or associations (see page 122).
- Design of the study (number of variables and groups involved).
- Type of data (so called measurement scale of the data: nominal, ordinal, interval or ratio).
- Frequency distribution of the data.
- Sample size.

Each significance test has its proper name (*e.g. t-test, one-way analysis of variance*), which it often takes after its inventor (e.g. *Wilcoxon, Pearson, Spearman*), as well as a letter symbol (e.g. *F* for the analysis of variance, *r* for Pearson's correlation coefficient, etc.).

While a statistical apprentice may feel anxious or even overwhelmed with this variety of statistical tests, it is worth bearing in mind that all of them share the same basic logic and structure (outlined in this chapter), so understanding one of them well helps a great deal in understanding all the others. Moreover, a huge number of sources (textbooks and webpages) exist that offer in-depth discussion of individual texts of significance, their applications and assumptions (i.e. the conditions that have to be met if the test is to be used validly).

5. **Finding out how probable your results are, assuming the null hypothesis is true**

At this stage, we need to compute the value of our statistical test of significance, and the probability associated with that value. This probability tells us how likely our set of results is to occur if the null hypothesis is actually true. Those calculations allow us to make the following statements:

Example 1: testing a hypothesis about the means of two populations (using t-test).

> Let's assume that that the null hypothesis is true: the two populations being studied have identical means (i.e. the

difference between those means is zero). If that is so, then the chances of drawing a sample of 30 participants from each population, comparing the means of those samples (using t-test), and finding out a difference of moderate size (t-test value of 2.92) are only 1 in 200 (i.e. very low). In other words, if I kept repeating my study, drawing samples of 30 participants from two populations whose means are equal, it would be only 1 study for each 200 carried out that would give me a t-test value as high as 2.92 or higher.

Example 2: testing a hypothesis about association between two variables (using Pearson's correlation coefficient).

Let's assume that the null hypothesis is true: in the population being studied, the variables X and Y are totally unrelated (i.e. the coefficient of correlation between those variables is zero). If that is so, then the chances of drawing a sample of 20 participants from that population, analysing the strength of correlation between variables X and Y in that sample (using Pearson's correlation coefficient) and finding this correlation coefficient to be 0.23 (i.e. weak) are 1 in 3 (that is, quite high). In other words, if I kept drawing samples of 20 people from a population where variables X and Y are totally uncorrelated, in 1 out of 3 such studies I would find a Pearson's correlation co-efficient that would be equal to, or higher than 0.23.

The probability of a given result, assuming the null hypothesis, is known as *significance level* (often abbreviated to *sig.*) or the *p value* (where *p* stands for *probability*). It plays a central role in null hypothesis significance testing, which we will explain below.

At this point, we would like to reassure the mathematics-averse readers! In this day and age the calculations of values of significance tests (t-tests, correlation coefficients, etc.) and their corresponding probabilities are all done using specialist software (e.g. Excel, SPSS, Statistica). Its user needs to understand the meaning of the values obtained, but need not worry about the mechanics of obtaining them.

6. **Decision-making: rejecting or not rejecting the null hypothesis**

The *p* value allows us to make a decision about the plausibility of the null hypothesis – and so, by implication, also the research hypothesis. The examples below illustrate this decision-making process.

Premise: calculations tell me that if the null hypothesis is true then the probability of obtaining my result is low (p=.006, i.e. 6 in 1000).

Reasoning: If the null hypothesis is true then I am unlikely to get my result. Alas, this is the result I did get! The null hypothesis does not look like a plausible explanation of this result. It is more likely that the null hypothesis is false and I got the result I did because the alternative (research) hypothesis is true.

Decision: *reject the null hypothesis, accept the alternative (research) hypothesis* as the explanation for the result.

Premise: calculations tell me that if the null hypothesis is true then the probability of obtaining my result is high (p=.20, i.e. 1 in 5).

Reasoning: If the null hypothesis is true I am likely to get my results. So, the null hypothesis is a plausible explanation of my result. I do not need to seek any further hypothesis to explain it.

Decision: *do not reject the null hypothesis*, take it as a plausible explanation for the result. (This decision is always provisional. You must be prepared to reject the null hypothesis in the future if some new data compel you to do so.)

The decision about the null hypothesis is binary (reject–not reject). This introduces a problem: where to draw a line between rejection and non-rejection? How improbable does our result have to be, under the assumption of the null hypothesis, to force us to reject this hypothesis? A widely adopted statistical convention states that the null hypothesis should be rejected only if the probability of our result, assuming the null hypothesis, is less than 0.05 (i.e. less than 5 in 100 or 1 in 20). It is worth remembering that this is just a convention which is, inevitably, arbitrary to a degree.

The null hypothesis is, then, rejected (and the alternative hypothesis accepted) when the *p* value is lower than 0.05 (in formal notation: $p<.05$). In such case we would conclude that our results are *statistically significant*. The lower (i.e. closer to zero) the p value is, the more significant our results are and the stronger our grounds for rejecting the null hypothesis.* Conversely, if the p value is higher than 0.05 ($p>.05$) the null hypothesis is not rejected. In such a case we would conclude that our results are *not significant*.

So, when p<.05 we reason:

> If the null hypothesis is true, the effect we find here could occur by chance, but only on fewer than 1 in every 20 occasions – a rather improbable event. It is therefore more reasonable to conclude that the observed effect did not occur by chance, but reflects a *real* effect in the population we study. As the presence of such population effect was predicted by the research (alternative) hypothesis, we have a reason to accept this hypothesis'.

When $p>.05$ we reason:

> If the null hypothesis is true, the effect we find here could occur by chance on more than 1 in every 20 occasions – a fairly probable event. It is therefore reasonable to conclude that the observed effect is just a random occurrence – there is no reason to postulate an alternative explanation. In other words, there is not sufficient evidence that would convince us that a real population effect is present, and compel us to accept the research (alternative) hypothesis that predicted that effect.

You can see that the NHST requires us to be very cautious about rejecting the null hypothesis. Our data have to be very improbable (not just a bit unlikely) in the light of the null hypothesis, before we are asked to reject it and embrace the alternative hypothesis. The default decision is always: do not reject it!

Hypothesis Testing and the Possibility of Error

There is a close similarity between the process of NHST and the process of reaching a verdict in a court of law. Each require

* Which means that when the p value is very *low* (p<.01) then the results are *highly* statistically significant!

a binary decision (guilty–not guilty; reject–do not reject the null hypothesis). Each start with a default hypothesis (not guilty; no effect) that is rejected only once the evidence against it becomes insurmountable. Finally, the decisions are probabilistic: whether you choose to reject the default (not guilty, or null) hypothesis, or not reject it, you run some risk of error (see Figure 7.1.).

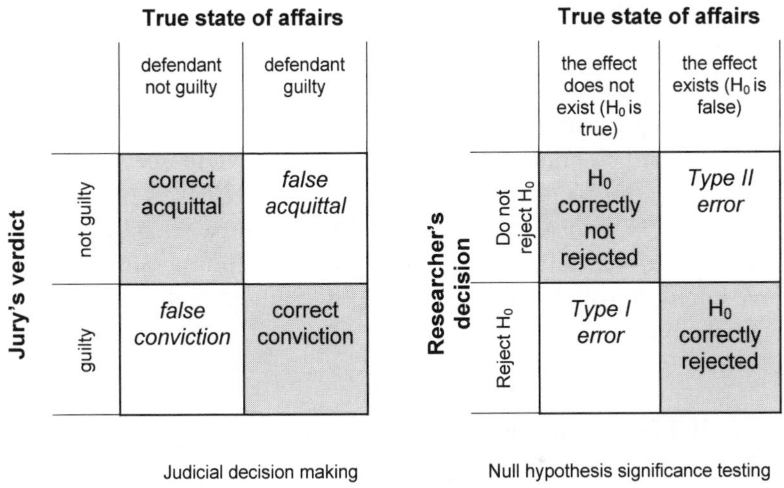

	True state of affairs	
	defendant not guilty	defendant guilty
Jury's verdict — not guilty	correct acquittal	false acquittal
Jury's verdict — guilty	false conviction	correct conviction

Judicial decision making

	True state of affairs	
	the effect does not exist (H_0 is true)	the effect exists (H_0 is false)
Researcher's decision — Do not reject H_0	H_0 correctly not rejected	Type II error
Researcher's decision — Reject H_0	Type I error	H_0 correctly rejected

Null hypothesis significance testing

Figure 7.1 Parallels between a Judicial Process and the NHST

If the researcher decides to reject the null hypothesis he runs a risk that it is actually true. Rejecting the null hypothesis that is in fact true is called *type I (one) error*. This is a statistical equivalent of false conviction. The risk of this error is usually small, however, given that the NHST requires strong evidence before the null hypothesis is rejected ($p<.05$ being the statistical equivalent of 'beyond reasonable doubt').

If the researcher decides not to reject the null hypothesis he risks that it is actually false. Not rejecting the null hypothesis that is in fact false is *type II (two) error*, a statistical equivalent of false acquittal. The probability of this error depends on:

- The actual magnitude of the population effect that is investigated: the smaller the effect the harder it is to detect, so the greater the risk of type II error.
- The amount of data available: the smaller the data set, the harder it is to see the real effect, thus the greater the risk of type II error.*
- The specific significance test that is used: some tests have greater *statistical power*, i.e. greater probability of detecting the effect if it really exists, thus lesser likelihood of producing type II error.

The researchers who study small population effects using small samples run a very high risk of type II error: their studies often fail to find any effect (even though it really does exist) because much more data would be required to see such an effect clearly. So, the best way to reduce the chances of type II error is to increase sample size. Many sources (e.g. Cohen, 1992) provide guidance regarding the minimum sample size required to offer an adequate (powerful enough) test of a research hypothesis.

Null Hypothesis Significance Testing: A Research Example

How are significance tests actually used in 'real research' to test hypotheses and reach a research conclusion? We illustrate this with a study published in an educational psychology journal.

STUDY: Stuart, M. (2004) 'Getting ready for reading: a follow-up study of inner-city second-language learners at the end of Key Stage 1'. *British Journal of Educational Psychology* 74, 15–36.

---

* To be precise, what matters here is the number of *degrees of freedom* (often abbreviated to *df*). Degrees of freedom represent the number of independent ('free to vary') data points that went into the analysis. The number of degrees of freedom is always slightly lower than the number of data points actually collected by the researcher. This is because, in the process of computing a statistical test of significance, a certain amount of information becomes no longer free to vary, but predetermined by the earlier stages of the calculation process.

RESEARCH PROBLEM: It has been debated whether children learning to read and write benefit from explicit and systematic phonics instruction (i.e. instruction in how letters and their combinations correspond to speech sounds). The study addresses this issue by comparing literacy skills of children taught with three distinct literacy programmes which differed in the amount and timing of systematic phonics instruction.

PARTICIPANTS: 101 7-year-old children living and attending schools in an inner-city London borough. 84 per cent of them learned English as a second language.

STUDY DESIGN: Experimental and longitudinal. The children were divided into three groups, each taught with a different programme, and followed from Reception (age 5) until Year 2 (age 7). Stuart (2004) reports only the final (Year 2) phase of the study; earlier phases were reported in a separate paper (Stuart, 1999).

INDEPENDENT VARIABLE: the method of literacy instruction. Three were compared:
-   Early systematic phonics (in Reception Year). This group used the Jolly Phonics programme (Lloyd, 1992).
-   Late systematic phonics (in Year 2). The Best Practice phonics scheme (Miskin, 1997) was used.
-   No systematic phonics; the Whole Language/Big Books approach (Holdaway, 1979).

DEPENDENT VARIABLE: Literacy. This was studied in several aspects: a) skills of segmenting words into their constituent sounds (phonemes); b) knowledge of correspondences between letters and phonemes; c) skills of decoding (sounding out) familiar and unfamiliar words, in and out of context; d) spelling skills; e) reading comprehension skills; f) skills demonstrated in formal literacy exam taken at the end of the initial stage of primary education; g) interest in reading, reading experiences and habits.

General spoken language ability was an additional variable measured.

OPERATIONALIZATION OF THE DEPENDENT VARIABLE: Several formal tests, a questionnaire and a formal school exam (Key Stage 1 SAT). Only two of those are discussed in detail here:

BAS Single Word Reading Test (Elliott *et al.*, 1983), a measure of single word reading accuracy.

Schonell Spelling test (Schonell and Schonell, 1952), a measure of spelling accuracy.

Performance on both tests is expressed in *age equivalents* (for definition see Chapter 8).

RESULTS: DESCRIPTIVE STATISTICS

Table 7.2 Results of BAS and Schonell Tests

| GROUP | N (sample size) | BAS reading age | | | Schonell spelling age | | |
		MEAN	STANDARD DEVIATION	RANGE	MEAN	STANDARD DEVIATION	RANGE
Early phonics	48	8.17	1.25	5.83–11.83	7.86	1.15	6.00–10.00
Late phonics	20	8.00	1.46	5.92–12.33	7.51	0.96	5.75–9.50
Big Books	33	7.54	1.47	4.67–10.50	6.89	1.31	4.50–9.33

RESULTS: INFERENTIAL STATISTICS. Average performance of the three groups was compared using one-way analysis of variance (ANOVA) with planned comparisons.

Reading: BAS reading ages did not differ significantly between the groups; $F(2,98)=2.09$, $p=.13$.

Spelling: Schonell spelling ages differ significantly between the groups; $F(2,98)=6.65$, $p<.01$. Planned comparisons analyses revealed that this was mostly due to the Early Phonics group significantly outperforming the Big Books group ($p<.05$). The differences between the Big Groups and Late Phonics, as well as between the Late Phonics and Early Phonics groups were not statistically significant.

STATISTICAL REASONING AND DECISION IMPLICIT IN THE SIGNIFICANCE TEST:

Reading: Let's assume that the three teaching methods are equally effective, i.e. result in exactly the same reading scores (the null hypothesis). If so, the probability of drawing samples of children taught with each method that are as large as ours (48, 20 and 33 participants) and differ in reading

Spelling: Let's assume that the three teaching methods are equally effective, i.e. result in exactly the same spelling scores (the null hypothesis). If so, the probability of drawing samples of children taught with each method that are as large as ours (48, 20 and 33 participants) and differ in spelling scores as much as ours (see Table 7.2) is 0.13 – that is, thirteen in a hundred. This is quite a high probability. Thus, the data we obtained are quite likely to occur if the null hypothesis is true (i.e. if the three teaching methods are equally effective). The null hypothesis provides a plausible account of the data; there is no reason to search for an alternative explanation. However, we must remember that new data may be collected in the future that will force us to reject the null hypothesis.

scores as much as ours (see Table 7.2) are less than 0.01 – that is, less than one in a hundred. This is a very low probability. Thus, the data we obtained are unlikely to occur if the null hypothesis is true (i.e. if the three teaching method are equally effective). So, it makes sense to reject the null hypothesis and accept the alternative (research) hypothesis (the three methods differ in effectiveness, resulting in different spelling scores) as a more plausible account of the data.

The same reasoning applies to the planned comparisons tests that followed the initial ANOVA test.

CONCLUSION:

There is no sufficient evidence that presence and timing of phonics teaching has impact on single word reading (as measured by the BAS test).

Systematic phonics teaching done *early* (in Reception Year) produces better spelling skills (as measured by Schonell test) than Big Book teaching. The late phonics results fall in between early phonics and Big Books; there is no sufficient evidence that late phonics is either better or worse than the other two approaches.

BROADER INTERPETATION: The results of other literacy tests reported in the paper (but not discussed here) indicate the phonics taught groups significantly outperformed the Big Books group on measures of phoneme blending, letter-sound knowledge, some measures of word reading (especially reading of unfamiliar words), and spelling. In most cases, the difference between early and late phonics groups was not significant, but *both* were significantly better than the Big Books group. The three groups did not differ on measures of reading comprehension, attitudes towards reading and reading habits.

CONCLUSIONS: Systematic phonics teaching (especially done early) is more effective than Big Books/Whole Language teaching. However, its advantage is limited mostly to lower levels of literacy: the ability to read and spell individual words. Even for word reading, the advantage is apparent on some tests only (e.g. not on BAS). Different teaching approaches appear equally effective in promoting reading comprehension and interest in reading.

LIMITATIONS:

(a) Population. The findings can be directly generalized only to the population of children from which the sample was drawn (British, inner-city, largely bilingual). The outcome could be different for different populations. (The author presented some additional analyses which tentatively suggested that the benefits of phonics teaching may be higher for monolingual English children.)

(b) Sample size. It was rather small, thus a risk of type II error was considerable. If larger samples could have been studied it is likely that more significant differences (undetectable with present numbers) could have been discerned (e.g. with respect to reading comprehension).

(c) Time span of the study. Differences between the groups may change as children grow older and develop their literacy skills further.

We hope it is apparent that, in the study summarized above, the NHST is not just an optional add-on, but an essential method of answering the research question.

Common Misinterpretations of the Null Hypothesis Significance Testing

NHST is often misinterpreted, even when it has been carried out correctly. Some of those misinterpretations may result from the conceptual complexity of the process. Others seem to be associated with the word 'significant', which, in the context of the NHST is used in a very specific, technical sense, quite different from its vernacular English meaning. Some of the most frequent misinterpretations are addressed below.

1. *Significance level (p value) is the probability of the null hypothesis being true.* Researchers who see a highly significant result (for example, $p=.004$) often reason along the following lines: 'My result is highly significant: $p=.004$. Therefore, there are only 4 chances in a 1000 that the null hypothesis is

true. So, there are 996 chances in a 1000 that my alternative (research) hypothesis is true. I should accept the research hypothesis – I am nearly certain it is true'. This reasoning is incorrect. The significance level (p value) does not represent the probability of the null hypothesis being true, but only *the probability of obtaining the data we did obtain if the null hypothesis were true*. These are not the same! To obtain the probability of the null hypothesis being true and, by implication, the research hypothesis being true (something the researcher ultimately wants to know) you need to consider not only your data, but also the a priori (pre-study) plausibility of your research hypothesis. It is only when those two pieces of information are considered together that the true probability of the null and research hypotheses can be computed (the procedure, called Bayesian analysis, is described in Nickerson, 2000). This, unfortunately, is usually not done. The reassuring news, however, is that scientists typically test research hypotheses whose a priori probability (estimated on the basis of existing evidence) is quite high, 50 per cent at least. If that is the case, then a statistically significant result can generally be interpreted as meaning 'the null hypothesis is probably false, so the research hypothesis is probably true'. This interpretation would be wrong, however, when testing research hypotheses whose probability is very low to start with. A good example is given by research into the existence of extrasensory perception (ESP) or the effectiveness of homeopathy. A single statistically significant result should *not* compel the researcher to reject the null and accept the research hypotheses ('ESP does exist'; 'Homeopathy has genuine healing powers'), because the a priori probability of those research hypotheses is extremely low.* A large number of studies, consistently producing highly significant

---

* We have no space to justify this claim fully. The most important reason is that the existence of ESP or the genuine healing power of homeopathy would clearly contradict much of what we know about the laws of nature. As such, their existence would violate the *principle of connectivity* (Stanovich, 2000).

results would be necessary before such hypotheses could be reasonably accepted. Putting it succinctly, extraordinary claims require extraordinary proof.

2. *'Statistically significant' means 'large'*. Not always! It is possible to observe the effect that is statistically significant (thus probably real) yet small, thus of little practical consequence. For example, it is known that people with large heads tend to have higher intelligence quotients (IQs) than those with small ones. This association between IQ and head size is probably genuine, since it came up as statistically significant in a number of studies (for a review, see Vernon *et al.* 2000; McDaniel, 2005). However, it is weak: only 3–7 per cent of individual differences in IQ can be predicted by differences in head size (Nguyen and McDaniel, 2000, in McDaniel, 2005). So, measuring head circumference in order to gauge someone's IQ would be highly impractical, as the resulting error of prediction would be huge!

    The distinction between *statistical* and *practical significance* is particularly important in the context of applied science. Think of a doctor who comes across a new method of treating a particular disorder and considers whether he should adopt it instead of the one he has been using so far. The compelling evidence for the superiority of the new method requires results that are better not only in the statistical sense, but also in the sense of being easily noticeable. A miniscule difference between the results of two competing therapies would provide no compelling reason for choosing one over another, even if that difference was statistically significant. The same would apply to a teacher making a choice between two competing teaching methods, or to any other practitioner who needs to make a choice considering the effectiveness of his or her work.

    Various statistical measures of practical significance (i.e. of magnitude of the observed effects) are available. They include *Cohen's d* (for measuring the magnitude of average difference between two groups or conditions) and *the coefficient of determination* (for measuring the strength or correlation between two variables) (Cohen, 1992; Kirk, 1996). It is absolutely essential that each study that reports statistical test of significance also reports measures of practical significance, or at least provides sufficient descriptive statistics to enable the readers to compute such measures themselves (Wilkinson and APA Task Force on Statistical Inference, 1999).

3. *'Statistically significant' means 'important', 'interesting' and 'revealing'*. Again, not always! Whether your findings are important, interesting or revealing is a function of how important and interesting your hypotheses were, and how sound the design of your study was – and not whether the results were statistically significant.

4. *A non-significant result means that my study has failed*. Far from it! Whether a study is a success or a failure depends on how interesting your research questions were, and how sound the methodology was. It is not a matter of squeezing significance out of your data! This misunderstanding runs quite deep: researchers tend to be less willing to submit null (non-significant) results for publications, and journals are less willing to publish them. This *file-drawer problem* may result in systematic bias in the published literature (Scargle, 2000).

As Vignette 4 hopefully illustrates, the null hypothesis significance testing can produce results that are interesting, important (and occasionally amusing!), whether they are statistically significant or not.

5. *If p=.049 then the result is significant. If p=.051 then it is not.* As we have mentioned earlier, NHST routinely uses the $p < .05$ as the criterion for rejecting the null hypothesis. In other words it is recommended that the probability of obtaining the data that were obtained if the null hypothesis is true must be less than 5 in 100, before we reject the null hypothesis. This criterion should not be adopted too mechanistically, however. If one test of significance produced the significance level of .049 ($p=.049$) and the other of .051 ($p=.051$) then, really and truly, their results are virtually identical and our conclusions regarding the null hypothesis should be the same. It is generally recommended that if we obtain the significance level lower than 0.10 ($p < .10$) but higher than 0.05, then this should be reported

as a 'difference approaching significance' and interpreted cautiously as (very weak) evidence in favour of rejecting the null hypothesis.

Beyond the Null Hypothesis Significance Testing

NHST is by far the most popular approach to statistical hypothesis testing in social sciences – but by no means the only one available. Other possibilities include: examination of confidence intervals, parameter estimation and model-fitting techniques, Bayesian analysis, and estimation of the probability of replicating the effect (so called p-rep) (Nickerson, 2000; Killeen, 2005). Arguably the best approach involves *research synthesis*: examining whether the effect we are interested in has been consistently replicated across independent studies (Torgerson, 2003).

The possibilities listed above need not be treated as alternatives to NHST and to each other, but rather as complementary approaches that can be integrated within the same research project.

Further Reading

Official advice on standards and conventions of reporting statistical information issued by the American Psychological Association (and adopted internationally; see Chapter 9):

American Psychological Association (2001) *Publication Manual of the American Psychological Association* (5th ed.). Washington DC: APA.

Wilkinson, A. and APA Task Force on Statistical Inference (1999) 'Statistical methods in psychology journals: guidelines and explanations'. *American Psychologist* 54, 594–603.

Practical tips on how to present and display descriptive statistics – and avoid being duped by dishonest presentations!

Huff, D. (1991) *How to Lie with Statistics*. London: Penguin.

Jones, G. E. (2006) *How to Lie with Charts* (2nd ed.). Charleston, S.C: Booksurge Llc.

Nicol, A., Nicol, A. M., and Pexman, P.M. (1999) *Presenting your Findings: A Practical Guide for Creating Tables*. Washington DC: American Psychological Association.

Nicol, A., Nicol, A. M., and Pexman, P.M. (2003) *Displaying your Findings: A Practical Guide for Creating Figures, Posters and Presentations*. Washington DC: American Psychological Association.

Vignette Four: Null Hypothesis Significance Testing: Some (Hopefully Interesting) Examples

Finding out that an effect, widely believed to exist, in fact does not can be very important. We need to know what therapies *don't* work, what factors *don't* cause diseases, and what variables share *nothing in common*. Thus, null results can be informative, providing they come from well-designed studies. Here is a handful of examples.

Table 7.3 Examples of Null and Significant Results

NULL RESULTS	SIGNIFICANT RESULTS
AUTISM	
There is no association between the MMR vaccine and the risk of developing autistic spectrum disorder (e.g. Demichelli *et al.*, 2005; Wilson *et al.*, 2003).	Individuals with autistic spectrum disorder have difficulties in reasoning about other people's minds (their beliefs, desires or intentions). This 'theory of mind' deficit is significantly greater than it could be expected given the (typically low) language skills and IQ of people with autistic spectrum disorder (Mitchell, 1997).
DYSLEXIA	
There is no association (or only a very weak association) between handedness and the risk of reading problems (Bishop, 1990).	Reading problems are strongly associated with the difficulties in processing speech sounds (Snowling, 2000).
SELF-ESTEEM	
There is no correlation between self-esteem and 'objective' physical attractiveness (i.e. one's self-esteem does nor relate to how physically attractive other people perceive one to be). Efforts to boost self-esteem of pupils do not improve their academic performance. High self-esteem does not prevent children from smoking, drinking, taking drugs or engaging in early sex (Baumeister *et al.*, 2003).	Self-esteem correlates very strongly with subjective physical attractiveness (i.e. the higher one's self-esteem, the higher one's perception of one's own physical attractiveness) (Baumeister *et al.*, 2003).

HAPPINESS

The following factors are not associated (or only weakly associated) with feeling happy: age, sex, 'objective' physical attractiveness, education (Layard, 2006).

The following factors are associated with feeling happy: family relationships, financial situation, work, community and friends, personal freedom (quality of government), personal values (philosophy of life) (Layard, 2006).

And finally . . .

There is 'no statistically significant correlation between shoe size and stretched penile length' (Shah and Christopher, 2002)

All other things being equal, athletes wearing red attire have significantly higher chance of winning than those wearing other colours (Hill and Barton, 2005).

8 Psychometrics: Measuring Traits and States

Etymologically, the term *psychometrics* means 'the measurement of the soul'. It describes the field of study and practice concerned with the measurement of human psychological characteristics. This measurement is achieved using a variety of instruments and procedures typically referred to as *tests*.

Even a cursory glance at any interdisciplinary catalogue of tests (e.g. Buros Institute of Mental Measurements, 2004) reveals a bewildering array of methods and variables measured. One can find tests of intelligence, various special abilities, attitudes (e.g. toward ethnic minorities), scholastic achievement, motor dexterity, speed of reaction, developmental disorders, and so on. Some tests require 'the testees' to perform certain tasks, others comprise a list of questions to be answered or statements to be evaluated, yet others are just detailed observational schedules. Yet beyond this variety lie core commonalities. All psychometric tests are concerned with individuals, not groups. All elicit and collect *samples of behaviour*. These behaviours are analysed and converted into a numerical value (score). The score is then used to infer something about individuals' *psychological characteristics* which are *latent* (i.e. directly unobservable). Finally, all psychometric tests worthy of their name must meet the same criteria of 'goodness': standardization, objectivity, reliability and validity – which we will discuss below.

While the psychological characteristics measured by psychometric test vary greatly, most are *psychological traits* – relatively stable characteristics of an individual (such as personality, intelligence, beliefs, attitudes, or specific skills). Some tests, however, measure current *psychological states*, which may fluctuate widely in the same person (e.g. current mood, level of alertness and so on).

Types of Tests

Most tests can be classified into a few broad categories, depending on the way in which data (i.e. behaviours) are elicited.

1. *'Objective' tests.* These instruments comprise series of purpose-built problems or tasks. The testee's performance on those tasks is taken as an index of some latent trait or state. Instruments of this type constitute 'tests' in the strictest, literal sense. Objective tests are typically used to measure either *potential for learning* (general ability or aptitude (i.e. intelligence), or specific abilities (e.g. musical, mathematical, linguistic, etc.)) or actual learning achievement (e.g. scholastic skills: reading, writing, arithmetic, etc.). There are many tests not typically thought of as 'psychometric' (e.g. tests of vision, hearing, or the driving test), which also effectively fall into that category.

    The term 'objective tests' is really a misnomer – all good tests ought to be objective, and so-called objective tests are not necessarily more objective than others. 'Performance test' is probably a better, if still not fully precise, label for that category of instruments.

2. *Questionnaires.* These instruments consist of lists of statements or (less often) questions. The testee has to indicate his or her degree of agreement with each statement, or answer each question. While most questionnaires require self-report (they are filled in by the 'testee'), some rely on 3rd-person reporters (e.g. a parent filling in a questionnaire assessing characteristics of his or her child).

    Questionnaires are the most commonly used method of assessing temperament, personality, beliefs and attitudes. They also play an important role in the diagnosis of mental disorders.

    Completing questionnaires requires adequate language comprehension and (unless they are delivered orally) adequate reading skills. This naturally limits their use in certain populations (e.g. children, functionally illiterate adults), though those limitations may be partly overcome by supplementing written items with their pictorial or symbolic equivalents (e.g. Brumfitt and Sheeran, 1999a, 1999b).

3. *Structured interviews.* Open-ended, unstructured or semi-structured interviews lie outside the domain of psychometrics, since they are not standardized (see below). However, structured interviews, consisting of scripted questions, may be considered psychometric methods. They are rather similar to questionnaires; adequate language skills are also a prerequisite of their successful completion.

4. *Projective techniques.* This type of assessment is closely linked with the psychodynamic theories of human mind, developed by Sigmund Freud and his followers. According to their proponents, projective techniques allow us to probe feelings, motives and conflicts that became unconscious (actively repressed by the mind) because of their threatening nature.

Projective tests involve presentation of some open-ended material, such as incomplete sentences (e.g. 'My mother always ...'), ambiguous pictures, or amorphous ink blots (used in the famous Rorschach test; see Figure 8.1). The testee is encouraged to freely 'interpret' the material (complete the sentences, tell the story about each picture, state what he/she 'sees' in the ink blots, etc.). Since the material is inherently ambiguous, the testee's responses are inevitably the 'projections' of the contents of his mind – hence the name of the technique. The responses are then classified, interpreted and scored according to some preset criteria.

Projective techniques are used most often to assess personality and emotions, or assist in the diagnosis of mental disorders. Their popularity, once great, seems to be on the wane. The main reason for this probably lies in the relative demise of the psycho-dynamic theories of mind, from which projective techniques originate. Additionally, their administration is often very time- and labour-consuming. Most   importantly   from   our methodological point of view, numerous studies have shown that projective techniques often lack objectivity and reliability, and provide little information that cannot also be gained by other, more straightforward, techniques, such as questionnaires or interviews (Lilienfeld, Wood and Garb, 2000, 2001).

Figure 8.1 First of the Ten Cards of the Rorschach Inkblot Test (Source: Rorschach inkblot test, 2007)

5. *Observational scales.* These are lists of categories that can be used to structure one's observation of a particular person or event. Observational data collected that way can then be scored. Observational scales are particularly useful in assessing young children (e.g. the quality of their play, communication with peers and adults) and may be used to identify developmental delays or disorders. Strictly speaking, such techniques do not constitute psychometric *tests*, since the behaviour is not elicited but merely observed. However, observational scales are used to measure psychological characteristics and they have to meet the same criteria of objectivity, reliability and validity as all other psychometric procedures.

The Use of Psychometric Tests: Criterion–Referenced versus Norm–Referenced Assessment

It is possible to use the results of psychometric assessments merely to describe the psychological characteristics of a testee (i.e. identify the skills he/she has or lacks, types of problems he/she can or cannot solve, etc.). However, this is not their main use. Typically, psychometric assessments are used to compare the performance of a testee against some external benchmark: a criterion or a set of norms.

In *criterion-referenced* assessment, performance is compared against a fixed standard, which is established before the assessment is carried out. The outcome of such assessment is typically binary (pass–fail) and the criterion represents the minimum level of skills or competencies deemed 'good enough' for passing. Examples include a driving test (which can only be passed when knowledge of the Highway Code and specific driving skills are demonstrated) or university admissions criteria (which require a certain profile of marks from high school graduation exams). Criterion-referenced assessments are used mostly in the context of selection, when a sample (usually small) of 'good enough' testees needs to be chosen from a larger pool of candidates.

A vast majority of tests used in the context of research or clinical (special needs) assessment fall into the *norm-referenced* category. Here, the testee's performance is compared with the performance of her peers (or, more technically, performance of other people from the same population). Statements such as 'John's intelligence is in the top 2 per cent of children of his age', 'Mary's language skills are age appropriate' or 'Tom's reading ability is below average' reflect norm-referenced assessment.

Needless to say, a norm-referenced test requires the *norms*, i.e. information on distribution of the scores obtained on this test by individuals from the population of interest. The process of collecting this information is called the *normalization of the test*. We will discuss it in the following section.

The Ingredients of a Good Psychometric Test

Standardization. The requirement of standardization stipulates that all aspects of a test (its instruction, materials, testing procedure, criteria for scoring the results) should be identical each time the test is used. The necessity of standardization is obvious if we remember that psychometrics is about making meaningful *comparisons* between scores obtained on the same test by different people (or the same person tested repeatedly). Unless the test was standardized it would be impossible to decide whether the observed difference in scores reflects genuine differences in the trait or state being measured, or is merely an artefact of using a somewhat different test.

To make the test standardized, its authors must produce directions for administering the test that are very clear and precise, leaving no scope for alternative interpretations. Even the exact wording of the instructions to be given to the testees should be specified.

Objectivity. This requirement concerns the interpretation of test results. If a test is objective, then two (or more) assessors examining the same filled-in test sheet should arrive at the same score, even though they work 'blind' (not communicating with each other, and not knowing the testee). To make the test objective, its authors must produce scoring criteria that are precise and unambiguous.

Reliability. If a test is reliable, then it measures *precisely*, i.e. it results in negligible *measurement error*. The simplest way to check reliability is to repeat measurement. A reliable measurement instrument should produce the same result each time the same object is measured. This principle is usually straightforward when we measure physical variables (length, mass, etc.). For example, if you were to measure the length of your living room repeatedly with a tape meter you would expect to obtain a virtually identical value each time. Substantially different readings would suggest that your instrument is unreliable (e.g. a tape measure made of elastic). However, checking reliability is much more complex when it comes to psychological traits. Since human beings learn and remember, repeating the assessment is bound to affect its results: for example, the scores may improve as a result of practice, or get worse as a result of boredom. So, while repeating the testing may still be a useful way of checking reliability in certain contexts, it is insufficient. Psychometricians have developed alternative procedures for ascertaining reliability, which bypass the need for repeated testing. Most of them involve examining the degree of agreement (consistency) between scores obtained on different parts of the same test. For example, the test may be 'split into halves' (by separately adding the scores obtained on even and odd items) to measure the consistency of those half-test scores. In a similar vein, we can examine responses given to each and every individual item the test is built of, and measure how well they 'agree'. Appendix 1 at the end of this book provides a longer and more technical summary of different ways of assessing test reliability.

The degree of reliability can be expressed mathematically as a reliability coefficient. It can vary between zero (a totally unreliable test, which picks up random 'noise' and does not really measure anything) and 1 (a hypothetical ideal instrument which measures with perfect precision). The reliability co-efficient represents the proportion of individual differences in test results that can be attributed to genuine differences on the variable being measured, and not to measurement error.* So, a test whose reliability coefficient is 0.80 is 80 per cent reliable, i.e. 80 per cent of individual differences picked up by it are down to true differences between things being measured, while the remaining 20 per cent constitute measurement error. This, naturally, begs a question: what constitutes a 'good enough' level of reliability? The answer, predictably, is not universal, but depends on the purpose of testing. This is the case not only with psychometric assessment but also with any other type of measurement: an engineer building a huge bridge requires more precise measurement than one building a bungalow. Some rules of thumb have been proposed, however. Nunnally

---

*Putting it more technically, reliability coefficient is the proportion of *variance* in test scores that is due to true differences on the variable being measured (Hammond, 2000).

(1978, in Hammond, 2000) suggests that the reliability coefficient needs to be at least 0.70 if the test is to be used as a research tool, and at least 0.90 if it is to be used for individual diagnosis or selection purposes. Nunnally's criteria are perhaps too strict; many instruments widely accepted as 'good enough' for the purpose of individual diagnosis fall short of 0.90 standard. What constitutes good enough reliability should perhaps be decided on a case-by-case basis, considering how precise a measurement is required (and feasible) in any given case. It should also be remembered that the limitations of imperfect perfect reliability can be overcome (to a degree) by using confidence intervals (see below).

Validity. If a test is valid, it measures what the users believe it measures, and not something else. In other words, validity is the degree to which a test is true to its name (i.e. if it is called 'a test of intelligence' it should measure intelligence and not, say, attention or motivation). Validity is the most important requirement of all psychometric tests; indeed, in its broader sense (ability to demonstrate that a theoretical claim is sustained by the data; Cohen, Manion and Morrison, 2000) it is an essential requirement of every scientific investigation (see Chapter 3).

Psychometric apprentices often confuse reliability and validity. The two are indeed related: reliability is a necessary but not a sufficient condition of validity. If a test is unreliable it cannot be valid (because it measures *nothing* precisely). However, even a very reliable test may be invalid (if it measures precisely something other than what the users believe it to measure). The following example is often used to illustrate the distinction: an ill-calibrated bathroom scale that overestimates the weight of everybody that stands on it by 10 pounds is reliable (its readings are consistent) but invalid (since it does not tell you what you want to know (your weight) but something else (your weight + 10 pounds)).

Establishing validity is usually trivial when it comes to measuring directly observable, physical variables: we know that a (properly calibrated) bathroom scale measures body weight, and not temperature, while the reverse is the case with a thermometer. However, the validity of the measurement of latent psychological variables is always a complex matter, for at least two reasons. First of all, such variables are hard to *operationalize*. A latent variable can only be measured indirectly, *inferred* from some directly observable behaviours that are its indices. Yet what behaviours one should look at is often far from straightforward (e.g. what behaviours are indicative of 'racist attitude'?) and bad choices made there will inevitably compromise test validity.

Secondly, human performance on any task, however simple it may seem, is always determined by *multiple causes* – so no psychometric test measures just one variable. For example, the result of a spelling test is (hopefully!) determined by the knowledge of words' spellings, but also by motor/handwriting skills (in the case of spelling to dictation), attitudes towards spelling and scholastic tasks generally, attention span and persistence on task (especially if the test is long), and so on. In the light of these constraints, the definition of test validity should perhaps be modified: a test is valid if its results are determined *primarily* by the variable we want it to measure, and much less by other variables.

Establishing validity is more complex than establishing reliability: it is not a matter of computing a single reliability coefficient. Validity has many facets and dimensions, so several research studies are needed to see whether a test is valid. The key aspects of psychometric validity are listed below; a more comprehensive summary is provided in Appendix 2 at the end of this book.

- *Face validity*. This criterion is met when the test *appears* to measure what it purports to measure. Needless to say, this criterion is subjective and insufficient in most contexts.
- *Criterion validity*. If a test indeed measures a particular variable, then its results should agree with other, external criteria of that variable, whose validity is not itself in dispute. For example, a psychometric test of creativity (e.g. Urban and Yellen, 1996), if valid, should produce much higher scores among professionals whose jobs require 'thinking out of the box' (e.g. painters, designers,

architects, filmmakers), in comparison with members of more 'conventional' professions.

- *Content validity.* A test that is valid in that respect has the content (tasks, questionnaire items) that represents the variable to be measured in a comprehensive way. For example, a test of reading comprehension for adults that checks only literal understanding of narrative prose has limited content validity, since adults read many types of texts (narrative prose, but also poetry, newspapers, textbooks, instructions, application forms, maps, guides, etc.), and should have the ability to extract their literal as well as inferential (hidden) meanings.

- *Construct (theoretical) validity.* If a test indeed measures a particular variable, then the results it produces should be consistent with what the scientific theory and existing empirical data tell us about that variable. For example, it has been established that intelligence is related to academic achievement (Neisser *et al.*, 1996; Gottfredson, 1997), but essentially unrelated to personality traits (Zeidner and Matthews, 2000). A new test of intelligence, if it is valid, should replicate that pattern of correlations.

All this means that establishing validity is not a matter of a single study, but a systematic research programme. Thus, conclusions about the validity of a test can only emerge slowly, as the evidence from various studies accumulates.

Normalization. The requirement of normalization applies to norm-referenced tests only, i.e. those that interpret the performance of a testee by comparing it with the performance of other members of the same population. To make such comparisons possible, we need the norms: a set of test scores obtained from a sample of people representative of the population we are interested in.

Valid (i.e. unbiased) norms require a representative sample: one that is sufficiently large and (most importantly) selected through probability sampling. Testing such a sample is not an easy task, especially if the target population is large and diverse. For example, to collect test norms truly representative of US adults one would have to test a sample whose structure would reflect the age, geographic, linguistic, ethnic and socio-economic structure of the US adult population. Needless to say this would be a complex task (requiring some type of stratified or cluster sampling; see Chapter 4), and its cost would be considerable. Inevitably, large-scale normalization studies (making the norms representative of a large population, e.g. of an entire country) are relatively rare. They are typically carried out by large test publishing companies, who can afford to hire the required team of testers and data analysts, and then recoup the costs through test sales. Even then subtle biases may creep into the normalization process; for example, it is usually the case that normalization samples under-represent people of lower socio-economic status, as such individuals are harder to access.

While an individual researcher or diagnostician is usually not in a position to collect the norms for the test he or she uses (unless dealing with a very small population, e.g. a single school), he/she is responsible for checking whether the norms used are valid (unbiased); that is, whether the testees *belong to the population on which the test was normed*. The answer can be found in a technical manual that accompanies each high-quality norm-referenced test, which describes the normalization process and the characteristics of the normalization sample (home language, place of residence, age, sex, education, etc.). The test user should also pay attention to the time when the norms were collected. Norms of some tests (e.g. of attitudes or scholastic achievement) age rather rapidly, becoming obsolete due to educational, economic, ethnic and other changes that affect the population of interest. Ideally, tests should be re-normed every decade or so.

Interpreting the Results of Norm-Referenced Tests: The Derived Scores

Once the test is normalized, it becomes possible to interpret its results. This is done through converting the *raw scores* (the direct result of testing: a number of correct answers, time taken to complete the tasks, etc.) into *derived scores* that allow us to make meaningful comparisons between performance of different individuals. Below we describe four types of derived scores that are used most frequently.

Age equivalents and grade equivalents. These derived scores interpret performance by identifying the chronological age (in the case of age equivalents) or the school grade (in the case of grade equivalents) for which a given raw score is typical (average). For example, if a raw score of 30 points on a reading test is average for 7-year-old children, then any person (no matter what their chronological age) who obtains such raw score is said to have a reading age of 7 years. Likewise, any person has a mental age of 11 years if, on an IQ test, they have achieved a raw score that is typical of 11-year-olds. By definition, a typically developing person would show no discrepancy between chronological age (and school grade) and performance measured in age or grade equivalents.

Age and grade equivalents are appealing through their intuitive simplicity: statements such as 'the score of your child would be typical for a 7-year-old' can be understood by non-professionals. Moreover, age and grade equivalents describe the *absolute level of attainment* since they identify the chronological age (or the school grade) for which a given score is typical. Other types of derived scores (percentile ranks and standard scores which we describe below) can describe only *relative level of attainment* – relative to attainment of other people of the same age.

Despite these advantages, valid applications of age and grade equivalents are very limited, and they are very prone to misinterpretations. For a start, they are hard to use when assessing adults, who are no longer in full-time education and whose performance typically 'plateaus' and changes little with age. Secondly, age and grade equivalents, which are merely descriptions of test performance, are routinely overinterpreted as statements regarding the nature and quality of underlying competence. So, while age equivalents allow us to say that 'on a reasoning test, John *obtained a score that is typical for 6-year-olds*', this is often understood to mean that 'John *reasons like a 6-year-old*'. Such interpretation is usually invalid: if John is an intellectually impaired 20-year-old individual who obtains a reasoning test score typical of a 6-year-old, then he probably does not reason anything like a typical 6-year-old; his way of going about solving intellectual problems is very different.

Finally, when we compare someone's age or grade equivalents with their chronological age or actual school grade, we may be tempted to make statements indicating developmental delay (e.g. 'the child is delayed in mental development by two years') or acceleration (e.g. 'the child is one year ahead of his/her age in reading'). The meaning of such a statement is imprecise, as it depends very much on a person's chronological age. An example taken from the TOWRE (Test of Word Reading Efficiency, Torgesen, Wagner and Rashotte, 1999), a measure of reading rate used widely in the US, illustrates this. Tables of norms included in the TOWRE manual tell us that, on that test, an average US child reads 27–30 words (during the allotted time of 45 seconds) at the age of 7 years, 56–7 words at 9 years, 88 words at 15 years, and 96 words at 17 years. So, a 9-year-old child who reads 30 words can be said to show a 'two year delay in reading skills' – and so can a 17-year-old who reads 88 words. However, the meaning of this 'two year delay' is very different in each case. For a 9-year-old it means a substantial discrepancy (53 per cent of the expected score), which is relatively rare (only 4 per cent of 9-year-olds read 30 words or fewer). For a 17-year-old the discrepancy is relatively minor, however (92 per cent of the expected score) and fairly common (23 per cent of 17-year-olds read 88 words or fewer). Thus, an apparently equivalent delay is nothing of the kind!

Because of their limitations, age and grade equivalents should not be used as the main tool of interpreting test performance, but only as an additional way of describing it. Good modern psychometric tests (like the Test of Word Reading Efficiency mentioned above) indeed limit their use to this auxiliary capacity.[*]

Percentile ranks. When we convert raw scores into percentile

---

[*] An alternative way of describing absolute level of performance that is far superior to age and grade equivalents is provided by so called *absolute scores* (e.g. Wilkinson, 1993). Since absolute scores are a relatively recent development, as yet rarely used, we do not discuss them here.

ranks, we state what per cent of people in our normalization sample performed *the same or worse*. If a raw score of 30 points corresponds to the 45th percentile, it means that 45 per cent of our normalization sample obtained a score of 30 points or worse, while the remaining 55 per cent of the sample a score of 30 points or better (the individuals who performed the same – 30 points in our case – are evenly divided into the 'worse' and 'better' categories). If a raw score of 57 points corresponds to the 77th percentile, then 77 per cent of our sample obtained a score of 57 or lower, while the remaining 33 per cent scored 57 or more points; and so on. Percentile ranks scale ranges from 1 to 99; the 1st and the 99th percentile represent the worst and the best performing 1 per cent of the population, respectively.

While age or grade equivalents are used to make comparisons across ages or grades (e.g. the performance of a 7-year-old may be likened to the performance of older or younger children, depending on how good or poor it is), percentile ranks are only used to make comparisons within the same cohort, i.e. against individuals falling within the same age or grade band. Thus, the comparisons are relative to that band, and not absolute (so the performance that represents the 99th percentile among 6-year-olds is excellent for a 6-year-old but probably not for a 16-year-old). Limiting the comparisons in that way is useful as it makes percentile ranks equally suitable for interpreting the performance of people of any age, children as well as adults. The greatest advantage of percentile ranks is that they express *how typical* (or not) a particular score is for a population of individuals of given age or grade. What they cannot tell us is how much any two individuals with unequal percentile ranks *actually differ in their performance*. This is because equal intervals of percentile ranks do not correspond to equal intervals in the performance being measured. For example, a difference between the 50th and the 55th percentiles may represent a negligible difference in actual performance (e.g. just one more correct answer), while the (numerically identical) difference between the 94th and the 99th percentile may represent a substantial performance discrepancy (e.g. 15 more correct answers). Putting it technically, percentile ranks constitute an ordinal measurement scale (that tells us who is better), but not an interval scale (that also tells us *how much* better). Appendix 3 at the end of the book illustrates this.

When making very fine distinctions in performance levels is unnecessary or impossible, percentile ranks can be replaced with *deciles* (10 ranks, each representing 10 per cent of the population) or *quartiles* (4 ranks, each representing 25 per cent of the population).

Deviation-based scores (standard scores). Standard scores inform us how much a particular raw score differs from the mean of the normalization sample. That difference is measured in standard deviation units, standard deviation being a descriptive statistics measure of how widely spread the scores are. Standard scores, like percentile ranks, describe relative attainment, i.e. allow us to make comparisons only within the same (narrow) age or grade band.

Raw scores can be converted into standard scores using the formula:

$$z = \frac{X - M}{SD}$$

where X is an individual raw score, M and SD are, respectively, the mean and the standard deviation of the raw scores in the normalization sample. Standard scores produced using this formula are called *z scores*.

To give an example: if the distribution of raw scores in the normalization sample has the mean of 25.00 and the standard deviation of 10.00, then a person who scores 30 points obtains a z score of 0.5 (i.e. half a standard deviation above the mean) when compared against that sample. A person who scores 10 points would obtain a z score of −1.5 (i.e. one and a half standard deviation below the mean).

It is customary to interpret scores falling within one standard deviation from the mean (±1z) as 'normal', 'typical', 'ordinary' or 'within average range'; those more than 1z away from the mean as 'high' or 'low' (depending on whether they are positive or negative), while those more than 2z away from the mean as 'very high' or 'very low'. By this convention, the first person in the above example demonstrates typical performance, slightly 'on the positive side' (high average), while the second person performed rather poorly. Naturally, one must always remember that this interpretative convention is partly arbitrary, though it makes sense if the raw scores are normally distributed (see below).

Unlike percentile ranks, standard scores constitute an interval scale of measurement: they can tell us how much any two participants differ in their performance. Equal intervals of standard scores translate into equal intervals in actual performance being measured: for example, two individuals whose z scores are, say, -1.0 and 1.0 differ in their performance exactly as much as those who score $1.5z$ and $3.5z$.

Standard scores in the form of z scores are rarely used in contemporary psychometrics, being replaced by *normalized standard scores*. They also interpret individual raw scores in terms of the distance away from the mean of the normalization sample (measured in standard deviations), but with two important modifications:

1. 'Normalizing' the distribution. As far as precision and ease of interpretation are concerned, the ideal distribution of raw data is *the normal distribution* ('the bell curve'), where exactly the same number of people perform above and below the mean, and most of them quite close to the mean (see Appendix 3). However, the distribution of 'real-life' data, collected from normalization samples, often departs somewhat from that ideal shape. To deal with this problem, the data are transformed into normal distribution: distances between the z scores are adjusted so that the resulting new distribution resembles the normal distribution as much as possible (for details of this rather simple procedure see e.g. Anastasi, 1990).

   Once the data have been transformed into the normal distribution we can use our knowledge of that distribution to translate standard scores into percentile ranks, or vice versa. For example, we know that, if the distribution is normal, the score of $-2z$ (2 standard deviations below the mean) corresponds to the 2nd percentile, the score of $-1z$ to the 16th percentile, $0z$ (i.e. the mean) to the 50th percentile, $1z$ to the 84th percentile, and so on (see

Appendix 3). These correspondences simply follow from the (mathematically defined) properties of the normal distribution. Once any set of raw data is transformed into the normal distribution, we can start using these correspondences, which is very helpful in interpreting individual test scores.

A slight disadvantage of 'normalizing' the distribution is that the subsequent measurements are no longer, strictly speaking, of the interval type: equal intervals between normalized standards scores do not correspond to exactly equal intervals in the actual performance being measured. This is the result of the adjustments to the distances between scores that were made to make the distribution normal. The departures from the interval measurement are small when the original distribution of the raw data was similar to the normal distribution to start with; if it was not, however, then the departures may be large.

2. Choosing convenient values of mean and standard deviation. When we use z scores, we have to use positive as well as negative values, and whenever we wish to describe finer differences in performance we must produce fractions. This is inconvenient and error prone. We can avoid this if we express normalized standard score on a scale whose mean and standard deviation values are chosen for our convenience. For example, we may decide that a score that is exactly average will be assigned a (conventional) value of 100, and there will be 15 points to every standard deviation. This was the convention adopted by American psychologist David Wechsler to express the results of intelligence tests he created, and now used (under the name of *Wechsler scores*) with numerous other tests. Since Wechsler scores have the mean (M) of 100 and the standard deviation (SD) of 15, this means that a person whose performance is exactly average is assigned a score of 100, a person performing one standard deviation above the mean gets a score of 115; someone performing half a standard deviation below a mean gets a score of (approximately) 93 and so on. There are no negative values, and no fractions.

Figure 8.2 illustrates the process of converting raw scores into normalized standard scores. Raw data (collected from a sample of 242 Polish Reception year children) represent reading rate scores (number of words read correctly per minute). They are

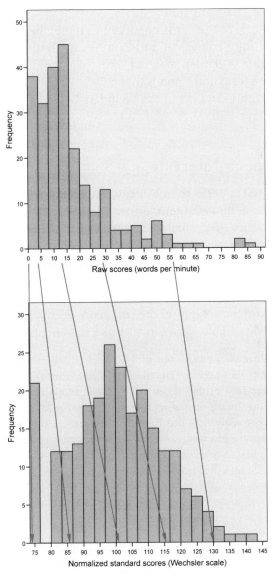

Figure 8.2 Converting Raw Scores into Normalized Standard Scores

transformed (so that their distribution approximates the normal distribution) and expressed as Wechsler scores (M=100, SD=15).

Apart from the Wechsler scores, other types of normalized standard scores are widely used (see Appendix 3). These include: *scaled scores* (M=10, SD=3), *T scores* (M=50, SD=10), *stanines* (or 'standard nines': M=5, SD=2), *stens* (or 'standard tens': M=5.5, SD=2). It is important to remember that all these scores are fully equivalent and express exactly the same information: the Wechsler score of 130 (two standard deviations above the mean) corresponds to the scale score of 16, T score of 70, 9th stanine, and lies at the boundary between 9th and 10th sten (see Appendix 3).

Confidence Intervals

Since no test is perfectly reliable, each psychometric assessment carries some measurement error. In other words, a testee's observed score (the actual score obtained on the test) may differ somewhat from the true score (the true level of the trait or state measured). However, this problem can be bypassed, at least to a degree. If we know the reliability coefficient of the test we use, we can build *a confidence interval* around the testee's observed score, in order to 'capture' the true score with a certain degree of probability. This allows us to make statements like this:

> Mary obtained an IQ score of 117. Such score may be labelled as 'high' (i.e. above the average range of performance). I would like to be 95 per cent certain about what Mary's true score is. Probability calculations (based on test reliability) tell me that, in order to capture Mary's true score with that degree of confidence, I must allow for 10 points margin of error. So, I can be 95 per cent certain that Mary's true IQ lies somewhere between 107 (i.e. 117−10) and 127 (i.e. 117+10) − so it lies either at the upper end of the average range of performance, or is indeed above that range. It is possible that Mary's true IQ is lower than 107 or higher than 127, but it is rather improbable (5 per cent chance).

All textbooks of psychometrics provide formulae for computing confidence intervals. However, test users rarely need to deal with them, since all good test manuals go one step further and inform the reader directly about the size of confidence intervals (i.e. they state the number of standard score points that have to be added to and taken away from the observed score in order to build a confidence interval of certain probability). 68 per cent, 80 per cent, 90 per cent and 95 per cent confidence intervals are used most often.

Using confidence intervals is an honest way of reporting psychometric data, as it explicitly acknowledges the uncertainty (measurement error) that goes with such methods. Moreover, using confidence intervals allows us to compare different scores (scores of different people, or the same person tested repeatedly) and see whether they differ significantly – that is, whether a difference in observed scores is likely to represent a genuine difference on the variable being measured, or just measurement error. This has many practical applications (e.g. measuring the effectiveness of educational or psychological intervention). Many textbooks of psychometrics as well as test manuals provide detailed instructions on using confidence intervals to examine the significance of the difference between two scores.

Advantages, Limitations (and Confusions) of Psychometric Assessment: The Case of IQ Testing

The huge advantage of psychometric methods is their convenience. Psychometric data can be obtained much faster, often cheaper, and are easier to interpret than data collected using alternative approaches. This, no doubt, is one of the main reasons for the huge popularity of psychometric methods. While convenience should never be the main criterion for choosing a research method, it naturally has to play a role.

Well designed psychometric tests can also be very reliable. For example, some tests designed to measure stable traits fulfil the expectations: individual differences they pick up persist over the period of several years and sometimes even decades. This has been demonstrated in several longitudinal studies, for example of reading ability (Scarborough, 1998), personality traits (Roberts and DelVeccio, 2000) and general intelligence (Deary et al., 2000).

Despite these advantages, psychometric assessment has attracted a great deal of (often quite heated) criticism and controversy. Of all areas of psychometrics, the assessment of intelligence appears to be a particular bone of contention. A dominant view of intelligence postulates the existence of a latent trait called 'general intelligence' or 'general mental ability' that influences our performance on all problem-solving tasks in all life contexts, so is highly relevant to our educational, professional and social success. This trait can be reliably measured using intelligence tests and expressed with a single number called IQ (intelligence quotient). These claims have their vocal supporters (e.g. Jensen, 1998; Herrnstein and Murray, 1994) and equally vocal critics (e.g. Gould, 1996; Richardson, 2000). Naturally, we do not hope to resolve this debate here, but we want to expose some (commonly made) claims about IQ and its assessment that we believe to be myths: not fully false perhaps, but imprecise and conceptually confused. The reader should bear in mind that our main interest lies with psychometric assessment generally (its advantages and limitations) and not with IQ testing per se. We use the latter as a convenient example of how claims regarding the psychometric assessment can be evaluated.

Myth 1: IQ tests measure intellectual potential that is fully innate and thus unmodifiable

It is definitely true that the *intention* of the designers of an IQ test is to measure intellectual potential – your ability to solve new problems and learn. Research confirms that they indeed measure such potential, to a degree: for example, IQ scores predict educational achievement, even after some other relevant factors (such as socio-economic status) are controlled for (Neisser *et al.*, 1996). However, this should not be taken to imply that the IQ test measures pure potential, 'uncontaminated' by one's background and experience – simply because the concept of context-free and experience-free intellectual potential is meaningless. Nor, indeed, is it possible for any test to measure just one 'pure' variable anyhow – the point we made earlier. So, a valid test of intelligence measures intellectual potential that is relevant for learning and problem-solving in the context of a particular culture.

As for the innateness (i.e. genetic determination) of such potential, no sensible debate about it is possible unless a distinction is made between *relative differences* in intelligence (relative standing in the age cohort one belongs to), and the *absolute level* of intelligence (absolute standing in the entire population of all ages). A person whose IQ score falls within the 10th percentile when measured at the age of 5, 35 and 65 maintains the same relative standing in relation to his or her same-age peers, yet her actual level of intellectual ability changes very substantially, being the highest at the age of 35 and the lowest at the age of 5. Typical IQ tests are very good at describing relative differences in intelligence (percentile ranks and standard scores are designed to do just that) but much worse in describing its actual level (this can be done using age equivalents, but their application beyond adolescence is limited, as we discussed earlier).

Numerous twin and adoption studies have shown that relative differences in intelligence (and, for that matter, in every other psychological trait that has been examined) are partially genetically determined. Between 40 and 80 per cent of individual differences in IQ can be attributed to the role of genes, while the remaining 20–60 per cent is attributable to the role of environment (biological as well as social) and to measurement error (Plomin and Spinath, 2004; McGue and Bouchard, 1998; Devlin, Daniels and Roeder, 1997). While this conclusion is still disputed by few (Rose, 1998), the evidence for it appears very compelling. Thus, the innate constraints on individual differences are substantial, but environment also plays a role, especially during childhood (Plomin and Spinath, 2004).

However, innateness of relative differences on a particular trait does not imply that the trait itself (its absolute level) is innate, or that it cannot be modified. Even if individual differences in intelligence were completely determined by the action of genes this would still not mean that the actual level of intelligence is genetically determined and cannot be modified (Sternberg and Grigorenko, 1999). This point is often lost on both critics and defenders of IQ testing. Individual differences in height are strongly genetically determined (as much as 90 per cent according to some studies), yet during the twentieth century the average height in the Western world was increasing from one generation to the next largely as a result of improvement in diet and health care. This was paralleled by improvement in the performance on IQ tests (so-called Flynn effect: Sundet, Barlaug and Torjussen, 2004; Flynn, 1987), probably brought about by a combination of several factors (improvements in diet, education, greater complexity of physical and social environment, etc.). Adoption studies also show that intelligence can be boosted through modifying the environment, providing that the modification is substantial and long lasting (van Ijzendoorn, Juffer and Poelhuis, 2005). It is even possible to teach intelligent thinking directly (Grotzer and Perkins, 2000), although only some interventions of this type really work. The unsuccessful ones may be too short or not intensive enough, or fail to target the key thinking and learning skills (Mayer, 2000).

A fallacious belief in immutability of intelligence level may have serious consequences, as demonstrated in a classic study of Rosenthal and Jacobson (1968a, 1968b; see also Rosenthal, 2003). The authors administered an intelligence test to all students of one US elementary school, ostensibly to identify 20 per cent of the students who showed 'unusual potential for intellectual growth' and were expected to 'bloom' in the following year. The teachers were informed about the outcome. In fact, the information they received was false: the children labelled as 'smart' were no different from the rest; their names were picked up at random from the school register. Eight months later, all children were reassessed. This time, the 'smart' group really did show better IQ scores than the rest – a stark example of a self-fulfilling prophecy, fulfilled no doubt through the positive change in teachers' behaviour towards positively labelled children. It is likely that, had the children been labelled negatively (as showing 'unusually low potential') their intellectual growth would have actually been hampered. False beliefs in what IQ tests measure do matter.

Myth 2: Problem-solving skills measured by IQ tests are of little relevance to 'real life'

It is certainly true that typical IQ tests require solving problems that, at first glance, appear rather remote from concerns of daily life: defining words, finding missing elements in complex visual patterns, memorizing strings of digits, and so on. They may resemble academic tasks encountered at school or university, but little else. Yet despite this, there is considerable evidence that IQ scores predict not only school performance and number of years of completed education, but also many other life outcomes, such as social status and income (even after controlling for socio-economic status 'inherited' from parents), job performance and even likelihood of engaging in juvenile crime (which is marginally yet significantly lower among youngsters with higher IQs) (Neisser *et al.*, 1996; Gottfredson, 1997). Clearly, IQ tests have some *ecological validity* – the problem-solving abilities that they measure, sterile as they may appear at the first glance, do have some relevance to 'real life'.

At the same time, there are types of problem-solving abilities that traditional IQ test do not measure, or measure very poorly, and which also matter a great deal. Recent work on practical intelligence (Sternberg *et al.*, 2000), emotional intelligence (Goleman, 1995) and multiple intelligences (Gardner 1983) suggest that intelligence measured by traditional IQ test is but one facet of what it means to be 'smart'. For example, success in managerial roles is only poorly predicted by the scores obtained on traditional IQ tests, but depends more on common sense, context-specific practical abilities to solve everyday problems, especially social problems – abilities dubbed 'practical intelligence' (Sternberg *et al.*, 2000). Such abilities can also be measured psychometrically, but only using instruments very different from traditional IQ tests. Typically, they are questionnaires that include descriptions of complex interpersonal problems, as well as various possible solutions to those problems. Testees are required to rate those solutions according to how good they consider them to be (e.g. Sternberg, 1998).

Myth 3: IQ tests are biased

It is certainly the case that not all groups perform equally on IQ tests. Average IQ scores differ according to education, occupation and (most controversially), race and sex (Loehlin, 2000).[*] But the mere presence of such differences is not in itself the evidence that tests are biased against the groups that tend to score less well – the differences may be genuine.

There are two (closely related) senses in which tests can be biased. First of all they can be *unfair*, in requiring the testee to demonstrate skills he or she had no opportunity to learn. Being tested in an unfamiliar language, with tasks and materials that are unknown in your culture would be blatantly unfair. Unfortunately, such unfair assessment tools have occasionally been used. Gould (1996) provides a striking example of the Army Beta, an intelligence test used in the US army before the Second World War. It included a picture completion subtest that required finding missing elements in a series of line drawings. While some of the pictures were fairly 'culture neutral' (e.g. human faces) others were anything but (e.g. a bowling alley, a tennis court, a lady's dressing table, a gramophone). Despite this, the test was frequently administered to recent immigrants who spoke little English, and often had little education. Needless to say, the chances that a semi-literate Polish or Italian farmer recently disembarked on Ellis Island had ever seen a bowling alley or a tennis court were rather slim. Fortunately, such obvious biases are not found in modern IQ tests. It is now well understood that a fair test must be a product of culture to which a testee belongs, and be normed on a population to which he or she belongs. Still, some would argue that even if these requirements are met, subtle unfairness still remains. For example, some IQ tests require testees to provide definitions of various words of their native language. Success on such a task depends not only on intellectual potential (ability to

---

[*] With respect to race, Asians tend to outperform Whites, who tend to outperform Blacks. Average IQs of men and women are very similar, but men tend to perform better on visuo-spatial tasks (especially those involving mental rotation of three-dimensional objects) while women tend to have an advantage on verbal tests (especially those involving fluent production of words) (Loehlin, 2000).

understand and memorize new words one comes across) but also on mere opportunity (the number of new words one is exposed to). Consequently, the test could be said to be unfair, as not everybody has equal opportunities to hear or read new words. But to claim this amounts to saying that life itself is unfair, as it does not offer everyone the same opportunities to thrive. To construct a pure test of intellectual potential, unaffected by life experiences, is an unrealistic goal, as we have discussed already. Inevitably, all tests must, to some degree, measure people's opportunities for learning.

The second sense in which a test can be biased is that *it measures different things in different groups* (i.e. its validity varies across groups). For example, if an IQ test measured problem-solving abilities in the White population but in the Black population it would merely reflect parental income (and thus chances of being sent to a good school), then it would be biased. However, evidence suggests that modern IQ tests are *not* biased in that sense (Loehlin, 2000). Firstly, IQ scores predict life outcomes (school achievement, delinquency, etc.) similarly in different populations. Secondly, the internal structure of IQ tests (patterns of relationship between different tasks comprising those tests) also tends to be similar across populations. Thirdly, the rank order of item difficulty (which test item is the hardest, the second hardest, etc.) also tends to be similar. These data imply that what IQ tests measure is similar across different populations.

The issue of group differences in IQ scores (and particularly sex and race-related differences) raises strong emotions. We believe that these emotions are partly fuelled by a misunderstanding of what those differences actually mean. To say that two groups differ (on average) in their IQ scores does not imply that this difference is fully innate, or that it cannot be altered. Naturally, neither does it mean that each and every person in the better-performing (on average) group is more intelligent than each and every person in the worse-performing group. To say this would be to forget completely about individual differences *within* each group, which are always considerable and more interesting and informative than differences between groups.

Summary: What is Good in Psychometrics?

There is little doubt that psychometric tests are very useful – indeed, indispensable – in certain research contexts (such as measurement of individual differences within a population, or monitoring of change), providing their results are not mis-interpreted. This is an important caveat, since the history of the discipline abounds in examples of misinterpretations. Tests are not 'culture free' and perfectly 'neutral'; and their results reflect nature as well as nurture. But, well designed and understood, they are not inherently biased and need not disenfranchise any testees. Ultimately, the results of psychometric tests need to be tested against the results collected using other methods, quali-tative and quantitative. Triangulation and seeking converging evidence are powerful safeguards against bias (see Chapter 3).

Further Reading

American Psychological Association and American Educational Research Association (1999) *Standards for Educational and Psychological Testing.* Washington DC: Author. The most authoritative source on theory and practice of testing (including its ethical aspects). Highly recom-mended – always to be consulted whenever in doubt on any testing matters!

Anastasi, A. (1990) *Psychological Testing* (6th ed.). New York: Macmillan.

Assessment and Evaluation on the Internet, http://ericae.net/nint-bod.htm, accessed 9 April 2007. 'Test locator' and 'assessment resources' options are especially worth checking.

Beech, J. R. and Harding, L. (1990) *Testing People: A Practical Guide to Psychometrics.* Windsor: NFER-Nelson.

Buros Institute of Mental Measurements (2004), http://www.unl.edu/buros/indexbimm.html, accessed 9 April 2007. The most compre-hensive source of information about specific tests we know of.

Domino, G. and Domino, M. L. (2006) *Psychological Testing: An Intro-duction* (2nd ed.). Cambridge: Cambridge University Press.

Edenborough, R. (1999), *Using Psychometrics: A Practical Guide to Testing and Assessment* (2nd ed.). London: Kogan Page.

Lyman, H. B. (1997) *Test Scores and What they Mean* (6th ed.). London: Allyn & Bacon.

Part 4: Presenting and Disseminating Research

9 Presenting and Reporting Research

A piece of research cannot be considered to be complete unless it 'enters the public domain' – its findings are disseminated. This is true of both 'applied' research (which tries to 'make a difference' by influencing practice or policy in an area) and more 'theoretical' research (which aims to influence thinking and theorizing in a field of study).

For some reason, dissemination is the aspect of research that is perhaps the least written about. This chapter discusses the different ways in which research is disseminated. We look at key features of 'good research reporting' and emphasize relevant standards and conventions recommended by professional bodies.

Ways of Reporting and Disseminating

There is a range of possibilities for disseminating and presenting research findings: some will involve spoken presentations (typically using visual aids); some will involve writing for conference proceedings, journals or book publishers; or a combination of spoken and written forms.

Different types of research publication serve different purposes. For example, conference presentations (oral or posters) are usually used to present 'work in progress'. This gives the researcher not only the opportunity to disseminate the 'fresh' findings, but also to get the valuable feedback from the audience (regarding data analysis, interpretation and presentation), which they can take on board in preparing a subsequent written publication (a peer-reviewed paper or a book).

Different types of publication also differ in their impact and

Table 9.1 Main Types of Research Publication (adapted from Wikipedia)

Articles ('papers') in peer-reviewed journals	With respect to their content, papers can be divided into: **Primary literature:** reports of new, previously unpublished data. **Narrative literature reviews:** critical summaries of a current state of knowledge on a given topic. **Quantitative literature reviews/meta-analyses:** 'pulling together' and statistical reanalysis of results of all (quantitative) studies on one particular topic, in order to draw a general conclusion about their outcome.
Books	With respect to authorship and editorial process, academic books may be divided into: **Scholarly monographs**: books addressing a single topic, written by one or few authors. **Edited books**: books where each chapter is written by different authors. Chapters are revised by editors, who take responsibility for overall consistency, coherence and cohesion. They usually address a single topic. With respect to content, academic books are typically narrative literature reviews, though they may also report primary findings or quantitative literature review/meta-analyses.
Presentations at conferences (organized by learned societies or professional organizations)	Different forms are possible: **Oral presentations**: oral accounts (typically using visual aids) of research in front of the peer audience. **Posters**: a 'single-page' summary of research, presented during poster sessions that are part of most conferences. **Conference proceedings**: printed summaries of research presented during conferences. May be very brief (abstracts) or more substantial (resembling research papers).
Commissioned scientific reports	The commissioning body may be the government, a charity, a quango, a commercial company, etc.
Other, e.g.	**Technical reports**: typically prepared for internal distribution (e.g. for a sponsor of the research project). **Working papers**: reports of work in progress, ahead of more formal peer-reviewed publication. They are often made available online. **Blogs**: blogs as the means of disseminating research findings have been increasingly adopted, e.g. by some scientists researching online communities.

prestige. Papers published in *peer-reviewed* journals typically enjoy the highest status (even higher than the books), since they undergo the most stringent scrutiny and may be easily be rejected if found wanting. This status is directly proportional to the *impact factor* of the journal in which the paper is published. Vignette 5 at the end of this chapter provides more information on peer review.

Several professional bodies and research foundations give advice to researchers on disseminating their work (e.g. choosing the appropriate mode of presentation, making the presentation 'audience-friendly', use of IT and visual aids, etc.). We provide relevant references at the end of this chapter.

What Counts as Good Research Writing?

Really good research writing is, like the proverbial elephant, easier to recognize than to pin down and define. Some, however, made a good attempt. For example, Woods (1999) provides an excellent discussion of what he calls successful writing. One of his criteria is 'attention to detail'. He quotes the novelist David Lodge who describes how he learnt to 'use a few selected details, heightened by metaphor and simile, to evoke character or the sense of place' (Wood, 1999, p. 13). This art, or craft, applies equally well to academic writing.

The ability to connect or synthesize ideas is an interesting aspect of creativity which sometimes shows itself in good writing and research. It might be the ability to connect and interrelate one's own findings with existing research or theory, it might be a synthesis of ideas from two completely different domains of knowledge, e.g. using literature from a seemingly unrelated area, or it might be the application of a theory or model from one field to a totally new area. Syntheses or connections of this kind can be risky, and require a degree of self-confidence, but they can be illuminating in a piece of writing. In some ways, they are a clear mark of originality in writing.

In discussing the writing up of qualitative research, Woods (1999, pp. 54–6) also talks of the importance of including 'other voices' in the text, besides that of the author. One of the objectives of social research is to give people a voice or a 'platform' and this must be reflected in the written medium by which the research is made public. Giving people a voice, however, leads to some difficult choices. Every write-up is finite. Do you include lengthy statements or transcripts from one or two people, or many shorter points from a larger variety? (See Woods, 1999, p. 56 for discussion.)

A final point made by Woods concerns the importance, when writing, of not missing the humorous side of research, e.g. by including an ironic comment from an interviewee.

Writing a Good Report – A Few Tips

In Table 9.2 we list a few more criteria of good academic writing – those which we believe are often neglected or pose a challenge to academic writers. Naturally, the same criteria apply equally when reading and evaluating published research.

Table 9.2 A Checklist for Good Reporting of Research

(a) Make your interests clear.
     State your place of employment, status in relation to the project (e.g. a project director, a research assistant employed on the project, PhD student reporting his/her work, etc.), and sources of funding. Any potential conflicts of interest must be declared (e.g. a researcher evaluating a test who is an employee of a company that publishes that test) since (unsurprisingly!) there is evidence that they can bias conclusions (Bekelman, Li and Gross, 2003).

(b) Attend to ethical issues.
     • Identify ethical issues involved in the study (e.g. obtaining informed consent, confidentiality, creating risk to participants) and describe how they were resolved (e.g. procedure for obtaining informed consent, safeguarding confidential information, minimizing risk, etc.).
     • Name the body (e.g. the university ethic committee) that carried out a formal ethical review of your project.

(c) Present your argument well.
     • Provide a precise definition (theoretical as well as operational) of all key terms. As much as possible, avoid using terms whose meaning is ambiguous (e.g. 'learning disability').
     • Provide justification for *every* statement you make. The

justification may come in the form of empirical data (your own or someone else's) or a clearly stated logical argument (your own or someone else's).

- Acknowledge the sources. Every idea or piece of information that you 'borrowed' from somebody should be clearly referenced to its source.

(d) Present your study well.

- Describe sample selection method (random, purposive, opportunistic, etc.) and procedure. This should be done in such detail as to enable the reader to replicate your sample selection process in another study.

- Describe participants' characteristics sufficiently. As a general rule, you should report sample size, and descriptive statistics regarding participants' age, sex, level of education, native language, ethnicity and place of residence. Depending on the nature of the study, other characteristics may also be essential (e.g. describing participants' handedness is essential in studies of motor skills but not of attitudes towards same-sex marriages). If a 'special relationship' exists between you and your participants (e.g. they are your colleagues or students) this must be mentioned. Sadly, a large proportion of published research is rendered practically useless because of insufficient sample characteristics. This makes it impossible to compare studies or reanalyse them (e.g. through meta-analysis).

- Describe the data collection methods and procedures in sufficient detail to enable the reader to replicate your study. Provide references to all research instruments. If you use an original, as yet unpublished instrument (e.g. your own questionnaire) consider reproducing it in its entirety in an appendix to your report.

- Report the data and describe the process of their analysis in sufficient detail to enable the reader to fully evaluate the validity of your conclusions. What this means in practice will vary depending on the nature of the study. In qualitative research, this may mean reproducing selected sections of interview data or narratives verbatim, as exemplars. In quantitative research, this means reporting 'informationally adequate statistics' (APA, 2001, p. 23).

- Acknowledge unforeseen problems (e.g. errors in data collection that resulted in missing data, sample attrition, etc.). Evaluate the impact of those problems on the validity of your findings. There is no reason to be shy here: no research has ever been done exactly according to the plan! Acknowledge all limitations of your study that you are aware of.

(e) Pay attention to style.
- Present ideas in an orderly way.
- Be precise and clear, eliminate all potential ambiguities.
- Be succinct. Follow George Orwell's maxim: 'If it is possible to cut out a word, always cut it out'.
- Use non-discriminatory language. Avoid labelling people by their disability (e.g. say 'people diagnosed with dyslexia' rather than 'dyslexics') and prefer emotionally neutral expressions (e.g. 'person who was sexually abused' rather than 'victim of sexual abuse'. Consult sources that provide advice on improving academic writing style (e.g. APA, 2001, Chapter 2; Barrass, 2002).

(f) Pay attention to detail.
- Check and re-check all your figures. Silly mistakes (e.g. $p=0.5$ instead of $p=.05$) are easy to make
- Consult the relevant sources regarding the publishing conventions that are adopted in your field (see later in the chapter). Follow those conventions.
- Adopt one referencing style and use it consistently. Check that no references are missing. Using referencing software (e.g. EndNote (Thomson Corporation, 2004)) may be helpful here.

Publishing Standards and Conventions

Academic writing is surprisingly well codified. Each academic journal issues its own 'instructions for authors', which state formal requirements for submitted manuscript (their length, structure, style, referencing, etc.). Those specific recommendations are based on more general publication quality guidelines issued by various professional organizations. Some prominent examples of those guidelines are listed below.

- *The Publication Manual of the American Psychological Association* (APA, 2001). This lengthy (400-page) book covers most aspects of academic writing in psychology (e.g. the structure of a research paper, appropriate style, reporting statistics, referencing, publication process). While ostensibly written for the US market, the Manual has effectively acquired an international status, since its recommendations (collectively referred to as 'the APA style') are now adopted by many social science journals across the world (not just those in psychology, but also in education and related disciplines).

The information on APA style can also be found, in an abridged form, in a large number of online publications. Many are listed on webpages of various university psychology departments, and also on the webpage of the American Psychological Association itself (www.apastyle. org).

- *The American Sociological Association Style Guide* (ASA, 1997). The sociologists' equivalent of the APA Manual described above. It covers much of the same ground, albeit less comprehensively (50 pages only). The Guide's recommendations ('ASA style') are also disseminated in a large number of webpages.
- *Good Practice in Educational Research Writing* (BERA, 2000) and *Revised Ethical Guidelines for Educational Research* (BERA, 2004). Brief documents produced by the British Association of Educational Research (and available on its website: www.bera.ac.uk/publications) which outline key principles of good research and good writing.

The guidelines highlight three major audiences for research writing (fellow researchers, policy-makers and practitioners) and give as the two main reasons for publishing: i) 'seeking critique' on the research; ii) 'Contribution to publicly available knowledge of theory, policy and practice'. They suggest that good practice involves 'lucid prose which communicates effectively to the intended audience' and avoids 'jargon and obscurantism' – two criteria which are not always, in our experience, met by every author (see Table 9.3).

With respect to ethics, the BERA guidelines emphasize people's entitlements to 'dignity and privacy' and stress the importance of academic integrity, e.g. in avoiding 'distortion of evidence' and unsubstantiated assertions in research writing.

Reaching Different Audiences

The main purpose of writing up social research is to communicate with other people (although this is not always obvious when reading it). It is hardly worth doing research if it is not disseminated. Communication can, and should, take place with a number of different audiences in mind: one's peers and fellow researchers, practitioners, policy-makers, curriculum planners and developers, teachers or lecturers, parents or the general public. Once again the ground rule is horses for courses: 'Different purposes and different audiences require different styles of writing' (Woods, 1999, p. 48). In addition, different aims and audiences require different *lengths* of writing.

An interesting author on 'writing for diverse audiences' is Richardson, who also writes very interestingly on writing strategies in general (1985, 1987, 1990, 2000). From a piece of research on single women in relationships with married men, she published both academic journal articles and a populist book (*The New Other Woman*). Peter Woods (1999, pp. 48–50) discusses the way she varied her language, her style, her tone and the structure in her writing for different audiences. Woods himself gives an example of writing for different audiences from his own research into 'critical events' in schools. This was disseminated via an academic journal article focusing on the theory emerging from the research; another journal article concentrating on the pupils' perspectives, including case study material; and a reader for students training to be primary teachers with a catchy title including the term 'exceptional educational events'. The latter included only eight references, the former contained over a hundred. One of our own experiences of writing for different audiences has been to convert a PhD thesis into a book (Wellington, 1989, on the links between education and employment). The book (about 60,000 words long) was considerably shorter than the thesis (about 100,000 words including all the appendices). The book omitted large chunks of qualitative data and most of the discussion on methodology which appeared in the thesis.

Writing for Journals: Tips for Improving Your Acceptance Chances

By and large, books are written for 'open markets', while journal articles are written for peers. Different rules of engagement apply.

We suggest the following tips for submitting a piece of writing to an academic journal:

- Decide on a journal you want to submit to before you write anything. The choice should depend on your intended audience (e.g. fellow researchers? practitioners? policy-makers?) and, naturally, the perceived quality of your work (the better you consider your work to be, the higher impact factor journal you should select). To make the choice wisely, leaf through a good number of back issues of potential journals (identifying recurring topics, debates or themes), and talk to more experienced colleagues. Remember that submitting the same paper to several journals at the same time is considered unethical.
- Read the journal's guidelines to authors (regarding manuscript structure, format, referencing, word length, a number of copies to be submitted, etc.) and follow them. This is essential: you don't want to write a 10,000 word long paper, only to discover that a word limit in your chosen journal is 6,000 words!
- Look for key traits/characteristics in your chosen journal and attempt to model them in your writing.
- Prepare your manuscript meticulously. Remember it must be a finished product, not a draft. Ask a critical friend to proofread it and comment on it before sending it off.
- Accompany your submission with an appropriate letter to the editor.

Then, prepare to wait (don't hold your breath). The next step is to deal with referees' comments. The outcomes of the refereeing process will be one of the following:

- Accept without revisions. In modern academic publishing this never happens, so no more needs to be said about this.
- Accept with minor revisions. Action: celebrate and just do them.
- Accept with major revisions. Action: strong drink, then take each point one by one.
- Reject. Action: it depends. You may change the manuscript (taking reviewers' comments on board) and then

send it to another journal. Or you may agree with the reviewers that your study is not good enough – and start working on a better one. Most reviewers try to be constructive, so a letter of rejection typically contains plenty of useful feedback that allows you to make your work better.

When making revisions bear in mind that you have to address *all* points raised by the reviewers. It is not sufficient to just make the required changes in the manuscript: they have to be presented in a separate letter to the editor, each change listed and linked to a specific point raised by a reviewer. The *APA Manual* (2001) gives useful suggestions regarding such correspondence with editors.

Finally, be patient: the whole process takes time. A two-year interval from the initial submission to the actual publication is not uncommon. Journals often provide information regarding average 'turnover' time – check it.

Submitting a Book Proposal

Book proposals require considerable thought, partly because, unlike journal articles or dissertations, books have to be sold, meaning that somebody must want to buy them. Our experience with publishers and their commissioning editors is that they are extremely helpful and will support a good idea, even if it will not result in tens of thousands of books sold (see Wellington, 2003, for more details on getting published). The editor who commissioned the book you are now reading offered the valuable guidelines to writing book proposals shown in Table 9.3.

Writing Up: Some Specific Suggestions

For the sake of brevity here, a list of eleven suggestions and guidelines on writing is given below, as concisely as possible (for further discussion, an excellent source is Becker, 1986).

1. Treat writing as a 'form of thinking' (Becker, 1986). Writing does not proceed by having pre-set thoughts which are then transformed onto paper. Instead,

Table 9.3 How to Submit a 'Perfect Book Proposal' (source: Anthony Haynes, former Commissioning Editor for Education, Continuum)

I've been asked several times what I want to see in a book proposal. Below is a pretty exhaustive guide. Not every point in it will apply to every proposal. Three sides of A4 is usually sufficient, four sides is usually ample.

1. Summarize the book in a few lines at the start, including a working title.
2. Outline the contents. It is often useful to do this chapter by chapter.
3. Say how long the book will be, to the nearest 5,000 words, and how many illustrations, tables, etc. it will include.
4. Identify the intended market(s).
   (a) Avoid Uncle Tom Cobleigh sentences ('This book is intended for classroom teachers, middle management, senior management, ITT students and their tutors and mentors, researchers, lecturers, advisers, administrators, policy-makers . . .). It may well be that your book would appeal to more than one of these groups, but it would be helpful to distinguish between main and subsidiary audiences.
   (b) Quantify the market as far as possible. For example, if your book is aimed at a certain type of degree course, how many such courses are there? And how many students are there on such courses?
   (c) Identify courses for which your book might make recommended or essential reading.
   (d) Explain how your book would appeal, e.g. through contributors, references, case studies, to different national markets, e.g. Scotland, Ireland, the EU, North America, Australia.
5. Analyse the competition:
   (a) What comparable books are there? How does your book compare/ contrast?
   (b) If there isn't a comparable book, suggest why there isn't.
6. Present yourself as author/editor.
   (a) Give your title, affiliation and relevant qualification.
   (b) Give a brief bibliography of your relevant publications, annotated to identify the kind of audience if this is less than obvious.
   (c) Mention any relevant networks you belong to (e.g. conferences you attend, associations to which you belong).
   (d) Explain your affective involvement: why does this matter to you? What is at stake for you?
7. By when could you submit the manuscript? Avoid good intentions here – be realistic.
8. What's in it for the reader? Finally, it is useful to summarize the benefits the book offers to the reader. Many of these will be implicit in much of the above, but it is worth spelling out what's in it for the reader.
9. Include contact numbers, including fax and email where available.

thoughts are created and developed by the process of writing. Daniel Dennett's (1991) confession 'I don't know what I think unless I say it' applies to writing even more than it does to talking. Writing up your work is an excellent, albeit slightly painful, way of thinking through and making sense of what you have done or what you're doing. This is a good reason for not leaving writing until the end; writing should begin immediately.

2. Edit 'by ear'; make sure it sounds right and feels right. Treat writing as somewhat like talking to someone, except that now you are communicating via the written word. Keep your readers in mind at all times, better still, one particular reader. What will they make of this sentence? It can help if you visualize your reader(s) as you are writing.

   But, unlike talking, the reader only has what is on paper. Readers, unlike listeners, do not have body language, tone of voice or any knowledge of you, your background or your thoughts. Writers cannot make the assumptions and short cuts that can be made between talkers and listeners.

3. Draft and redraft; write and rewrite – and don't either expect or try to get it right first time. Writing up, especially with a word processor, should not be treated as a 'once and for all' activity. Getting the first draft on to paper is just the first stage.

4. Remove unnecessary words; make each word work for a living. After the first draft is on paper go back and check for excess baggage, i.e. redundant words and circumlocution.

5. Avoid tired/hackneyed metaphors like 'cutting edge' and 'huge terrain', and overdone sayings like 'falling between two stools' and 'the bottom line'.

6. Think carefully about when you should use an active voice in your sentences and when a passive voice may or may not help (see Holliday, 2002, ch.6; APA, 2001). The passive voice can be a useful way of depersonalizing sentences but sometimes naming the 'active agent' helps clarity and gives more information, e.g. 'Jane Smith, the

ICT coordinator, bought three new computers' (active voice), compared with 'three new computers were bought' (passive).

7. Vary sentence length; use a few really short ones now and again, e.g. four words. These can have a real impact.

8. Expose it to a friend; find a reader/colleague whom you can trust to be reliable and just, but critical. Look for somebody else, perhaps someone with no expertise in the area, to read your writing and comment on it. They, and you, should ask: is it clear? Is it readable? Is it well structured, e.g. do you need more subheadings? Use other people, use books (e.g. style manuals, books on writing). And don't do your own proofreading.

9. Readers need guidance, especially to a large thesis or book. In the early pages, brief the readers on what they are about to receive. Provide a map to help them navigate through it.

10. Break a large piece of writing down into manageable chunks or pieces which will gradually fit together. We call this the 'jigsaw puzzle' approach – but an overall plan is still needed to fit all the pieces together. The pieces will also require linking together. The job of writing link sentences ('metasentences') and link paragraphs joining section to section and chapter to chapter, is vital for coherence and fluency.

11. Above all, get it 'out of the door' (Becker, 1986) for your friendly reader to look at. Don't sit on it for months, 'polishing' it. Get it off your desk, give it to someone to read, then work on it again when it comes back.

Finally, two of the common problems in writing are (a) getting started; (b) writing the abstract. You can avoid the first by not trying to find the 'one right way' first time round (Becker, 1986), and the second by leaving the abstract until last.

A Few Parting Thoughts: The Complex Connection between Research, Dissemination, Policy and Practice

Of course, dissemination is not without its problems. The idea that researchers simply need to make their work public and accessible and then policy-makers or practitioners will be influenced by it, is naive. Similarly, a crude interpretation of 'evidence-based practice' would seem to assume that all that researchers in (say) medicine, social work, speech therapy or education need to do is present their research evidence and then practitioners or policy-makers will act upon it. This idea is flawed for several reasons:

1. Practice in the social world is as much a matter for judgement and interpretation as it is of fact (very much as refereeing a sport can be at times). Value judgements are as important as the 'facts'. It is thus a very simplistic model to assume that all we need to do is to collect the 'evidence' (even if that were possible in something as complicated as the social world) and then deduce the 'practice' from it. There is a gap (as the philosopher David Hume pointed out) between what *is* the case and what *ought* to be done about it (the 'is–ought' distinction as it is often known).

2. Simply presenting a practitioner with the evidence and research on an area and then expecting them to change their practice as a result of it is a false expectation. Practitioners' beliefs are influenced by a variety of factors, such as first-hand experience, intuition ('sixth sense') or tacit knowledge that would be hard for most practitioners to explain let alone put into writing.

3. Equally, people's practices are extremely resilient and difficult to shift. Simply 'giving' them research evidence

and expecting them to go away and begin to change their working practices is naive. A huge amount of work needs to go into changing and adapting practice – it may require mentoring and coaching for example. In some cases, change may never occur because a practitioner may have good, very personal reasons (though not always rational ones) for *not* changing their practice.

4. The notion also assumes that evidence (or the 'facts') are themselves unproblematic. While the research evidence often *is* relatively clear and conclusive (e.g. regarding the safety of the MMR vaccine or mobile phones, or ineffectiveness of homeopathic remedies), it can sometimes be inconclusive, contentious or simply unavailable due to the lack of relevant studies.

Thus the notion of evidence-based practice is problematic for several reasons. However, this is not to deny the value of basing practice on the best available evidence and research that has been published. Practice can be informed and greatly improved by basing it on research and evidence. But it is important to question the idea that practice can be, or ever will be, crudely based on evidence and follow directly on from it. Evidence-*informed* practice is probably a better term.

Another issue of course is the fact that practitioners in most, if not all, professions are extremely busy people – when do they have the time and opportunity for reflection that will allow them to read or hear about research, let alone evaluate it, adapt it and change their own practice as a result? Practitioners may also be highly sceptical, perhaps cynical about the 'research fraternity' and perhaps dismiss them as having nothing to do with practice or being stuck in the ivory tower.

Equally, policy-makers, even if research findings reach them loud and clear, may have numerous reasons for leaving it on the shelf, or simply ignoring it. There will be myriad other pressures – such as budgets, ideologies, more senior civil servants or the government minister – which have a far greater influence in shaping policy than a piece of research, however well conducted. For example, many policy-makers may wish to hear 'good news stories' about a particular innovation or programme that they have been involved in, rather than (say) a research evaluation which shows that the innovation had little or no impact, or was not well received or put into practice 'on the ground'. Whether evidence informs practice depends not only on the willingness of practitioners, but also on external constraints (resources, systems one works within, legislation). Subsequently, if the evidence-based (or evidence-informed) practice is to happen, the evidence has to inform all relevant levels (not only bottom-rank practitioners).

Despite these remarks on the complex connections between research, dissemination and practice, there are good grounds for optimism! Research, and practice based upon it, have made a difference over the last century or more. In this century, the possibilities for dissemination, given the advances in the technology of communication (i.e. ICT) have never been more varied nor as capable of reaching a global audience in as short a time. Dissemination continues to be as important as ever and, from a technical point of view, easier than ever.

Who would possibly argue against evidence-*informed* practice and policy, which is informed by the best available and most current research? By what else could or should practice and policy be informed: whim, faith, fashion, hearsay, anecdote, astrology or divine intervention?

Further Reading

American Psychological Association (2001) *Publication Manual of the American Psychological Association* (5th ed.). Washington, DC: APA.

American Sociological Association (1997), *The American Sociological Association Style Guide*. Washington, DC: ASA

Barrass, R. (2002) *Scientists must write*. Abingdon: Routledge Falmer.

Becker, H. (1986) *Writing for Social Scientists: How to Start and Finish your Thesis, Book or Article*. Chicago: University of Chicago Press.

British Educational Research Association (2000), *Good practice in Educational Research Writing*. Southwell: BERA

Richardson, L. (1990) *Writing Strategies: Reaching Diverse Audiences*. London: Sage.

Wellington, J. (2003) *Getting Published*. London: Routledge Falmer.

Woods, P. (1999) *Successful Writing for Qualitative Researchers*. London: Routledge.

Vignette Five: Is Peer Review Important? And is it Fallible?

The Story of Sokal's Submission

In 1996, an American professor of physics, Alan Sokal, played a cunning and clever hoax on the editorial staff and the readers of a prestigious journal in the humanities called *Social Text*. He submitted an article filled with spoof language which he claimed was 'liberally salted with nonsense' but was intended to 'sound good' and would flatter the editors' 'ideological preconceptions': the literary equivalent of the Emperor's new clothes perhaps? The article claimed that quantum theory had political implications and that 'emancipatory mathematics' must be developed for a 'post-modern science' – and more language and statements of a similar ilk throughout. The paper was accepted (without peer review, since *Social Text* had abandoned the process) and later published.

On the day of its publication, Sokal announced in another journal (*Lingua Franca*) that his article was a hoax. He called his paper 'a pastiche of left-wing cant, fawning references, grandiose quotations and outright nonsense'. His own writing was structured around what he called 'the silliest quotations' he could find about mathematics and physics by humanities academics.

Claims and Counter-Claims

Sokal claimed that his hoax showed that the journal editor had published an article on quantum physics without bothering to consult anyone who knew anything about it. He claimed that they published articles on the basis of who had written them and how they sounded.

The journal defended itself, accusing Sokal of unethical behaviour and defending their earlier decision to abandon peer review as an attempt to promote more original, less conventional research – they had placed trust in authors and presumably felt that in this case Sokal had betrayed their trust in the integrity and honesty of the author.

It seems that the affair did promote some debate about peer review, a debate which still has considerable mileage, especially in the context of recent trends to publish journals online, in some cases without thorough peer review.

Peer Review under Scrutiny

In fact, the case had a precedent which also raised important questions about the process of peer review. In 1982, Peters and Ceci carried out a similarly controversial study subtitled 'The fate of published articles submitted again'. Thirteen articles by US authors from 'high status' institutions, which had been published in reputable psychological journals, were resubmitted, in disguised form, to exactly those journals that had originally published them. Fictitious names and institutions were given in the new covering letters. Only three were spotted as being resubmissions and were therefore rejected, while nine were rejected on other grounds. Only one article was accepted for publication. Among the rejections, the most commonly mentioned weakness was 'serious methodological flaws'.

Peters and Ceci suggested that the second group of reviewers may be less competent than the first, or that there was a clear bias towards submissions from authors based in 'high status' institutions.

Peters and Ceci's is not the only study that seems to point to reviewer unreliability; several more are reviewed by Armstrong (1997). Among them, the experiment carried out by Lloyd (1990) is a particularly striking example. Lloyd submitted identical psychology manuscripts to several journals; the only thing that was changed was the author's (fictitious) name. She found that female reviewers accepted significantly more manuscripts whose authors appeared female (62 per cent) than male (10 per cent), while male reviewers showed no significant bias (accepting 21 per cent and 30 per cent of female-authored and male-authored manuscripts, respectively.)

Some of the Questions We Would Pose about the 'Sokal Affair' and the Peer-Review Studies

- Is the 'hoax paper submission method' used by Sokal (1997), Peters and Ceci (1982) or Lloyd (1990) an ethical one? Perhaps editors (and reviewers) have the right to assume that the papers submitted to them (and the identities of their authors) are genuine, and this relationship of trust was abused?
- Where should the balance of responsibility lie in publishing – what proportions rest with the author, the peer reviewers and/or the editor?
- Would the quality of *Social Text* papers improve if they were peer-reviewed? Would it prevent the journal from publishing Sokal's hoax paper?
- Are the editors of *Social Text* right in claiming that the peer review process stifles originality and innovation? (Interestingly, Armstrong (1997), who writes from a very different perspective, seems to partly agree.)
- Are there any (scientifically more rigorous) alternatives to peer-reviews?
- How can the quality of peer review be improved? Blinding the reviewers to the identity of authors seems one obvious suggestion; providing the reviews with explicit evaluation criteria may be another (for more suggestions see Armstrong, 1997).

(Incidentally, our own answers to the questions posed in the title of this vignette are Yes! and Yes!)

References

Armstrong, J. S. (1997) 'Peer review for journals: evidence on quality control, fairness and innovation'. *Science and Engineering Ethics* 3, 63–84. Retrieved 26 February 2007 from Cogprints Archive http://cogprints.org/5197/.

Editors of Lingua Franca (2000) *The Sokal Hoax: The Sham that Shook the Academy*. Lincoln, NE: University of Nebraska Press.

Gross, P. R. and Levitt, N. (1994) *Higher Superstition: The Academic*

Left and Its Quarrels With Science. Baltimore: Johns Hopkins University Press. [Sokal claimed that reading this book had prompted him to write the spoof article.)

Peters, D. and Ceci, S. (1982) 'Peer review practices of psychological journals: the fate of published articles, submitted again'. *The Behavioural and Brain Sciences* 5, 187–255.

Sokal, A. D. (1996) 'Transgressing the boundaries: towards a transformative hermeneutics of quantum gravity. *Social Text* 46/47, 217–52. Retrieved 26 February 2007 from author's website http://www.physics.nyu.edu/faculty/sokal/transgress_v2/transgress_v2_singlefile.html.

—— and Bricmont, J. (1998) *Fashionable Nonsense: Postmodern Intellectuals' Abuse of Science*. New York: Picador, USA.

Sokal Affair. In *Wikipedia, The Free Encyclopedia*. Retrieved 26, February 2007 from http://en.wikipedia.org/w/index.php?title=Sokal_Affair &oldid=110623768.

Part 5: Extras

References

Allport, G. (1947) *The Use of Personal Documents in the Psychological Sciences*. New York: Social Science Research Council.

Altman, D. G. (1994) 'The scandal of poor medical research'. *British Medical Journal* 308, 283–4.

American Psychological Association (2001) *Publication Manual of the American Psychological Association* (5th ed.) Washington DC: APA.

—— and American Educational Research Association (1999) *Standards for Educational and Psychological Testing*. Washington DC: Author.

American Sociological Association (1997) *ASA Style Guide* (2nd ed.). Washington DC: American Sociological Association.

Anastasi, A. (1990) *Psychological Testing* (6th ed.). New York: Macmillan.

Anderson, B. (1990) *Methodological Errors in Medical Research*. Oxford: Blackwell.

Anderson, G. (1998) *Fundamentals of Educational Research*. Basingstoke: Falmer Press.

Angell, R. C. and Freedman, R. (1953) 'The use of documents, records, census materials and indices', in L. Pestinger and D. Katz, *Research Methods in the Behavioral Sciences* (1st ed.). New York: Holt, Rinehart and Winston, ch. 7, 300–26.

Armstrong, J. S. (1997) 'Peer review for journals: evidence on quality control, fairness and innovation'. *Science and Engineering Ethics* 3, 63–84. Retrieved 26 February 2007 from Cogprints Archive http://cogprints.org/5197/.

Armstrong, M. (1980) *Closely Observed Children*. London: Writers and Readers.

Ary, D., Jacobs, L. C. and Razavieh, A. (1985) *Introduction to Research in Education* (3rd ed.). New York: Holt, Rinehart and Winston.

Assessment and Evaluation on the Internet, http://ericae.net/nintbod.htm. Retrieved 7, April 2007.

Atkinson, J. (1968) *The Government Social Survey: A Handbook for Interviewers*. London: HMSO.

Atkinson, P. and Delamont, S. (1985) 'Bread and dreams or bread and circuses? A critique of "case study" research in education', in M. Shipman (ed.) *Educational Research, Principles, Policies and Practices*. London: Palmer Press. [A useful, critical look at case-study research, including a strong critique of Simons, 1981, cited below.]

Atkinson, R. (1998) *The Life Story Interview*. London: Sage.

Baker, M. (1994) 'Media coverage of education'. *British Journal of Educational Studies* 42(3), 286–97.

Ball, S. J. (1981) *Beachside Comprehensive*, Cambridge: Cambridge University Press.

—— (1990) 'Self-doubt and soft data: social and technical trajectories in ethnographic fieldwork'. *Qualitative Studies in Education* 3(2), 157–71.

Barrass, R. (2002) *Scientists Must Write* (2nd ed.). London: Routledge.

Bassey, M. (1990) 'On the nature of research in education, part I'. *Research Intelligence* (BERA Newsletter) 36, 35–8. (See also Bassey's Part II and Part III articles in *Research Intelligence*, autumn 1990 and winter 1991, nos 37 and 38.)

Baumeister, R.F., Campbell, J,D., Krueger, J.I. and Vohs, K.D. (2003) 'Does high self-esteem cause better performance, interpersonal success, happiness and healthier lifestyle?' *Psychological Science in Public Interest* 4(1), 1–44. Retrieved 10 February 2007 from http://www.blackwell-synergy.com/loi/PSPI.

Becker, H. S. (1970) *Sociological Work: Method and Substance*. Chicago: Aldine.

—— (1986) *Writing for Social Scientists*. Chicago: Chicago University Press.

Beech, J. R. and Harding, L. (1990) *Testing People: A Practical Guide to Psychometrics*. Windsor: NFER-Nelson.

Bekelman, J. E., Li, Y. and Gross, C. P. (2003) 'Scope and impact of financial conflicts of interest in biomedical research: a systematic review'. *Journal of the American Medical Association* 289, 454–65.

Bell, J. (1993) *Doing Your Research Project: A Guide for First-time Researchers in Education and Social Science*. Buckingham: Open University Press. [A concise, valuable guide for new researchers, now in its 3rd edition.]

BERA (2004) *Revised Ethical Guidelines for Educational Research*, Retrieved June 21, 2007, from: *http://www.bera.ac.uk/publications/guides.php*.

BERA (2000) *Good Practice in Educational Research Writing*, Retrieved June 21, 2007, from: *http://www.bera.ac.uk/publications/guides.php*.

Best, J. (1981) *Research in Education* (4th ed.). New Jersey: Prentice-Hall.

—— and Kahn, J. V. (1986) *Research in Education* (5th ed.). Englewood Cliffs: Prentice-Hall.

Blass, T. (1999) 'The Milgram paradigm after 35 years: some things we now know about obedience to authority. *Journal of Applied Social Psychology* 25, 955–78.

Bogdan, R. and Biklen, S. (1982) *Qualitative Research for Education.* Boston: Allyn & Bacon.

Bonnett, A. (1993) 'Contours of crisis: anti-racism and reflexivity', in P. Jackson and J. Penrose (eds), *Construction of 'Race', Place and Nation.* London: UCL Press.

Borg, W. R. and Gall, M. D. (1989) *Educational Research: An Introduction.* New York: Longman.

Brenner, M., Brown, J. and Canter, D. (eds) (1985) *The Research Interview: Uses and Approaches.* London: Academic Press.

Brumfitt, S. and Sheeran, P. (1999a) *VASES: Visual Analogue Self-Esteem Scale.* Brackley: Speechmark Publishing.

—— (1999b) 'The development and validation of the Visual Analogue Self-Esteem Scale (VASES)'. *British Journal of Clinical Psychology* 38, 387–400.

Bulmer, M. (1979) *Beginning Research.* Milton Keynes: Open University Press.

—— (1982a) *The Uses of Social Research.* London: George Allen & Unwin.

—— (ed.) (1982b) *Social Research Ethics: An Examination of the Merits of Covert Participant Observation.* London: Macmillan.

Burgess, R. G. (1981) 'Keeping a research diary'. *Cambridge Journal of Education* 11(1), 75–83.

—— (1982a) 'The unstructured interview as a conversation', in R. G. Burgess (ed.), *Field Research: A Sourcebook and Field Manual.* London: Allen & Unwin.

—— (ed.) (1982b) *Field Research: A Sourcebook and Field Manual.* London: Allen & Unwin. [The companion volume to the above text consisting of readings on all phases of the research activity.]

—— (1983) *Experiencing Comprehensive Education.* London: Methuen.

—— (1984) *In the Field: An Introduction to Field Research.* London: Allen & Unwin. [Over the years, one of the most widely cited books on fieldwork; it covers the main issues and problems involved in the 'field' research approach.]

—— (ed.) (1984) *The Research Process in Educational Settings: Ten Case Studies.* Lewes: Falmer Press. [Ten 'first-person accounts' of real-life research.]

—— (ed.) (1985a) *Strategies of Educational Research: Qualitative Methods.* London: Falmer Press.

—— (ed.) (1985b) *Field Methods in the Study of Education.* Lewes: Falmer Press.

—— (ed.) (1989) *The Ethics of Educational Research.* London: Falmer Press.

Buros Institute of Mental Measurements (2004) *Test viewers online* http://www.unl.edu/buros/indexbimm.html. Retrieved 9 April 2007.

Capra, P. (1983) *The Tao of Physics*. London: Fontana.

Carr, W. (2000) 'Partisanship in Educational Research', *Oxford Review of Education* 26(3/4), 495–501.

—— (2006) 'Education without theory'. *British Journal of Educational Studies* 54(2), 136–59.

—— and Kemmis, S. (1986) *Becoming Critical: Education, Knowledge and Action Research*. Lewes: Falmer Press.

Carroll, J. B. (1997) 'Psychometrics, intelligence and public perception'. *Intelligence* 24(1), 25–52.

Chagnon, N. A. (1968) *Yanomamo: The Fierce People*, London: Holt, Rinehart & Winston.

Chall, J. S. (1967) *Learning to Read: The Great Debate*. New York: McGraw Hill.

Chalmers, A. F. (1982) *What Is This Thing Called Science?* Milton Keynes: Open University Press.

Clarke, Adele (2005) *Situational Analysis: Grounded Theory after the Postmodern Turn*. London: Sage.

Clifford, G. (1973) 'A history of the impact of research on teaching', in R. Travers (ed.), *Second Handbook of Research on Teaching*. Chicago: Rand McNally.

Codd, J. (1988) 'The construction and de-construction of educational policy documents'. *Journal of Educational Policy* 3(3), 235–47.

Coffey, A. and Atkinson, P. (1996) *Making Sense of Qualitative Data*. London: Sage.

Cohen, J. (1992) 'A power primer'. *Psychological Bulletin* 112, 155–9.

—— (1994) 'The Earth is round ($p<.05$)'. *American Psychologist* 49(12), 997–1003.

—— and Manion, L. (1994) *Research Methods in Education* (4th ed.). London: Routledge.

—— and Morrison, K. (2000) *Research Methods in Education* (5th ed.). London, New York: Routledge Falmer.

Collins, H. (1985) *Changing Order: Replication and Induction in Scientific Practice*. London: Sage.

Corey, S. (1953) *Action Research to Improve School Practices*. New York: Columbia University.

Crick, F. H. C. (1979) 'Thinking about the brain'. *Scientific American* 241, 219–32.

Davies, P. (1999) 'What is evidence-based education?'. *British Journal of Educational Studies* 47, 108–21.

Dean, I. P. and Whyte, W. (1969) 'How do you know if the informant is telling the truth?', in G. McCall and J. Simmons (eds), *Issues in Participant Observation*. Reading, MA: Addison-Wesley.

Deary, I. J., Whalley, L. J., Lemmon, H., Crawford, J. R., and Starr, J. M. (2000) 'The stability of individual differences in mental ability from childhood to old age: follow up of the 1932 Scottish Mental Survey'. *Intelligence* 28(1), 49–55.

Delamont, S. (1992) *Fieldwork in Educational Settings*. Basingstoke: Palmer Press.

Demicheli, V., Jefferson, T., Rivetti, A. and Price, D. (2005) 'Vaccines for measles, mumps and rubella in children'. *Cochrane Database of Systematic Reviews* 4.

Dennett, D. (1991) *Consciousness Explained*. London: Penguin Books.

Dennis, W. (1941) 'Infant development under conditions of restricted practice and of minimal social stimulation'. *Genetic Psychology Monographs*, 23, 143–89.

Denscombe, M. (1998) *The Good Research Guide*. Buckingham: Open University Press.

Denzin, N. K. (1970) *The Research Act*. Chicago: Aldine.

—— and Lincoln, Y. S. (1994) *Handbook of Qualitative Research*. London: Sage.

—— (1998) *Collecting and Interpreting Qualitative Materials*. London: Sage.

—— (2000) 'The discipline and practice of qualitative research', in Denzin, N. K. and Lincoln, Y. S. (eds), *Handbook of Qualitative Research* (2nd ed.). Thousand Oaks, CA: Sage.

Derrida, J. (1978) *Writing and Difference*. London: Routledge.

Devlin, B., Daniels, M. and Roeder, K. (1997) 'The heritability of IQ'. *Nature* 388, 6641, 468–71.

Diamond, M. and Sigmundson, H. K. (1997) 'Sex reassignment at birth: long-term review and clinical implications'. *Archives of Pediatric and Adolescent Medicine* 151, 298–304.

Domino, G. and Domino, M. L. (2006) *Psychological Testing: An Introduction* (2nd ed.). Cambridge: Cambridge University Press.

Douglas, I. (1985) *Creative Interviewing*. CA: Sage.

Economic and Social Research Council (ESRC) (2005) *Research Ethics Framework* Newbury Park, Retrieved 23 April 2007 from http://www.esrc.ac.uk/

Edenborough, R. (1999). *Using Psychometrics: A Practical Guide to Testing and Assessment* (2nd ed.). London: Kogan Page.

Editors of Lingua Franca (2000) *The Sokal Hoax: The Sham that Shook the Academy*. Lincoln, NE: University of Nebraska Press.

Edwards, D. and Mercer, N. (1993) *Common Knowledge*. London: Routledge.

Edwards, J. (1994) *The Scars of Dyslexia*. London: Cassell.

Eichler, M. (1988) *Nonsexist Research Methods: A Practical Guide*. London: Hyman. [Puts forward a well argued 'guide' to identifying and eliminating sexist bias in educational research.]

EndNote® Computer Software. Thompson Corporation. www.endnote.com.

Faraday, A. and Plummer, K. (1979) 'Doing life histories'. *Sociological Review* 27(4), 773–98.

Farrell, E., Peguero, G., Lindsey, R. and White, R. (1988) 'Giving voice to high school students: pressure and boredom, ya know what I'm saying?'. *American Educational Research Journal* 25(4), 489–502.

Faulkner, R. (1982) 'Improvising on a triad', in I. van Maanen (ed.), *Variations of Qualitative Research*. Newbury Park, CA: Sage, pp. 65–102.

Fetterman, D. (ed.) (1984) *Ethnography in Educational Evaluation*. London: Sage.

Feyerabend, P. (1993) *Against Method*. London: Verso.

Fielding, N. (1981) *The National Front*. London: Routledge.

———. and Lee, R. (eds) (1991) *Using Computers in Qualitative Research*. London: Sage.

Fink, A. (1995) *How to Ask Survey Questions*. London: Sage.

Fisher, Box Joan (1978) *R. A. Fisher: The Life of a Scientist*. New York: Wiley.

Fisher, R. A. (1925) *Statistical Methods for Research Workers*. Edinburgh: Oliver & Boyd (many editions since).

——— (1935) *The Design of Experiments*. Edinburgh: Oliver & Boyd (many editions since).

Flynn, J. R. (1980) *Race, IQ and Jensen*. London: Routledge & Kegan Paul.

——— (1987) 'Massive IQ gains in 14 nations: what IQ tests really measure'. *Psychological Bulletin* 101, 171–91.

Fontana, A. and Frey, J. H. (2000) 'The interview: from structured questions to negotiated text', in Denzin, N. and Lincoln, Y. (eds), *Handbook of Qualitative Research* (2nd ed.). London: Sage.

Frankfort-Nachmias, C. and Nachmias, D. (1992) *Research Methods in the Social Sciences* (4th ed.). London: Edward Arnold.

Fullan, M. (1991) *The New Meaning of Educational Change*. London: Cassell.

Gardner, H. (1983) *Frames of Mind: The Theory of Multiple Intelligences*. New York: Basic Books.

——— (1993) *Intelligence Reframed. Multiple intelligences for the 21st century*. New York: Basic Books.

Gay, L. R. (1981) *Educational Research: Competencies for Analysis and Application* (2nd ed.). Cleveland, OH: Charles E. Merrill.

Giddens, A. (1976) *The New Rules of Sociological Method*. London: Hutchinson.

Gill, J. and Johnson, P. (1997) *Research Methods for Managers*. London: Paul Chapman.

Gilroy, D. P. (1980) 'The empirical researcher as philosopher'. *British Journal of Teacher Education* 6(3), 237–50.

Glaser, B. and Strauss, A. (1967) *The Discovery of Grounded Theory*. London: Weidenfeld & Nicolson.

Gleick, J. (1988) *Chaos: Making a New Science*. London: Heinemann.

Goertz, J. and Le Compte, M. (1981) 'Ethnographic research and the problem of data reduction'. *Anthropology and Education Quarterly* 12, 51–70.

—— (1984) *Ethnography and Qualitative Design in Educational Research*. Orlando, FL: Academic Press.

Goffman, E. (1961) *Asylums*. New York: Doubleday.

Goleman, D. (1995) *Emotional Intelligence: Why It Can Matter More than IQ*. New York: Bantam.

Gomm, R. and Woods, P. (eds) (1993) *Educational Research in Action*. London: Paul Chapman.

Goodson, I. (1999) 'The educational researcher as a public intellectual'. *British Educational Research Journal* 25(3), 277–97.

Gottfredson, L. S. (1997) 'Why g matters: the complexity of everyday life'. *Intelligence* 24(1), 79–132.

Gould, S. J. (1996) *The Mismeasure of Man*. New York: Norton.

Greenbank, P. (2003) 'The role of values in educational research: the case for reflexivity'. *British Educational Research Journal* 29(6), 791–801.

Grotzer, T. A. and Perkins, D. N. (2000) 'Teaching intelligence: a performance conception', in R. J. Sternberg (ed.), *Handbook of Intelligence*. Cambridge: Cambridge University Press, 492–518.

Guilford, J. (1967) *The Nature of Human Intelligence*. New York: McGraw-Hill.

Hagen, R. L. (1997) 'In praise of the null hypothesis significance testing'. *American Psychologist* 52(1), 15–24. (This paper attracted several comments, to which the author replied. The correspondence was published in *American Psychologist* 53(7), 796–803.)

Hall, C. (2006) *A Picture of the United Kingdom Using the National Statistics Socio-Economic Classification*. Office for National Statistics. Retrieved 4 April 2007 from http://www.statistics.gov.uh/articles/population_trends/PT125Hall.pdf.

Halpin, D. and Troyna, B. (eds) (1994) *Researching Educational Policy: Ethical and Methodological Issues*. London: Falmer Press.

Hammersley, M. (1987) 'Some notes on the terms "validity" and "reliability" '. *British Educational Research Journal* 13(1), 73–83.

—— (1995) *The Politics of Social Research*. London: Sage.

—— (ed.) (1993) *Educational Research: Current Issues*. London: Paul Chapman.

—— and Atkinson, P. (1983) *Ethnography: Principles in Practice*. London: Tavistock.

Hammond, S. (2000) 'Using psychometric tests', in G. M. Breakwell, S. Hammond and C. Five-Schaw, *Research Methods in Psychology* (2nd ed.). London: Sage.

Hannon, P. (1998) 'An ecological perspective on educational research', in J. Rudduck and D. McIntyre (eds) *Challenges for Educational Research*. London: Paul Chapman.

Harding, S. (ed.) (1987) *Feminism and Methodology*. Milton Keynes: Open University Press. (A collection of readings on feminist research methods.)

Hargreaves, A. (1994) *Changing Teachers, Changing Times*. London: Cassell.

Hargreaves, D. H. (1967) *Social Relations in a Secondary School*. London: Routledge & Kegan Paul.

—— (1999) 'Revitalising educational research: lessons from the past and proposals for the future'. *Cambridge Journal of Education* 29(2), 239–49.

Harrison, D. (1999) 'A guide to using bibliographies, abstracts and indexes', in M. Scarrott (ed.), *Sport, Leisure and Tourism Information Sources*. Oxford: Heinemann.

Heisenberg, W. (1958) *The Physicist's Conception of Nature*. London: Hutchinson.

Helmer, O. (1972) 'On the future state of the Union'. *Report* 12–27. Menlo Park, California: Institute for the Future.

Herrnstein, R. J., and Murray, C. (1994) *The Bell Curve: Intelligence and Class Structure in American Life*. New York: Free Press.

Hill, R. A. and Barton, R. A. (2005) 'Red enhances human performance in contests'. *Nature* 435, 293.

Hockey, J. (1991) *Squaddies*. Exeter: Exeter University Press.

Holdaway, S. (1985) *Inside the Police Force*. Oxford: Basil Blackwell.

Holliday, A. (2002) *Doing and Writing Qualitative Research*. London: Sage. [This book moves from a discussion of conducting qualitative social research to guidelines and debate on presenting data, the 'writer voice' and the importance of caution in 'making claims'. It cites and uses a range of exemplars].

Howard, K. and Sharp, J. (1983) *The Management of a Student Research Project*. Aldershot: Gower.

Huff, D. (1991) *How to Lie with Statistics*. London: Penguin.

Janowitz, M. (1972) *Sociological Models and Social Policy*. Morristown, NJ: General Learning Systems.

Jensen, A. (1998) *The g Factor: The Science of Mental Ability*. Westport, CT: Praeger.

Jensen, A. R. (1973) *Educability and Group Differences*. London: Methuen.

Jones, G. E. (2006) *How to Lie with Charts* (2nd ed.). Charleston, SC: Booksurge

Joynson, R. B. (1989) *The Burt Affair*. New York: Routledge.

Kaplan, A. (1973) *The Conduct of Inquiry*. Aylesbury: Intertext Books.

Killeen, P. R. (2005) 'An alternative to null hypothesis significance test'. *Psychological Science*, 16(5), 345–53.

Kimmel, A. J. (1988) *Ethics and Values in Applied Social Research*. Newbury Park, CA and London: Sage.

Kirk, R. E. (1996) 'Practical significance: a concept whose time has come'. *Educational and Psychological Measurement* 56(5), 746–59.

Kluckhohn, C. and Murray, H. A. (eds) (1948) *Personality in Nature, Society and Culture*. New York: Alfred A. Knopf.

Krippendorf, K. (1980) *Content Analysis*. London: Sage.

Krueger, R. (1994) *Focus Groups: A Practical Guide for Applied Research*. Newbury Park, CA: Sage. [A detailed book on the conduct of focus group research, its value and the issues around it; clearly written; numerous practical points and guidance.]

Kuhn, T. S. (1970) *The Structure of Scientific Revolutions*. Chicago: University of Chicago Press.

Lacey, C. (1970) *Hightown Grammar*. Manchester: Manchester University Press.

Lagemann, E. C. (1997) 'Contested terrain: a history of educational research in the United States 1890–1990'. *Educational Researcher* 26(9), 5–17.

—— (2000) *An Elusive Science: The Troubling History of Education Research*. Chicago: University of Chicago Press.

Lakoff, G. and Johnson, M. (1980) *Metaphors We Live By*. Chicago: University of Chicago Press. [A classic text on how metaphors have become embedded and unnoticed in everyday life, thought and language.]

Lather, P. (1986) 'Research as praxis'. *Harvard Educational Review* 56, 257–77.

Latour, B. and Woolgar, S. (1979) *Laboratory Life: The Social Construction of Scientific Facts*. London: Sage.

Lave, J. (1986) *Cognition in Practice*. Cambridge: Cambridge University Press.

Layard, R. (2006) *Happiness*. London: Penguin Books.

Layder, D. (1993) *New Strategies in Social Research*. Cambridge: Polity Press.

Le Compte, M. and Goertz, J. (1981) 'Ethnographic data collection in education research', in Fetterman, D. (ed.), *Ethnography in Educational Evaluation*. London: Sage.

—— and Preissle, J. (1984) *Ethnography and Qualitative Design in Educational Research*. London: Academic Press.

Lewin, K. (1946) 'Action research and minority problems'. *Journal of Social Issues* 2(34–6), 286.

—— (1952) *Field Theory in Social Science: Selected Theoretical Papers*. ed. Dorwin Cartwright. London: Tavistock.

Lilienfeld, S. O., Wood, J. M. and Garb, H. N. (2000) 'Scientific status of projective techniques'. *Psychological Science in the Public Interest* 1(2), 27–66. Retrieved 20 February 2007 from http://www.psychologicalscience.org/journals/.

'What's wrong with this picture'. *Scientific American* 284, 81–7.

Limerick, B., Burgess-Limerick, T. and Grace, M. (1996) 'The politics of interviewing: power relations and accepting the gift'. *Qualitative Studies in Education* 9(4), 449–60.

Lincoln, Y. S. and Guba, E. G. (1985) *Naturalistic Inquiry*. Newbury Park, CA and London: Sage.

Lloyd, M. E. (1990) 'Gender factors in reviewer recommendations for manuscript publications'. *Journal of Applied Behaviour Analysis* 23, 539–43.

Locke, J. (1690) (ed. A. D. Woozley, 1964) *An Essay Concerning Human Understanding*. London: Fontana.

Loehlin, J. C. (2000) 'Group differences in intelligence', in R. J. Sternberg (ed.), *Handbook of Intelligence*. Cambridge: Cambridge University Press, 176–97.

Lyman, H. B. (1997) *Test Scores and What they Mean* (6th ed.). London: Allyn & Bacon.

Lyotard, J. F. (1984) *The Postmodern Condition: A Report on Knowledge*. Minnesota: University of Minnesota Press.

McCulloch, G. (2004) *Documentary Research in Education, History and the Social Sciences*. London: Routledge.

McDaniel, M. (2005) 'Big-brained people are smarter: a meta–analysis of the relationship between *in vivo* brain volume and intelligence'. *Intelligence* 33, 337–46.

McGue, M. and Bouchard, T. J. (1998) 'Genetic and environmental influences on human behavioural differences'. *Annual Review of Neuroscience* 21, 1–24.

McNiff, J. (1992) *Action Research: Principles and Practice.* London: Routledge.

Mahler, E. (1986) *Research Interviewing: Context and Narrative.* London: Harvard University Press.

Mann, C. and Stewart, C. (2000) *Internet Communication and Qualitative Research.* London: Sage.

May, T. (2001) *Social Research – Issues, Methods and Process.* Maidenhead: OUP.

Mayer, R. E. (2000) 'Intelligence and education', in R. J. Sternberg (ed.), *Handbook of Intelligence.* Cambridge: Cambridge University Press, 519–33.

Maykut, P. and Morehouse, R. (1994) *Beginning Qualitative Research: A Philosophic and Practical Guide.* London: Falmer Press.

Medawar, P. (1963) 'Is the scientific paper a fraud'. *The Listener,* September.

—— (1979) *Advice to a Young Scientist.* New York: Harper & Row.

Merton, R., Fiske, M. and Kendall, P. (1956) *The Focused Interview: A Manual of Problems and Procedures.* Chicago, ILL: Free Press.

Miles, M. B. and Huberman, A. M. (1984) *Qualitative Data Analysis: A Sourcebook of New Methods.* Newbury Park, CA. and London: Sage. (An imaginative book on different ways of analysing qualitative data.)

—— (1994) *Qualitative Data Analysis: An Expanded Sourcebook* (2nd ed.). Newbury Park, California and London: Sage.

Milgram, S. (1963) 'Behavioral study of obedience'. *Journal of Abnormal and Social Psychology.* 67, 371–8. Reproduced at http://www.radford.edu/~jaspelme/gradsoc/obedience/Migram_Obedience.pdf (retrieved 29 January 2007).

—— (1974a) *Obedience to Authority; An Experimental View.* London: HarperCollins.

—— (1974b) 'The perils of obedience'. *Harper's Magazine.* Reproduced at http://home.swbell.net/revscat/perilsOfObedience.html (retrieved 29 January 2007).

The Milgram Experiment: A lesson in depravity, peer pressure, and the power of authority. Retrieved 29 January 2007 from http://www.new-life.net/milgram.htm.

Milgram's experiment (2007) In *Wikipedia, The Free Encyclopedia.* Retrieved 29 January 2007 from http://en.wikipedia.org/wiki/Milgram_experiment.

Mitchell, J. C. (1983) 'Case and situation analysis'. *Sociological Review* 31(2), 187–211.

Mitchell, P. (1997) *Introduction to Theory of Mind: Children, Autism and Apes*. London: Edward Arnold.

Morgan, D. (1988) *Focus Groups as Qualitative Research*. Newbury Park, CA and London; Sage. (Short guide to the conduct and applications of focus groups.)

Mortimore, P. (2000) 'Does educational research matter?'. *British Educational Research Journal* 26(1), 5–24.

Moser, C. A. (1958) *Survey Methods in Social Investigation*. London: Heinemann.

Mouly, G. (1978) *Educational Research: The Art and Science of Investigation*. Boston: Allyn & Bacon.

National Cancer Institute (2007) Cancer starts fact sheets: cancer of the breast. www.cancer.gov, 22 January, 2007.

Neisser, U., Boodoo, G., Bouchard, T.J., Boykin, A.W., Brody, N., Ceci, S.J. *et al.* (1996) 'Intelligence: knowns and unknowns'. *American Psychologist* 51(2), 77–101.

Neuman, L. W. (1994) *Social Research Methods* (2nd ed.). Boston: Allyn & Bacon.

Nickerson, R. S. (2000) 'Null hypothesis significance testing: a review of an old and continuing controversy'. *Psychological Methods* 5(2), 241–301.

Nicol, A., Nicol, A. M. and Pexman, P. M. (1999) *Presenting your Findings: A Practical Guide for Creating Tables*. Washington DC: American Psychological Association.

—— (2003) *Displaying your Findings: A Practical Guide for Creating Figures, Posters and Presentations*. Washington DC: American Psychological Association.

Nisbet, J. and Broadfoot, P. (1980) *The Impact of Research on Policy and Practice in Education*. Aberdeen: Aberdeen University Press.

—— and Entwistle, N. (1970) *Educational Research Methods*. London: University of London Press.

Nixon, J. (ed.) (1981) *A Teacher's Guide to Action Research*. London: Grant McIntyre.

Nunan, D. (1992) *Research Methods in Language Learning*. Cambridge: Cambridge University Press.

Odendahl, T. and Shaw, A. M. (2002) 'Interviewing elites', in Gubrium, J. F. and Holstein, J. A. (eds), *Handbook of Interview Research: Context and Method*. London: Sage.

Oppenheim, A. N. (1966) *Introduction to Qualitative Research Methods*. London: Wiley.

Parsons, D. (1984) *Employment and Manpower Surveys: A Practitioner's Guide*. Aldershot: Gower.

Patrick, J. (1973) *A Glasgow Gang Observed*. London: Eyre-Methuen.

Patton, M. (1990) *Qualitative Evaluation and Research Methods*. Newbury Park, CA: Sage.

Payne, S. L. (1951) (paperback edn, 1980) *The Art of Asking Questions*. Princeton, NJ: Princeton University Press. An amusing guide aimed at stopping people from asking silly questions.

Perry, W. (1970) *Forms of Intellectual and Ethical Development in the College Years*. New York: Holt, Rinehart & Winston.

Peters, D. and Ceci, S. (1982) 'Peer review practices of psychological journals: the fate of published articles, submitted again'. *The Behavioural and Brain Sciences* 5, 187–255.

Peters, R. S. and White, J. P. (1969) 'The philosopher's contribution to educational research'. *Educational Philosophy and Theory* 1, 1–15.

Piaget, J. (1929) *The Child's Conception of the World*. London: Routledge & Kegan Paul.

Platt, J. (1981a) 'Evidence and proof in documentary research: 1'. *Sociological Review* 29(1), 31–52.

—— (1981b) 'Evidence and proof in documentary research: 2'. *Sociological Review* 29(1), 53–66.

Plomin R. and Spinath, F.M. (2004) 'Intelligence: genetics, genes and genomics'. *Journal of Personality and Social Psychology* 86(1), 112–29.

Plummer, K. (1983) *Documents of Life: An Introduction to the Problems and Literature of a Humanistic Method*. London: George Allen & Unwin.

Polanyi, M. (1967) *The Tacit Dimension*. Chicago: University of Chicago Press.

Popper, K. (1963) *Conjectures and Refutations: The Growth of Scientific Knowledge*. London: Routledge & Kegan Paul.

Powney, J. and Watts, M. (1987) *Interviewing in Educational Research*. London: Routledge & Kegan Paul.

Rice, S. A. (ed.) (1931) *Methods in Social Science*. Chicago: University of Chicago Press. [One of the early books describing focus group research in social science.]

Richardson, K. (2000) *The Making of Intelligence*. New York: Columbia University Press.

Richardson, L. (1985) *The New Other Woman: Contemporary Single Women in Affairs with Married Men*. New York: Free Press.

—— (1987) 'Disseminating research to popular audiences: the book tour'. *Qualitative Sociology*, 19(2), 164–76.

—— (1990) *Writing Strategies: Reaching Diverse Audiences*. London: Sage.

—— (2000) 'Writing: A Method of Inquiry' in Denzin, N. and Lincoln, Y. (eds), *The Handbook of Qualitative Research* (2nd edn): London: Sage.

Richardson, S., Dohrenwend, B. and Klein, D. (1965) *Interviewing: Its Forms and Functions*. New York: Basic Books.

Riley, J. (1990) *Getting the Most from your Data: A Handbook of Practical Ideas on How to Analyse Qualitative Data*. Bristol: Technical and Educational Services Ltd.

Riley, K. P., Snowdon, D. A., Desrosiers, M. F. and Markesbery, W. R. (2005) 'Early life linguistic ability, late life cognitive function, and neuropathology: findings from the Nun Study'. *Neurobiology of Aging* 26(3), 341–7.

Roberts, B. W. and DelVeccio, W. F. (2000) 'The rank order consistency of personality from childhood to old age: a quantitative review of longitudinal studies'. *Psychological Bulletin* 126, 3–25.

Robson, C. (1993) *Real World Research: A Resource for Social Scientists and Practitioner-Researchers*. Oxford: Basil Blackwell (a 510-page resource covering almost everything from design to data collection and 'making an impact').

Roizen, J. and Jepson, M. (1985) *Degrees for Jobs: Employers' Expectations of Higher Education*. Windsor: SRHE/NFER-Nelson.

Rorschach inkblot test (2007) in *Wikipedia, The Free Encyclopedia*. Retrieved 15 February 2007 from http://en.wikipedia.org/w/index.php?title=Rorschach_inkblot_test&oldid=107384515.

Rose, D. and Pevalin, D. J. (with O'Reilly, K.) (2005) *The National Statistics Socio-Economic Classification: Origins, Development and Use*. Office for National Statistics. Retrieved 4 April 2005 from http://www.statistics.gov.uk/methods_quality/ns_sec/downloads/NJ-SEC_Origins.pdf.

Rose, S. (1998) *Lifelines: Biology, Freedom and Determinism*. Harmondsworth: Penguin.

Rosen, W. and Donald, A. (1995) 'Evidence-based medicine: an approach to clinical problem solving'. *British Medical Journal* 310: 6987, 1122–5.

Rosenthal, R. (1973) *On the Social Psychology of the Self-Fulfilling Prophecy: Further Evidence for Pygmalion Effects and their Mediating Mechanisms*. New York: MSS Modular Publications.

—— (2003) 'Covert communication in laboratories, classrooms, and the truly real world'. *Current Directions in Psychological Science* 12(5), 151–4.

—— and Jacobson, L. (1968a) *Pygmalion in the Classroom*. New York: Holt, Rinehart & Winston.

—— (1968b) 'Teacher expectations for the disadvantaged'. *Scientific American* 218, 19–23.

Rowbottom, D. P. and Aiston, S. J. (2006) 'The myth of "scientific method" in contemporary educational research'. *Journal of Philosophy of Education* 40(2), 137–56.

Rowland, S. (1984) *The Enquiring Classroom.* Lewes: Falmer Press.

Rubin, H. and Rubin, I. (1995) *Qualitative Interviewing: The Art of Hearing Data.* London: Sage.

Rudduck, J. (1985) 'A case for case records? A discussion of some aspects of Lawrence Stenhouse's work in case study methodology', in R. G. Burgess (ed.), *Strategies of Educational Research: Qualitative Methods.* London: Falmer Press, 101–19.

Ryle, G. (1949) *The Concept of Mind.* London: Hutchinson.

Sackman, H. (1976) 'A sceptic at the oracle'. *Futures* 8, 444–6.

Sanger, J., Wilson, I., Davis, B. and Whittaker, R. (1997) *Young Children, Videos and Computer Games.* London: Falmer Press.

Scarborough, H. (1998) 'Predicting the future achievement of second graders with reading disabilities: contributions of phonemic awareness, verbal memory, rapid naming, and IQ'. *Annals of Dyslexia* 68, 115–36.

Scargle, J. D. (2000) 'Publication bias: the "file drawer" problem in scientific inference'. *Journal of Scientific Exploration* 14(1), 91–106.

Schattzman, L. and Strauss, A. (1973) *Field Research: Strategies for a Natural Sociology.* Englewood Cliffs, NJ: Prentice-Hall.

Schoenborn, C. A. (2004) 'Marital status and health: United States, 1999–2002'. Advance data from *Vital and Health Statistics* 351, 1–36.

Schon, D. (1971) *Beyond the Stable State.* London: Temple Smith.

—— (1983) *The Reflective Practitioner.* London: Temple Smith.

Schratz, M. (ed.) (1993) *Qualitative Voices in Educational Research.* London: Falmer Press.

Scott, D. (1990) *A Matter of Record: Documentary Sources in Social Research.* Cambridge: Polity Press.

—— and Usher, R. (eds) (1996) *Understanding Educational Research.* London: Routledge.

—— (1999) *Researching Education: Data, Methods and Theory in Educational Inquiry.* London: Cassell.

Selwyn, N. and Robson, K. (2002) 'Using e-mail as a research tool'. *Social Research Update* 21 University of Surrey.

Shah, J. and Christopher, N. (2002) 'Can shoe size predict penile length?' *British Journal of Urology International* 90(6) 586–7.

Shayer, M. and Adey, P. (1981) *Towards a Science of Science Teaching.* London: Heinemann.

Sherif, M., Harvey, O. J., White, B. J., Hood, W. R. and Sherif, C. W. (1961) *Intergroup Cooperation and Competition: The Robberts Cave Experiment.* Norman, OK: University Book Exchange.

Shils, E. (1961) 'The calling of sociology', in T. Parsons, E. Shils, K. D. Naegele and I. R. Pitts (eds), *Theories of Society*. New York: Free Press, pp. 1405–8.

Shipman, M. (1988) *The Limitations of Social Research* (3rd ed.). Harlow: Longman. [A critical look at social science research, discussing issues like reliability, generalizability, validity and 'credibility'.]

Shulman, L. (1987) 'Knowledge and teaching: foundations of the new reforms'. *Harvard Educational Review* 57(1), 1–22.

Silverman, D. (1993) *Interpreting Qualitative Data: Methods for Analysing Talk Text and Interaction*. London: Sage. [Concentrates on the study of language in qualitative research by discussing the analysis of interviews, texts and transcripts.]

Simons, H. (1981) *Towards a Science of the Singular: Essays About Case Study in Educational Research and Evaluation*. CARE occasional paper, no. 10. Centre for Applied Research in Education, University of East Anglia. [A set of papers presenting what was then a new approach to educational research.]

—— (1989) 'Ethics of case study in educational research and evaluation', in R. G. Burgess (ed.), *The Ethics of Educational Research*. London: Falmer Press.

—— (2003) 'Evidence-based practice: panacea or over-promise?'. *Research Papers in Education* 18 (4), 303–11.

Skilbeck, M. (1983) 'Lawrence Stenhouse: research methodology'. *British Educational Research Journal* 9(1), 11–20.

Smith, I. M. (1972) *Interviewing in Market and Social Research*. London: Routledge & Kegan Paul.

Snowling, M. J. (2000) *Dyslexia*. Oxford: Blackwell.

Social Research Association (SRA) (2003) *Ethical Guidelines* retrieved April 23, 2007 from http:// www.the-sta.org.uk/ethical.htm

Sokal, A. D. (1996) 'Transgressing the boundaries: towards a transformative hermeneutics of quantum gravity. *Social Text* 46/47, 217–52. Retrieved 26 February 2007 from author's website http:// www.physics.nyu.edu/faculty/sokal/transgress_v2/ transgress_v2_singlefile.html.

—— and Bricmont, J. (1998) *Fashionable Nonsense: Postmodern Intellectuals' Abuse of Science*. New York: Picador, USA.

Sokal Affair. In *Wikipedia, The Free Encyclopedia*. Retrieved 26 February 2007 from http://en.wikipedia.org/w/index.php?title=Sokal_Affair &oldid=110623768.

Sparkes, A. (1994) 'Life histories and the issue of voice: reflections on an emerging relationship'. *Qualitative Studies in Education* 1(2), 165–83.

Spindler, G. D. (ed.) (1982) *Doing the Ethnography of Schooling: Educational Anthropology in Action*. New York: Holt, Reinhart & Winston.

Spradley, J. P. (1979) *The Ethnographic Interview*. New York: Holt, Rhinehart & Winston.

—— (1980) *Participant Observation*. New York: Holt, Rhinehart & Winston.

Stake, R. E. (1994) 'Case studies', in N. Denzin and Y. Lincoln, *Handbook of Qualitative Research*. London: Sage.

—— (1995) *The Art of Case Study Research*. London: Sage.

Stanovich, K. (2000) *How to Think Straight About Psychology* (7th ed.). Boston: Allyn & Bacon, Pearson Education.

Stenhouse, L. (1975) *An Introduction to Curriculum Research and Development*. London: Heinemann.

—— (1978) 'Case study and case records: towards a contemporary history of education'. *British Educational Research Journal* 4(2), 21–39.

—— (1979) 'The problem of standards in illuminative research'. *Scottish Educational Review*, 11 January.

—— (1984) 'Library access, library use and user education in sixth forms: an autobiographical account', in R. I. Burgess (ed.), *The Research Process in Educational Settings: Ten Case Studies*. Lewes: Falmer Press, 211–33.

—— (1985) 'A note on case study and educational practice', in R. G. Burgess (ed.) *Field Methods in the Study of Education*. Lewes: Falmer Press, 263–71.

Sternberg, R. J. (1998) 'How intelligent is intelligence testing?' *Scientific American* 9(4), 12–17.

—— and Grigorenko, E. (1999) 'Myths in psychology and education regarding the gene-environment debate'. *Teachers College Record* 100(3), 536–53.

—— Forsythe, G.B., Hedlund, J., Horvath, J.A., Wagner, R.K., Williams, W.M. *et al.* (2000) *Practical Intelligence in Everyday Life*. New York: Cambridge University Press.

Stuart, M. (2004) 'Getting ready for reading: a follow-up study of inner-city second-language learners at the end of Key Stage 1'. *British Journal of Educational Psychology* 74, 15–36.

Sundet, J. M., Barlaug, D. G. and Torjussen, T. M. (2004) 'The end of the Flynn effect? A study of secular trends in mean intelligence test scores of Norwegian conscripts during half a century'. *Intelligence* 32, 349–62.

Suppes, P. (ed.) (1978) *Impact of Research on Education: Some Case Studies*. Washington DC: National Academy of Education.

Swets, J. A., Dawes, R. M. and Monahan, J. (2000) 'Psychological science can improve diagnostic decisions'. *Psychological Science in the Public Interest* 1(1), 1–26. Retrieved 20 January 2006 from http://www.blackwell-synergy.com/loi/PSPI.

Taylor, S. and Bogdan, R. (1984) *Introduction to Qualitative Research Methods*. New York: Wiley.

Taylor, W. (1973) 'Knowledge and research', in W. Taylor (ed.), *Research Perspectives in Education*. London: Routledge & Kegan Paul.

Terman, L. M. (1931) 'The gifted child', in C. Murchison (ed.), *A Handbook of Child Psychology*. Worcester, MA: Clark University Press.

Tesch, R. (1990) *Qualitative Research: Analysis Types and Software Tools*. London: Falmer Press.

Thomas, G. and James, D. (2006) 'Reinventing grounded theory: some questions about theory, ground and discovery'. *British Educational Research Journal* 32(6), 767–95.

Thorndike, E. L. (1918) 'The nature, purpose and general methods of measurement of educational products', in the *Seventeenth Yearbook of the National Society for the Study of Education*. Part II. *The Measurement of Educational Products*. Bloomington, IL: Public School Publishing Company.

Tooley, I. and Darby, D. (1998) *Educational Research: A Critique: A Survey of Published Educational Research*. London: Office for Standards in Education.

Torgerson, C. (2003) *Systematic Reviews*. London, New York: Continuum.

Torgesen, J., Wagner, R. and Rashotte, C. (1999) *Test of Word Reading Efficiency (TOWRE)*. Austin, TX: ProEd.

Tripp, D. (1993) *Critical Incidents in Teaching*. London: Routledge.

Troyna, B. (1994) 'Reforms, research and being reflective about being reflexive', in Halpin, D. and Troyna, D. (eds), *Researching Educational Policy: Ethnical and Methodological Issues*. London: Falmer Press.

Turkle, S. (1984) *The Second Self*. London: Granada.

United Kingdom Government (2002) *Iraq's Weapons of Mass Destruction. The Assessment of the British Government*. Retrieved 9 April 2007 from http://www.number-10.gov.uk/files/pdt/iraqdossier.pdf.

Urban, K. K and Yellen, H. R. (1996) *Test for Creative Thinking Drawing Production*. Oxford: Harcourt Assessment.

Usher, R. (1996) 'Textuality and reflexivity', in D. Scott and R. Usher (eds), *Understanding Educational Research*. London: Routledge.

—— and Edwards, R. (1994) *Postmodernism and Education*. London: Routledge.

van Ijzendoorn, M. H., Juffer, F. and Poelhuis, C. W. K. (2005) 'Adoption and cognitive development: a meta-analytic comparison of adopted and non-adopted children's IQ and school performance'. *Psychological Bulletin* 131(2), 301–16.

Verma, G. and Mallick, K. (1999) *Researching Education: Perspectives and Techniques*. London: Falmer Press.

Vernon P. A., Wickett, J.C., Bazana, P.G. and Stelmack, R.M. (2000) 'The neuropsychology and psychophysiology of human intelligence', in R. J. Sternberg (ed.), *The Handbook of Human Intelligence*. New York: Cambridge University Press, 245–64.

Walford, G. (ed.) (1991) *Doing Educational Research*. London: Routledge. A set of semi-autobiographical accounts from thirteen well-known researchers in education, including Ball, Mac and Ghaill, and Tizard and Hughes, in which they reflect on the problems, methods, publication and impact of their own particular projects/studies.]

—— and Miller, H. (1991) *City Technology College*. Buckingham: Open University Press.

Walker, R. (1980) 'The conduct of educational case studies: ethics, theory and procedures', in W. B. Dockrell and D. Hamilton (eds), *Rethinking Educational Research*. London: Hodder & Stoughton.

—— (1985a) *Doing Research: A Handbook for Teachers*. London: Methuen. [Practical and readable.]

—— (ed.) (1985b) *Applied Qualitative Research*. Aldershot: Gower. [Collection of readings on qualitative methods, taking a practical approach.]

—— and Adelman, C. (1972) *Towards a Sociography of Classrooms*. Final Report. London: Social Science Research Council.

Warburton, T. and Saunders, M. (1996) 'Representing teachers' professional culture through cartoons'. *British Journal of Educational Studies* 43(3), 307–25.

Watson, F. (1953) 'Research in the Physical Sciences'. *Phi Delta Kappa, Bloomington*, Bloomington, IN.

Webb, R. (ed.) (1990) *Practitioner Research in the Primary School*. London: Falmer Press. [Collection of personal accounts of research done by practitioners in primary schools.]

Webb, S. and Webb, B. (1932) *Methods of Social Study*. London: Longman, Green.

Weiss, C. (ed.) (1977) *Using Social Research in Public Policy Making*. Farnborough: Saxon House.

Wellington, J. (2000) *Educational Research: Contemporary Issues and Practical Approaches*. London: Continuum.

—— (2003) *Getting Published*. London: Routledge.

—— Bathmaker, A., Hunt, C., McCulloch, G. and Sikes, P. (2005) *Succeeding with Your Doctorate*. London: Sage.

Wellington, J. J. (1989) *Education for Employment: The Place of Information Technology*. Windsor: NFER-Nelson.

White, J. (1998) *Do Howard Gardner's Multiple Intelligences Add Up?* London: Institute of Education.

Whyte, W. F. (1943) *Street Corner Society: The Social Structure of an Italian Slum*. Chicago: University of Chicago Press. [Oft-quoted study by an 'upper middle-class' Harvard researcher who spent an extended period, in the late 1930s, in the Italian quarter of an 'Eastern City', chosen because it 'best fitted my picture of what a slum district should look like'! Written almost like a novel; focuses mainly on the males of the society, their groups, politics and racketeering.]

Wilkinson, A. and APA Task Force on Statistical Inference (1999) 'Statistical methods in psychology journals: guidelines and explanations'. *American Psychologist* 54, 594–603.

Wilkinson, G. S. (1993) *Wide Range Achievement Test – Revision 3 (WRAT3)*. Wilmington, DE: Wide Range, Inc.

Willis, P. (1977) *Learning to Labour: How Working Class Kids Get Working Class Jobs*. Farnborough: Saxon House.

Wilson, K., Mills, E., Ross, C., McGowan, J. and Jadad, A. (2003) 'Association of autistic spectrum disorder and the measles, mumps and rubella vaccine. A systematic review of current epidemiological evidence'. *Archives of Pediatric and Adolescent Medicine* 157, 628–34.

Wittrock, B. (1991) 'Social knowledge and public policy: eight models of interaction', in P. Wagner, C. H. Weiss, B. Wittrock and H. Wollman (eds), *Social Sciences and Modern States*. Cambridge: Cambridge University Press.

Wolcott, H. (1990) *Writing Up Qualitative Research*. Newbury Park, CA: Sage.

Wolcott, H. F. (1995) *The Art of Fieldwork*. London: Sage.

Woods, P. (1985) 'Conversations with teachers: some aspects of life-history method'. *British Educational Research Journal* 11(11), 13–26.

—— (1986) *Inside Schools: Ethnography in Educational Research*. London: Routledge & Kegan Paul.

—— (1993) *Critical Events in Teaching and Learning*. London: Falmer Press.

—— (1999) *Successful Writing for Qualitative Researchers*. London: Routledge.

Woolgar, S. (1988) *Science: The Very Idea*. London: Tavistock.

Wright, C. (1992) *Race Relations in the Primary School*. London: David Fulton.

Yin, R. K. (1983) *The Case Study Method: An Annotated Bibliography*. Washington DC: Cosmos.

—— (1984, 2nd ed. 1989) *Case Study Research: Design and Methods*. Newbury Park, CA: Sage. [Valuable book on the design and analysis of case studies.] For a later version see Yin, R. K. (1994) *Case Study Research: Design and Methods*. Beverly Hills, CA: Sage.

Young, B. and Tardif, C. (1992) 'Interviewing: two sides of the story'. *Qualitative Studies in Education* 5(2), 135–45.

Youngman, M. B. (1986) *Designing and Analysing Questionnaires*. University of Nottingham: Nottingham Rediguides.

Zeidner, M. and Matthews, G. (2000) 'Intelligence and personality', in R. J. Sternberg (ed.), *Handbook of Intelligence*. Cambridge: Cambridge University Press.

Zimbardo, P. G. (2007) *The Stanford Prison Experiment, a Situation Study of the Psychology of Imprisonment Conducted at Stanford University*. Retrieved 29 January 2007, http//www.prisonexp.org/.

Zimmerman, D. and Wieder, D. (1977) 'The diary: diary-interview method'. *Urban Life* 5(4), January, 479–98.

Glossary of Terms Used in Social Research

a posteriori: coming after; following from and dependent upon experience and observation, i.e. *after* experience.

a priori: coming before; prior to, and independent of, experience or observation, i.e. *before* experience.

action research: a term coined by social psychologist Kurt Lewin (1890–1947) in the 1940s. Lewin suggested the action research 'spiral' of: planning, acting, observing, reflecting. Action research is usually undertaken by a person who is both the researcher and practitioner/user. For example, researchers might aim to explore how and in what ways certain aspects of their teaching are 'effective'; this research could then inform and improve their current practice. Carr and Kemmis (1986) argued that all action research has the key features of involvement (practitioners are involved in all phases, i.e. planning, acting, observing and reflecting) and improvement (in the understanding practitioners have of their practice and the practice itself) (see *applied research, ecological validity*).

applied research: research directed towards solving a problem or designed to provide information that is directly useful and applicable to practice (see *action research, ecological validity*).

attitude test: a test (usually a self-report questionnaire) designed to measure a person's attitudes (their emotional, cognitive and behavioural components) toward social situations or people. Attitude tests are often criticized for being relatively crude instruments, whose results are heavily influenced by the social desirability factor (tendency to present ourselves in the best possible light).

audiences: individuals, e.g. lecturers/teachers, groups or organizations (e.g. pressure groups, schools) who might use the findings produced by a researcher.

bias: the conscious or subconscious influence of a researcher's attitudes and convictions on the research process. Bias can affect: the choice of topics/problems/questions to research; research planning and design; methods of data collection; data analysis; interpretation of results; conclusions drawn. Frequently recommended 'remedies' against bias include: *reflexivity*, *peer-review* process, and independent replication.

biased sample: the result of a sampling strategy which systematically includes or excludes certain individuals or groups. A sample may be biased for good reasons (see *purposive sampling*).

case study: the study of single 'cases' or 'units of analysis', e.g. a person, an event, a group (e.g. a family, an organization, a classroom, a town). Case studies are commonly used in law, medicine and education. Becker (1986) urges that case-study researchers should continually ask: 'What is this a case *of?*' Case study is often chosen to explore how or why questions and situations in their natural setting when the researcher is not attempting to control or intervene in them (Yin, 1984). Cases are often chosen to deepen understanding of an event, a problem, an issue, a theory, a model (Stake, 1995). A set of related case studies that are reported together is called a case series.

confounding variable (confound): a variable beyond the researcher's control, that may affect the results of the study (i.e. the dependent variable). Confounding variables are potential independent variables that the researcher chose not to study (either deliberately or through omission). Random confounds introduce 'noise' (i.e. increase measurement error) but do not invalidate the study. Systematic confounds, on the other hand, create *bias* and effectively invalidate the conclusions. A valid study must control (i.e. neutralize) all systematic confounds, either by appropriate design (e.g. matching of groups) or by statistical means (statistical 'partialling out' of the effects of the confound) (see *variable, independent variable, dependent variable*).

connectivity: The principle of connectivity stipulates the criteria for assessing the plausibility of a scientific claim (a hypothesis, a general law, or a theory). The claim is plausible if it 'connects to' (i.e. does not contradict) the hypotheses, laws and theories that are well established (reasonably proven) already. The principle allows us to reject certain claims (e.g. young Earth creationism, homeopathy, extrasensory perception) as a priori implausible. See *converging evidence*, a priori.

control group: the group of people (or plants or animals) in an experiment who do not experience the treatment given to an experimental group but are otherwise as identical as possible to the experimental group. The purpose of a control group is to show what would have happened to the experimental group if it had not been exposed to the experimental treatment (see *experimental group*).

converging evidence: The principle of converging evidence stipulates the criteria of scientific proof. It states that a claim (a hypothesis, a general law, a theory) can be said to be reasonably proven if it is consistent with a body of evidence that comes from different sources (different researchers), different populations, and is collected using a variety of methods. The evidence must have provided numerous opportunities for falsifying that law or theory, and those attempts must have been unsuccessful. Triangulation is one of many ways of seeking converging evidence (see *triangulation, falsifiability*).

deconstruction: a way of examining texts (i.e. 'taking apart'). By searching for the unspoken or unformulated messages of a text, it can be shown to be saying something more than or different to what it appears or purports to say. Texts say many different things, i.e. there is not one essential meaning (Derrida, 1978).

dependent variable: the responses produced by the object of our study. The results of the study, the data collected. Also called the *response variable* or the *outcome of the study* (see *variable, independent variable, confounding variable*).

discourse analysis: a general term used to encompass a range of approaches to analysing talk, text, writing etc; mainly concerned with analysing *what* is being communicated and *how*, looking for codes, rules and signs in speech or text.

document analysis: the strategies and procedures for analysing and interpreting the documents of any kind important for the study of a particular area. Documents might be public (government documents, media cuttings, television scripts, minutes of meetings, etc.) or private (letters, diaries, school records, memoirs, interview transcripts, transcripts prepared from video records or photographs, etc.).

ecological validity: an ecologically valid finding is applicable to 'real-life' situations. Researchers that emphasize the importance of ecological validity often carry out their work in naturalistic contexts, and are concerned with practical applications (see *applied research, action research*).

empirical research: (as opposed to deskwork or 'armchair' research, or 'thought experiments') inquiry involving data collection, e.g. by interviewing, observation, questionnaire, experimentation. People can do empirical research without adopting empiricism as their epistemological stance (see *empiricism, epistemology*).

empiricism: the belief that *all* knowledge is ultimately dependent upon and derived from *sensory experience (data)*, thus empirical research is the only way to verify any claims. The strict form of empiricism is *logical positivism*, which maintains that the only sensible sentences are either purely logical (e.g. mathematical theorems) or verifiable by sensory data. This would rule out most social science, all of theology and metaphysics, ethics and morals, and most theory of any kind. Logical positivism is now widely rejected but is often (wrongly) confused with positivism or with 'being scientific' and 'evidence-based'; all three are based on different ideas.

epistemology: theory of knowledge; the study of the nature and validity of knowledge. It is concerned with truth, belief, justification and verification. The two traditional camps have been: *rationalism,* which stresses the role of human reason in knowing; and *empiricism* which stresses the importance of sensory data. Some epistemologists (e.g. Immanuel Kant) argued for the synthesis of the two approaches.

ethnography: a methodology with its roots in anthropology (literally, the study of people); aims to describe and interpret human behaviour within a certain *culture*; uses extensive fieldwork and participant observation, aiming to develop rapport and empathy with the people studied.

experimental group: the group of people (or animals or plants) in an experiment who experience the experimental treatment or intervention (see *control group*).

falsifiability: according to some epistemologists (e.g. Karl Popper, 1902–94) falsifiability is a necessary logical property of all claims in empirical sciences. A claim is *falsifiable* if it allows for the data that would contradict it (if ever observed). If such data are really observed then the claim is *falsified* (i.e. proven false). The claim 'all swans are white' is falsifiable (that is, scientific), since it allows for the data that would contradict it (swans of other colours), if ever observed. The claim 'all swans are white' also happens to have been falsified, since black swans have been observed. The claim: 'there are some creatures we will never be able to detect' is non-falsifiable (that is, non-scientific) since any attempt to falsify it is logically impossible (it is impossible to think of any data that would prove it false).

formative evaluation: evaluation carried out in the early or intermediate stages of a programme, a course or an intervention, while changes can still be made; the formative evaluation shapes and informs those changes. Its opposite is *summative evaluation*, which is carried out at the end of a programme or intervention to assess its impact.

generalizability: the extent to which research findings in one context can be transferred or applied to other contexts or settings. No findings, even those based on a *probability sample*, can be generalized with complete certainty.

grounded theory: a methodological approach to social science developed by Barney Glaser (b. 1930) and Anselm Strauss (1916–96). It postulates that a researcher should approach a research problem without a preconceived theory; theory should gradually emerge from the data collected in a research study by the process of induction. This approach contrasts sharply with the standard model of 'the scientific method', which starts with an explicit theory and then verifies it against the data.

Hawthorne effect: initial (transient) improvement in performance following any newly introduced change. The name is based on a 1924 study of productivity at the Hawthorne factory in Chicago. Two carefully matched groups (experimental and control) were isolated from other factory workers. Factors in the working conditions of the experimental group were varied, e.g. illumination, humidity, temperature, rest periods. No matter what changes were made, including negative ones such as reduced illumination or shorter rest periods, its productivity showed an upward trend. Just as surprisingly, although no changes were made to the conditions of the control group, its output increased steadily. Hawthorne effect needs to be taken into consideration when assessing the effectiveness of any intervention in a natural setting (e.g. introduction of a new teaching method).

hermeneutics: the art or science of interpretation, a term first coined by William Dilthey (1833–1911). The term may now apply to the interpretation of a text, a work of art, human behaviour, discourse, documents and so on. Hans–Georg Gadamer (1900–78) proposed hermeneutics as a form of practical philosophy or methodology; the aim is to interpret and understand the meaning of social actions and social settings.

hypothesis: a tentative claim (usually derived from the theory the researcher wishes to verify) put forward for examination. A hypothesis can be used to guide and direct research along certain lines with certain procedures so that the hypothesis is 'put to the test' (see *theory*).

independent variable: variable the effect of which is studied; whose impact (on the dependent variable) is studied. Also called *explanatory variable*, *factor* or (in the context of correlational studies) *predictor*. In experimental research, independent variables are those directly controlled (manipulated) by the researcher (see also *variable*, *dependent variable*, *confounding variable*).

induction: the process of inferring a general law from the observation of particular instances. Criticized as logically flawed by David Hume (1711–76) and Karl Popper (1902–94), who pointed to the 'fallacy of induction': a general law (e.g. 'all swans are white') can never be proven, no matter how many particular instances consistent with that law (e.g. 1000 white swans) have been observed. See *falsifiability*.

instrument: any specific technique or tool that a researcher uses, e.g. a questionnaire, an interview schedule, observation framework, a standardized test, etc.

interpretative approach: argues that human behaviour can only be explained by referring to the subjective states of the people acting in it; this approach can be applied to the study of social actions/activity and texts or documents; opposed to positivism which claims that social life can only be explained by the examination of directly observable entities (see *empiricism*).

interview schedule: a set of questions used in interviewing; questions may be *open* (respondents give their 'free' answers) or *closed* (the possible range of responses is limited, e.g. 'yes' or 'no'). Interviews may range from unstructured to semi-structured to completely structured (a face-to-face questionnaire), i.e. from totally open to completely predetermined.

logical positivism: see *empiricism*

longitudinal research: research in which data are collected from the same entities (individuals, families, schools, businesses, etc.), at different points over an extended period of time, and the relationship between those different 'waves' of data is then examined. The approach is epitomized in Michael Apted's '7-Up' series of documentary films which examined the lives of a carefully chosen sample of 7-year-old children and then followed them up at age 14, 21, 28, 35 and 42.

methodology: the study of the methods, designs and procedures used in research. Methodology is sometimes called 'the science of doing good science'.

N: the number of people or other entities studied in a research project; e.g. $N = 1$, signifies a single case study.

Ockham's razor (also spelled *Occam's razor*): the principle of scientific succinctness or parsimony, named after William of Ockham (1285–1349). It states that 'entities should not be multiplied beyond necessity', that is, we should strive for the simplest possible explanations, and introduce new factors into our theories only if they are absolutely necessary to account for the data. Ockham's principle implies that, if we face the choice between two competing theories that explain a particular phenomenon equally well, we should select the simpler one. The principle can be usefully stretched further, e.g. chopping excessive words from a paper or thesis.

ontology: a branch of philosophy concerned with being or existence; the study or theory of 'what is', of core characteristics of reality.

paradigm: a term which became fashionable following Thomas Kuhn's (1922–96) book *The Structure of Scientific Revolutions*. Kuhn used the term in the sense of a (partly implicit) set of assumptions regarding what science should be concerned with and how it should be done, assumptions that are shared by the community of researchers over a particular period of time. The term is now often extended to mean perspective or view of the world, methodological position, viewpoint, community of researchers, cognitive framework, and so on. Researchers often speak of 'the qualitative and quantitative paradigms', as if they were separate and mutually exclusive; or the 'positivist paradigm' as a widely held and dangerous tendency. In experimental research, the term is often used in a very narrow sense, largely synonymous with 'procedure' (e.g. 'the Stroop paradigm' – the experimental procedure for investigating the automaticity of information processing invented by John Ridley Stroop (1897–1973)). The dictionary definitions of paradigm are: *pattern*, *example*, *exemplar*.

participant observation: a methodology or practice with its roots in early twentieth-century anthropology; it entails a researcher spending a prolonged period of time participating in the daily activities of a community or a group, e.g. a tribe, a gang, a school, the armed forces; and observing their practices, norms, customs and behaviour (either overtly or covertly). The researcher becomes socialized into the group being studied. The method therefore demands that a fine line be drawn between empathy/rapport with the group and overfamiliarity/total involvement. In some situations, participant observation raises both practical concerns (e.g. safety) and ethical concerns (e.g. pretending to be something you are not).

population: the entire set of units (people, objects, events, group entities, etc.) we are interested in. In social sciences, 'population' typically means 'population of people' (e.g. all children living in Sheffield), but populations of other units can be studied, too (e.g. all schools in Sheffield, all words of the English language, etc.). Where the boundaries of the population are drawn depends on the focus and scope of the research (e.g. population of Sheffield children in one study, population of all UK children in the other).

positivism: a philosophy (developed by Auguste Comte (1798–1857)) which claims that the only true knowledge is the scientific knowledge. Positivism also postulates that 'hard sciences' (physics, chemistry, biology, etc.) should become the model for 'soft sciences' (psychology, sociology, etc.); in other words, there is a common set of methodological principles ('the scientific method') that should be adopted by all sciences. 'Positivistic' is not synonymous with 'scientific' (one can do science without subscribing to positivist philosophy).

postmodernism: a widely used term, impossible to define, encompassing a broad range of amorphous ideas. It signals the end of universal truths, totalistic explanations and 'grand narratives' (Lyotard, 1984), giving way to little narratives (*petits récits*) and local knowledge, adequate for particular communities. Key words are: *difference, heterogeneity, fragmentation* and *indeterminacy*.

probability sampling: drawing on the members of a given population in such a way that every member of that population has a *known chance* of being selected. There are several subtypes of probability sampling, including simple random sampling (where every member has an *equal chance* of being selected), cluster sampling, stratified sampling, etc. Probability sampling eliminates systematic bias in selecting a sample (see *bias*, *population*, *purposive sampling*).

purposive sampling: sampling done with deliberate aims in mind as opposed to relying on chance. Members of the target population can be selected for a variety of reasons, e.g. for being typical or extreme or deviant or unique or exemplary or revelatory. See *probability sampling*, *population*.

qualitative: of or relating to quality or kind (from Latin *qualis*); adjective describing methods or approaches which analyse non-numeric data (narratives, images, etc.). See *quantitative*.

quantitative: of quantity or number; methods or approaches which involve measurement, i.e. collect and analyse numeric data. A false dichotomy is often drawn between a qualitative and a quantitative 'paradigm', as if the two approaches could not be used to complement and enrich each other. Also, use of quantitative data is often (wrongly) labelled 'positivism' (while positivism advocates quantitative research, one can carry out quantitative research without adopting positivist philosophy). See *qualitative*, *positivism*.

reflexivity: introspection and self-examination, i.e. the act of reflecting upon and evaluating one's own impact on the situation being studied; also involves researchers in examining their own assumptions, prior experience and bias in conducting the research and analysing its findings.

reliability: the term describing the quality of measurement instruments and procedures. If a measurement is reliable it results in negligible measurement error. Reliability is the extent to which a research method or procedure functions consistently and accurately by yielding the same results at different times or when used by different researchers. It is largely synonymous with 'repeatability' and 'precision' (of measurement). Research is said to be reliable if it can be repeated or replicated by another researcher and/or at a different time.

sample: a smaller number of units selected from a much larger population of such units. The process of selection is called sampling. See *probability sampling, purposive sampling, population*.

summative evaluation: see *formative evaluation*

theory: a systematic, formal account of why a specific type of phenomena happen as they do; a model of those phenomena. Theories seek patterns, relationships (especially causal relationships), correlations, associations or connections. The function of theories is to describe, explain and predict. Ability to make predictions is often seen as a key distinction between scientific and non-scientific theories, though this is contentious.

triangulation: the business of giving strength or support to findings/conclusions by drawing on evidence from other sources: (i) other methods (methodological triangulation), e.g. interviews, observations, questionnaires; (ii) other researchers; (iii) other times, e.g. later in a project; (iv) other places, e.g. different regions. Thus the same area of study is examined from more than one vantage point. See *converging evidence*.

trustworthiness: a criterion offered by Lincoln and Guba (1985) as an alternative to the traditional 'reliability' and 'validity' in judging the quality of research. Trustworthiness has four parts: (i) credibility; (ii) transferability; (iii) dependability; (iv) confirmability (the latter two being parallel to reliability). See *reliability, validity*.

validity: in its broadest sense, validity is a measure of the confidence in, credibility of, plausibility of and generalizability of a piece of research. As such, it is the ultimate criterion of the 'goodness' of a piece of research. Validity has several aspects; the key distinction is that between *internal validity* (the degree to which a claim made in a research study is sustained by the data reported in that study) and *external validity* (the degree to which a claim made in a particular study can be generalized beyond that study). In a more narrow sense (used in psychometrics), validity is the degree to which a particular method or procedure (e.g. a standardized test) measures what it purports to measure, and not something else; the degree to which a method is 'true to its label'. See *trustworthiness, ecological validity*.

variable: any attribute of an object, person or event that can be measured (at least in principle). See *independent variable, dependent variable, confounding variable*.

Appendix 1

Procedures for Establishing Reliability: A Brief Overview

METHOD	DEFINITION AND OPERATIONAL DEFINITION	ADVANTAGES	LIMITATIONS	TYPICALLY USED ESTIMATES (CO-EFFICIENTS)
Test-retest reliability	Stability of scores across repeated testing. Participants complete the same test twice. The second testing follows the first one immediately (so called **credibility**) or happens some time later (so called **absolute stability**). The correlation between participants' scores on 1st and 2nd testing is analysed.		Results of the second testing may be affected by: • learning/practice; • tiredness/demotivation (especially in measuring credibility).	• Pearson's r.
Parallel tests reliability	Stability of scores across equivalent tests. Two equivalent (parallel) tests are developed. Participants complete both tests, either in immediate succession, or with some intervening time period (so called **relative stability**). The correlation between participants' scores on both tests is analysed.	Reduces the effects of learning/practice inherent in test-retest method. The most conservative way of establishing reliability – it produces the lowest of all possible reliability co-efficients.	Tests must be parallel, that is: • they must be designed to measure the same variable; • their scores must have similar distribution (i.e. similar mean and standard deviation).	Estimating the reliability of each parallel test used on its own: • Pearson's r. Estimating the reliability of both parallel tests combined: • Spearman–Brown split half ('prophecy co-efficient'); • Guttman split-half.

Split-half reliability	Stability of scores across two halves of the same test. Each participant is tested just once. The test is then split into halves (typically by separating odd and even items). The correlation between participants' scores on both halves is analysed.		Cannot be used with tests that impose time limit. Both halves must be parallel (see above).	Estimating the reliability of each half: • Pearson's *r*. Estimating the reliability of the whole test: • Spearman–Brown split half ('prophecy co-efficient'); • Guttman split-half.
Internal consistency	Stability of scores across individual items of the same test. Degree to which individual items of the test measure the same variable. Mean of all possible split-half reliability co-efficients. Each participant is tested just once. The correlations between participants' scores on each and every item of the test is analysed.	The most reliable measure of reliability!	Cannot be used with tests that impose time limit. All items must be parallel (see above).	• Kuder-Richardson (KR 20 and KR 21 co-efficients). • Cronbach's alpha.
Inter-rater reliability	Agreement between the evaluations of two or more raters or 'judges'.	Suitable for evaluating the reliability of categorical classification schemes or ordinal ranking scales.		Estimating agreement between two 'judges' independently classifying items or people into one of several mutually exclusive categories: • Cohen's kappa. Estimating agreement between two or more raters ranking items or people on an ordinal scale: • Kendall's W ('co-efficient of concordance').

Appendix 2

Procedures for Establishing Validity: a Brief Overview

TYPE	WHAT DOES IT TELL YOU?	SUBTYPE	DEFINITION	EXAMPLE
Face validity	Does the test *look like* it measures what it is supposed to measure?		Informal examination of a test to find out whether it *apparently* matches its label.	A test of reading comprehension has face validity if it involves reading texts and answering questions about them.
Criterion validity	Are test results confirmed by another, independent measure of the same variable? (e.g. another test, clinical diagnosis, agreement of competent judges)	*Postdictive* validity	A valid test of variable X must produce results that are consistent with measurements of X collected *in the past* using different methods.	Validity of a case-history interview (in which a patient is asked when and how his/her problems occurred and developed) can be demonstrated through presenting corroborating evidence (e.g. medical records, interviews with family members).
		Concurrent validity	A valid test of variable X must produce results that are consistent with measurements of X collected at *(more or less) the same time* using different methods.	If a new test of non-verbal reasoning is valid, then scores on this test should correlate with scores on Raven's Progressive Matrices (an established measure of non-verbal reasoning).
		Predictive validity	A valid test of variable X must predict people's performance on the same test (and on other measures of variable X) *in the future.*	A valid test of intelligence for children must produce consistent results when taken at 6 and 12. It must also predict adult intellectual productivity (level of education completed, books written, patents obtained, etc.).
				An early screening test for the risk of dyslexia should identify children who will subsequently develop dyslexia.

Content (internal) validity	Do behaviours demanded by the test constitute a representative sample of all behaviours that exist in the domain we want to measure?		A valid test of variable X requires behaviours that are an adequate *operationalization* of this variable.	If my test is to measure driving skills, what tasks should I include? Is it sufficient, e.g., to look just at the ability to drive on country roads? If my test is to measure intelligence, what tasks should I include? Is it sufficient, e.g., to look just at reasoning based on abstract non-verbal material?
Construct (theoretical) validity	Does a test produce results that are expected given what we know about a variable X the test is supposed to measure?	*Group differences*	A valid test of a variable X must show between-group differences that are expected to occur for variable X.	If a questionnaire measures pupil's attitudes towards school, then 'good pupils' and persistent truants should score differently.
		Correlation matrices and factor analysis	A valid test of a variable X must correlate with other tests of X (and tests of different variables that are known to be related to X), but not with tests of variables that are known to be unrelated to X.	If a test measures intelligence, then its results should correlate with the results of other intelligence tests but not with the results of personality questionnaires.
		Studies of internal structure	If a test measures a single variable X, then it should have high internal consistency.	If a questionnaire measures a single personality trait (e.g. extraversion) then responses to all items of this questionnaire should be strongly intercorrelated.
		Studies of change over occasion	If a test measures variable X then experimental intervention should produce changes in test scores predicted for variable X.	If a test measures current anxiety level, then an experimental manipulation that reduces or induces anxiety should change the scores in the predicted direction.
		Studies of process	If a test measures variable X then the process of completing the test (style of problem-solving, type of errors, etc.) should differ between people in a way expected for variable X.	If a test measures narrative skills, then typically developing children and those diagnosed with specific language impairment should produce responses that are different not only quantitatively (overall accuracy of story recall, mean length of utterance) but also qualitatively (type of phonological, morphological and syntactic errors).

Appendix 3

The Relationship Between Percentile Ranks and Normalized Standard Scores

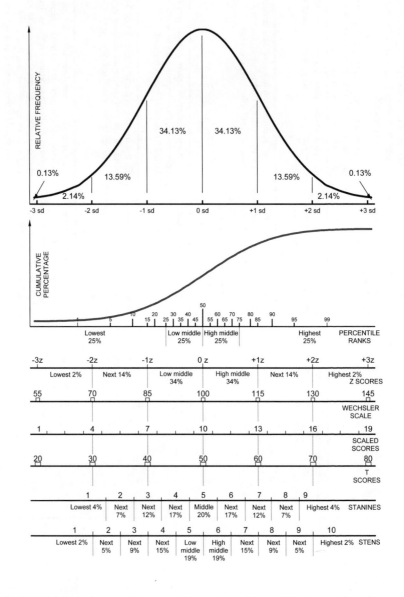

Index

access 57–58, 59, 67–70, 110
action research 24–25, 27. 214
age equivalents 152–154
algorithm 118
analysis of variance 132
analyzing qualitative data 100–114
ANOVA see analysis of variance
applied research 214
attitude test 214
a prori 9, 41–43, 105–107, 135, 214
a posteriori 9, 41–43, 105–107, 214

Bayesian analysis 135, 138
bias 215
blog 172
book proposals 180–181

case-study 91–95, 215
connectivity, principle of 17, 136, 216
converging evidence 36, 168, 216
cumulative research 42, 44
chaos theory 51, 70
coefficient of determination 137
confidence intervals (inferential
    statistics) 138
confidence intervals (psychometrics)
    149, 160–161
control group 21–23, 216
covert research 51–52
codes of conduct 61–63
computer analysis 108
connotation 112
conference presentation 172
criterion-referenced tests 146
criticality 13, 48–49

causal explanations 16, 23, 57
causality 16, 23, 57

data analysis 101–114
deconstruction 109–114, 216
degrees of freedom 130
denotation 112
descriptive research 56
descriptive statistics – see statistics
discourse analysis 109–114
disseminating research 171–190
documentary analysis 100, 109–114,
    217

ecological validity 8, 217
emergent theory 42
emotional intelligence 165
empirical research 217
empiricism 217
epistemology 217–218
error
    measurement error 119
    sampling error 119, 124
    systematic error 124
    type I 129
    type II 130
ethical dilemmas 71–75
ethical review committees 63
ethics 8, 23, 32, 58–63, 111
ethnography 52, 54, 218
evidence 184–186
evidence-based practice 185–186
experimental approach 21–23, 218
experimental group 21–23, 218
explanatory research 56–57

exploratory research 56–57

falsifiability, falsification 213, 218
focus groups 87–91
formative evaluation 218

gaining access 57–58, 59, 67–70
generalizability 95–98, 218
grade equivalents 152–154
grounded theory 42, 49, 218
group interviewing 87–91

Hawthorne effect 23, 219
hermeneutics 112, 219
heuristics 118
history of social research 6–8
hypothesis 219, 120–121
    null hypothesis 122–141
    research hypothesis 122–141
hypothesis testing 11, 122–141

ideographic 19
impact factor 173, 179
induction 9, 42, 106, 220
informed consent 59, 62
intelligence 8, 44, 161–167, see also
    IQ
interpretative approach 220
inter-subjectivity 51, 55, 61
interview schedule 84–85, 220
interviewing 81–91, 220
IQ 8, 46, 123, 161–167, see also
    intelligence

key informants 82

labels in social research 41
latent characteristics 142, 149–150, see
    also psychological traits and states
life-story method 55
literature review 172
literature reviewing 48–49
literature searching 46–48
longitudinal research 220–221

measurement error – see error
meta-analysis 172, 175, see also sys-
    tematic review
metaphor 38–39, 40, 70, 108
'methodological pragmatism' 34
methodology 33–50, 221
methods 79–99
model fitting 138
models of the research process 26–28,
    29, 58
morals 58–62
multiple intelligences 9, 165

naturalistic approach 21, 23
nomothetic 19, 118
normal distribution 157
normalization 146, 151–152
normalization of distribution 157–158
norm-referenced tests 146
norms 146
null hypothesis significance testing
    119, 121–141
null results 137, 140–141

objectivity in research 12, 51, 142, 147
observation 39, 42, 80–81, 93, 145
Ockham's Razor 49, 221
online questionnaires 96–97, 99
ontology 221
operationalization 132, 150, 174

p value 126
p-rep 138
paradigms in social research 18, 221–
    222
parameter estimation 138
participant observation 80–81, 222
partisanship 52
peer review 171–173, 188
peer-review 44, 55, 171, 172, 173,
    188–190
percentile ranks 154–156, 230
'philosophies' in research 19
pilots 84, 98
placebo effect 23

population 120, 121
populations 63–64, 222
   population effect 122, 123
   population parameters 119
positionality 53–55
positivism 222
postmodernism 222
power – see statistical power
practitioner research 24
primary sources 79–99
principle of connectivity 136
probability 135
psychological states 142
psychological traits 142
psychometrics 142
   psychometric tests 142–145
publishing conventions 176–177

qualitative research 11, 18–21, 79–
   114, 223
quantitative research 11, 18–21, 28,
   117–168, 223
quartiles 156
questioning 85–87, 97–98
questionnaires 95–99, 143–144

randomized controlled trials (RCTs)
   22–23, 59
reading research 4
recording interviews 85–87
reflectivity 49, 52–54
reflexivity 49, 52–54, 223
reliability 45, 109, 114, 142, 147–149,
   223, 226–227
replicability 45, 106
reporting research 171–190
research in the media 4–6
research process, the 55–58
research synthesis 138
response rates 96

sample 175
sample 119, 120, 121
   biased sample 215, 224
   normalization sample 151–152, 156

sample statistics 119
sampling
   non-probability 64–67
   probability 64–67, 150–151, 223
   purposive 223
   secondary sources 79
   structure in interviewing 83–85
sampling error – see error
'scientific method' 10–11, 14–15
scores (psychometrics) 152–160 see also
    percentile ranks, age equivalents
   absolute scores 154
   derived scores 152
   deviation-based scores 156–157
   normalized standard scores 157–
    160, 230
   observed scores 160
   raw scores 152
   standard scores 156–157
   true scores 160
   Wechsler scores 158, 230
   z scores 156–157, 230
significance
   practical significance 136–137
   significance tests 124–125
   significance level 126
   statistical significance 136
situated cognition 8
snowball searching 47
standardization 142, 147
statistical power 130
statistics 118
   descriptive statistics 119–120, 175
   inferential statistics 119–120
systematic enquiry 13
systematic error – see error
systematic review 22 see also meta-
   analysis

tests – see psychometric tests, significance tests
tests of significance – see significance
   tests
theorizing 9, 10, 36–43
theory 9, 10, 36–43, 50, 224

theory-laden observation 39, 42
transferable skills 7, 8
triangulation 34–36, 113–114, 168, 224
trustworthiness 224
type I error – see error
type II error – see error

uncertainty principle 51

validity 8, 43–44, 109, 114, 149–152, 224, 228–229
validity
    criterion validity 150, 228
    construct (theoretical) validity 151, 229
    content validity 150–151, 229
    ecological validity 165, 217
    external validity 224–225
    face validity 150, 228
    internal validity 224
variable 19, 44, 131225
    confounding (confound) 215
    dependent (response), 131, 216
    independent (explanatory) 131, 219
'voice' 105, 173–174

writing 174–184
writing a book proposal 180–181
writing for different audiences 177–178, 186
writing for journals 178–180